Columbus

& Cortez,

Conquerors for Christ

Columbus

& Cortez,

Conquerors for Christ

by
John Eidsmoe

New Leaf Press

First Printing: June 1992
Second Printing: February 1993
Third Printing: July 1993

Library of Congress Catalog Number: 92-81425
ISBN: 0-89221-223-3

Cover Art by Pamela Anzalotti, Greer, SC 29650

Dedication

This book is dedicated to two professors
who influenced me profoundly:

The late Colonel Theodore M. Velde,
Professor of Air Force ROTC at St. Olaf College,
who taught me duty, honor, and country;

and

Pastor Omar Gjerness,
Professor of Christian Dogmatics and Apologetics
at Lutheran Brethren Seminary,
who taught me to love sound doctrine
and to contend earnestly for the faith.

Contents

Foreword

In these last years of the twentieth century we Americans find ourselves in the midst of a titanic struggle for the soul of our nation. Never since the Civil War has the peril been greater, or the future of the nation more in doubt. For with the collapse of international communism as a system of world revolution, we can no longer pretend that our primary problems are external. Congress is virtually nonfunctional, public education is an abysmal failure, marriages and families are disintegrating, the economy is extremely shaky, and adult Americans are addicted to an entertainment industry deliberately touting adultery, homosexuality, and abortion as acceptable norms of behavior. The moral and spiritual dry rot within our nation is so far advanced that our society's basic timbers are collapsing.

It is my long-term conviction that this collapse stems from the loss of America's moral and spiritual foundations. We no longer have any awareness of who we are, or why we exist as a people. As President Woodrow Wilson pointed out, "A nation which does not remember what it was yesterday, does not know what it is today, nor what it is trying to do. We are trying to do a futile thing if we do not know where we came from or what we have been about." Saddened and disheartened over the refusal of Congress to ratify the League of Nations Treaty, Wilson himself died shortly after the end of the Great War, and mercifully never lived to see what he had warned against come to pass. The needless slaughter of hundreds of thousands of British, French, German, and Russian soldiers in the war produced a revulsion against patriotism, and even on this side of the Atlantic American pulled back into itself and the indulgence of the Roaring Twenties. Pre-war idealism gave way to disillusionment, and in the post-war cynicism of the

1920s the ideals of duty, honor, and country fell out of fashion among the educational elite. Many pseudo-sophisticated academics of "higher learning" came to doubt the authenticity of our forefather's stories of their heroes, and their experiences of God's miraculous interventions in our past — stories such as the Indian named Squanto who saved the Pilgrims' lives, the self-sacrifice of patriot Ceasar Rodney, or the miracle of fog that saved the Continental Army at Brooklyn Heights, New York.

And so these stories were no longer told or written in the history books. Those who educated our parents were themselves educated in that era, and the new American history books they wrote did not include the stories of the Christian faith and motivation of men like Christopher Columbus, George Washington, Samuel Adams, Patrick Henry, John Quincy Adams, Abraham Lincoln, and so many others. Thus three generations have grown up in America with little idea of our Christian roots.

In his customary careful and thorough manner, John Eidsmoe has pierced through the obfuscating fog of twentieth century humanist bias and judgments that have obscured the truth about two of the most controversial figures in American history, Christopher Columbus and Hernando Cortez. Using earlier sources, he has presented us with a well-researched, even-handed, and fair treatment of both their Christian motives for their incredible exploits, and the very real mistakes they made. This is a valuable contribution toward restoring a true Christian perspective on our American past.

But this book does more than rediscover the truth about Columbus and Cortez. So eroded is the traditional biblical base of American society that we find ourselves in the midst of a vicious culture war, produced by a secularized educational system that rejects the Bible as the source of absolute truth. As Alan Bloom wrote some years ago, "There is one thing a professor can be absolutely certain of: almost every student entering the university believes, or says he believes, that truth is relative." When God is rejected as the source of truth for both belief and conduct, when openness is the only sure virtue, then no particular culture has greater value than any other. So the humanist views the attempt on the part of Columbus and Cortez to impose Christian values on the cannibalistic and demonic culture of the Caribs and Aztecs as the European rape of a pristine paradise.

When biblical absolutes are rejected "anything goes," or what "goes" is whatever the majority of the American public will tolerate. So the disintegration of American society proceeds apace, and the possibility of our nation becoming "a city on a hill," or as Lincoln put it, "a beacon of hope for all men of all time to come" slips further and further away.

Tragically, as George Roche has pointed out, a society without absolutes can produce neither heroes nor happiness. And the cynical humanism which has increasingly prevailed in American education has systematically debunked and torn down all our national heroes. If heroes are those who rise above the crowd to exhibit extraordinary courage, valor, or greatness because of the dangers or challenges of the hour . . . if heroes scale the peaks of a society's absolute standards, and thus point the way for the rest of us, then America is in desperate need of heroes today.

The good news is that our American past is full of genuine heroes and heroines. There is a wonderful American heritage waiting for us to reclaim. And reclaim it we must, for "without a vision the people perish."

In this work on Christopher Columbus and Hernando Cortez, John Eidsmoe has recovered an important piece in the mosaic of our past American heroes. I commend it to you.

— Peter Marshall

Dr. Marshall, a graduate of Yale University and Princeton Theological Seminary, is the author of *The Light and the Glory* and *From Sea to Shining Sea*.

Chapter One

THE ASSAULT
ON WESTERN CULTURE

Stanford University, California, Autumn, 1990: Demonstrators chant, "Hey, Hey! Ho, Ho! Western Culture's Got To Go!"

University of Minnesota, September 16, 1992: Columbus found guilty in mock war crimes trial, sentenced to 50 years' community service.

Headquarters, National Council of Churches, May 1990: The NCC releases a three-page document titled "A Faithful Response to the 500th Anniversary of the Arrival of Christopher Columbus." The document states the following:

> What some historians have termed a "discovery" in reality was an invasion and colonization with legalized occupation, genocide, economic exploitation, and a deep level of institutional racism and moral decadence.[1]

Is this the same Christopher Columbus many Americans have learned to respect and admire as the discoverer who opened America to European exploration and settlement?

Is this the same Christopher Columbus of whom Dr. Samuel Eliot Morison, long considered the "dean" of Columbus scholars, closes his classic volume by paying "homage to Christopher, the stout-hearted son of Genoa, who carried

Christian civilization across the Ocean Sea?"[2]

Is this the same Christopher Columbus who planted the cross of Christ on American soil and gave the places he visited names like San Salvador (Holy Saviour), Vera Cruz (True Cross), and La Navidad (Nativity or Christmas)?

And why, as the 500th anniversary of Columbus's voyage approaches, are people so intent on vilifying this once-beloved figure?

A scholarly desire to correct the historical record is not the primary reason. People don't engage in impassioned street demonstrations over historical facts that are half-a-millennium old.

No, the attack is directed toward **values** — biblical values and the Christian civilization that is based on biblical values. Values on which flawed-but-believing Christians, however imperfectly, tried to build civilization and culture, first in the Middle East, then in Northern Africa, then in Europe. Values which Christopher Columbus and those who came after him, and a few who came before him, tried to transplant to the Western world.

To bring Christianity to a non-Christian society, it is said, is cultural genocide. And from the secular point of view of many historians and social scientists, that makes sense.

For if Christian belief and profession have no eternal significance, then transplanting Christianity to America merely imposes one society's culture upon another. Perhaps it replaces one religion or culture with a better one; perhaps not, depending on your point of view.

But suppose Jesus Christ truly is the eternal Son of God. Suppose, by His atoning death on the Cross, He truly paid for the sins of the whole world. Suppose eternal salvation is available to those who believe on Him and only those who believe on Him. And suppose Jesus therefore commanded believers to "Go ye therefore, and teach all nations . . ." (Matt. 28:20; Mark 16:15).

If these suppositions are objectively true, then the efforts of these explorers to bring Christianity to the Western world take on an entirely different significance, both as to the explorers' motives and as to the eternal effect of their actions on those who received the gospel at their invitation.

You may be saying to yourself, "History is boring!" Yes, all too often it is.

But it doesn't have to be.

The reason many of us find history boring is that we fail to see the sovereign hand of God at work as history unfolds. The way you look at history depends in large part upon your world view.

If your world view is that of the nihilist — one who sees no real meaning in life — you will regard history as an endless series of meaningless, unconnected, random facts — facts that fit no discernable pattern whatsoever.

If you hold a Hindu world view, you will see history as an endless series of repetitious cycles that continue predictably ad infinitum but lead nowhere.

If you are an environmental determinist, you will regard historical events as shaped and caused by environmental factors — the river theory of civilization that cultures build up along rivers, the climate theory that colder climates stimulate people to greater productivity and ingenuity, etc.

An evolutionary historian is likely to view history as the evolutionary development of the human race, involving such features as survival of the fittest, natural selection, and the steady improvement of humanity and culture.

To the Hegelian, history progresses as a result of conflict between ideas. The main idea that society accepts at a certain time is called a thesis. Then an opposite idea arises, called an antithesis. Conflict between the thesis and the antithesis takes place, and eventually the best of both ideas emerges as a synthesis. This synthesis then becomes the thesis of the next era of history. Another antithesis arises, a new synthesis, and so on.

To a Marxist, history is the record of the class struggle between the rich and the poor and the inevitable triumph of the working classes.

For the Christian, history is, or should be, the unfolding of God's plan for the human race.

For the Christian, the discovery, exploration and settlement of the Western Hemisphere takes on a whole new dimension of meaning as God works through imperfect vessels like Columbus, Cortez, Magellan, Champlain, Marquette, and others who bring salvation to the inhabitants of the Western world through the knowledge of Jesus Christ.

Why are the Christian motivations of the early explorers not emphasized today? The reasons vary.

Some secular-minded historians recreate the explorers in their own image. These historians find nothing positive about Christianity; therefore, the explorers must not have found anything positive about Christianity either. When these historians are confronted with the letters and journals of the explorers in which they clearly express Christian convictions, they conclude that these professions must have been insincere statements made to impress someone because that is the only reason they (the secular historians) would have made such statements.

But who were they trying to impress? Obviously, someone worth impressing must have been sincere about Christianity!

Unless one assumes, absent evidence to the contrary, that historical figures meant what they said and said what they meant, then historical scholarship becomes meaningless. I could just as easily claim that the explorers were tongues-speaking charismatics or secret Satanists or closet Jehovah's Witnesses, but they kept quiet about their beliefs because they would not have been accepted at the time. Instead of engaging in such wild speculation, I will present the explorers' words as they stated them and their deeds as they happened, and take them at face value.

Others are uncomfortable with public expression of Christian faith and don't know how to handle it. Fearful of offending their readers or publishers, and not wanting to either promote Christianity or attack it, these writers decide that the best way to be neutral about Christianity is to avoid mentioning it. The result is an incomplete and innaccurate picture of the explorers — what they believed, what they did, why they did it, and what was its lasting impact.

Still others object that the study of Western civilization is overly Euro-centric. They argue that other cultures have contributed to the development of Western civilization and that their contributions are ignored and forgotten today. A number of black historians maintain that advanced civilizations (in many cases, Christian civilizations) existed in black Africa during the Middle Ages and before and that these have influenced Western culture.[3] Some Native Americans point to the advanced cultures of the Mayas, Aztecs, and Incas and also claim that the Iroquois had an advanced system of confederate republican government that influenced the thinking of Benjamin Franklin, Thomas Jefferson, and other American founding fathers.[4] These claims deserve further exploration, and to the extent they are based upon sound scholarship rather than merely "politically correct" thinking, they deserve recognition. But it is unnecessary to vilify Christianity in the process.

And then, some are determined to remake America into a secular or pagan society. To do so, they must move this nation away from its Christian foundations.

But if it can be proven that these Christian foundations never existed or that they were corrupt from the beginning, then their task becomes much easier.

Hence the attack on the founding fathers. Despite thorough and irrefutable proof to the contrary, the myth is still perpetrated that the framers of our Constitution and Declaration of Independence were Deists, Unitarians and skeptics rather than committed Christians. With a few exceptions like Franklin and Jefferson, this is pure fiction.[5]

And hence the attack on the explorers. If the Christian professions of Christopher Columbus and others can be proven insincere, if their deeds can be downplayed and their sins and shortcomings magnified, then this element of America's Christian past can be discredited and set aside.

And best of all, the explorers have been dead for centuries. They cannot rise up and defend themselves!

But in a way they can. Their words and deeds live on, available for all to read and hear. And they tell a different story from what is being told today.

When I speak of the explorers as Christians, I do not mean they did no wrong. Like me and the rest of us, they were flawed, sinful human beings. But if I, despite my sin, can call myself a Christian because Christ died for me and I trust His atoning grace, then I can be somewhat charitable toward the shortcomings of the explorers.

Yes, they did wrong. Sometimes their actions had unfortunate consequences, such as the spreading of disease. But this was an innocent mistake. No one at that time understood how disease is transmitted. No one could forsee that the Spanish explorers, having developed an immunity toward disease over many centuries, would unwittingly bring disease to Native Americans who, having no such immunity, would die by the thousands. But if the explorers can be blamed for this unforseeable consequence, then they should also be credited for the great medical advances that have taken place in America, the land they explored and settled.

And if the explorers are to be blamed for the shortcomings of Western culture — some of which represent the degeneration and rejection of Western culture rather than Western culture itself — then let us credit them for its achievements and contributions: art, music, architecture, ethics, liberty, law, government, a Constitution that has served as a model across the world, an economic system that has produced the greatest good for the greatest number and the highest level of prosperity the world has ever known, and a spirit of ingenuity and achievement that led to unparalleled medical and technological advances.

Some of the explorers' shortcomings were not innocent mistakes; some were downright sins. Slavery, even though widely accepted at the time, was wrong. So was land-stealing. So was promise-breaking. Part of the reason some people have turned against Christianity today is that our deeds sometimes do not live up to our words.

Neither do I suggest that spreading the gospel was the explorers' only motive. Their motives were a mixture of God and gold, with perhaps a dash of power and adventure thrown in as well. Remember, though, that they had to make their voyages profitable to satisfy the investors back home who financed their expeditions, and to pay the high costs of ships, crews, and provisions.

And I do not mean to convey the impression that the

explorers did nothing all day but pray, preach, and quote Scripture. Like the rest of us, much of their lives were consumed by day-to-day tasks.

When I say the explorers were Christians, I mean they believed the basic doctrines of Christianity and tried to practice its tenets, and the spread of Christianity was a major motivating factor for their voyages of discovery.

In this brief volume I have not attempted to present comprehensive biographies of these explorers. Rather, I have tried to present an aspect of their lives that is neglected in most accounts today and that is in danger of being badly maligned and distorted in the current attacks on the explorers, European civilization, Western culture, and the Christian religion on which they are based.

With Leif Ericson and his Norse adventurers we will sail among the icebergs of Greenland to the rocky coast of Baffin Island and Labrador. With the Crusaders we will ride through Jerusalem in blood up to the bridles of our horses. With Christopher Columbus we will endure storm, shipwreck, mutiny, and war with cannibals. And with Hernando Cortez we will march through scenes of carnage and gore that would make Conan the Barbarian tremble with fear.

Some readers may question the need for such graphic detail. I have included the stultifying battle scenes so the reader will know what these soldiers of Christ endured for the spread of Christian civilization; and I have passed on the conquistadors' descriptions of the bloodstained Aztec temples with their holocaust of human sacrifice, so the reader will know the true nature of the Aztec society the conquistadors fought so hard to displace. It is unfair to sit in judgment upon the explorers without considering what they were up against. The reader who believes I have included too much detail may take comfort in the knowledge that there is much I left out.

There is a reason for the extensive use of quotations. The accounts the explorers themselves present of the preaching they did and the adversaries they faced are so different from what is passed off as history today, that if I were to simply retell their story in my own words it would lack authority. I would rather you hear what Columbus himself says in his letters and journals and what his son Ferdinand says about him in his biography, what Cortez says in his own letters and how his foot soldier Bernal Diaz describes the conquest of Mexico in his five-volume eyewitness account as one of the conquerors. That way you can judge the credibility of their story on its own merit rather than having it filtered through me.

So with this background in mind, let us meet the early explorers!

ENDNOTES

[1]National Council of Churches, "A Faithful Response to the 500th Anniversary of the Arrival of Christopher Columbus," May 1990.

[2]Samuel Eliot Morison, *Admiral of the Ocean Sea* (Boston: Little, Brown & Co., 1942), p. 671.

[3]Basil Davidson, *Africa: A Voyage of Discovery*, four 57-minute videotapes (Chicago: Public Media Video, 1984).

[4]Bruce E. Johansen, *Forgotten Founders: How the American Indian Helped Shape Democracy* (Boston: Harvard Common Press, 1982).

[5]For a thorough, documented refutation of the myth that the framers of the U.S. Declaration of Independence and Constitution were Deists, see my volume, *Christianity and the Constitution* (Grand Rapids: Baker, 1987, 1991).

CHAPTER TWO

EXPLORERS BEFORE COLUMBUS: FOR ODIN OR CHRIST?

In 1976, while America celebrated the 200th anniversary of the Declaration of Independence, I enjoyed a three-week backpacking trip to Greenland. It was a thrilling experience — climbing the mountains, camping on the glaciers, hiking across flower-strewn mountain meadows.

Greenland is a land of rugged and savage beauty. The foehn winds blow off the glaciers and off the Atlantic, often with a force in excess of 100 mph, and temperatures in northern Greenland can reach -80 F. On the barren east coast mountains rise 12,000 feet right out of the sea, and passage is in some areas blocked by ice floes. Eighty percent of Greenland is under an icecap up to two miles thick. But no place on earth is more magnificent and awe-inspiring than Greenland on a sunny afternoon.

A special highlight for me was the visit to the old Norse ruins. I stood among the ruins of the old Norse church at Hvalsoy, the bishop's residence at Gardar, and the foundations of the great hall of Eric Thorvaldson, known today as Eric the Red. In my imagination the Vikings of old lived again and feasted in Eric's great hall, retelling their sagas of battles won and lost, of Valhalla and the gods.

And here in Eric's hall, nearly a thousand years ago,

plans were laid for Leif Ericson's voyage to the West, and Thorfinn's colonization of the western land called Vinland.

And I reflected *Here, on this windswept, mountainous coast of Greenland, is a birthplace of America.*

The Norse were not the first people to discover America. They may not have even been the first Europeans. Native Americans, somewhat misleadingly called Indians, have been here for thousands of years. The most common belief is that they crossed the Bering Strait from Siberia to Alaska and spread southward, though others have theorized that they crossed the Pacific by way of the Polynesian islands or that they came from the Middle East or even Africa. By whatever means they came, they are the true discoverers of America.

Dr. Barry Fell, professor emeritus of biology at Harvard, believes others besides Indians have visited and colonized America for thousands of years. In his detailed book *America B.C.* he discusses rock inscriptions, artifacts and other evidence indicating the presence of Celts, Phoenicians, Carthaginians, Egyptians and others dating long before Columbus, before the Viking explorations, and in some instances even before the birth of Christ.[1]

Charles Michael Boland, in his book *They All Discovered America*, presents evidence of a Roman voyage shortly after the birth of Christ and a Chinese voyage to America's Pacific coast in the fifth century A.D. He also narrates the Irish legend of St. Brendan the Bold and his expedition across the Atlantic to discover the fabled Fortunate Isle.[2] While some dismiss St. Brendan's voyage as fable, others take it seriously, and in 1976 five young adventurers left Ireland in a leather boat to re-enact St. Brendan's 4,000-mile voyage.

Evidence exists to support each of these voyages; in some cases the evidence is stronger than others. In this chapter on pre-Columbian voyages to America I have singled out the Norse expeditions because, of all the visits before Columbus, only the Viking expedition is undisputably accepted as fact.

For generations the Viking legends of Leif Ericson and Vinland have been told, but scholars were uncertain whether to believe them. But in 1961 Dr. Helge Ingstad discovered the sites of early settlements at L'Anse aux Meadows on the coast of Labrador. Norse artifacts have been discovered at this site and have been carbon dated to around A.D. 1000, the year of Leif Ericson's voyage according to the sagas.[3] Largely because of these discoveries, the presence of Norsemen in America is now accepted by all.

But while the L'Anse aux Meadows sites proved that the Norse had been to America and established a settlement around A.D. 1000, they do not prove that Leif Ericson was that settler, that L'Anse aux Meadows was actually the site of Leif's shelters, or that the Viking sagas are correct in every detail. The sagas, it must be remembered, were passed down by oral tradition for many generations before they were written down. The information about Norse America comes to us from several sagas, one of which is the *Saga of Olaf Trygvasson* which was written down by an Icelandic historian, Snorri Sturluson in the 1200s in his work known as *Heimskringla: The Sagas of the Norse Kings.*[4] Another is the *Kristni Saga*, which was written down in the 1200s and which tells of the Christianization of Iceland and mentions Vinland.[5] Others include the *Graenlendinga Saga (Saga of the Greenlanders)* contained in a work known as the Flatyjarbok written around A.D. 1307, *Eirik's Saga (Saga of Eric the Red)* which is contained in a fourteenth century work by Hauk Erlendsson known as *Hauksbok, the Saga of Einar Sokkason,* and the *Islendingabok (Book of the Icelanders),* which also contains accounts of Greenland and references to Vinland, compiled by Ari Thorgilsson around A.D. 1127).[6] Other pre-Columbian references to Vinland come from the German priest-historian Adam of Breman around A.D. 1075,[7] the English monk Nicholas of Lynn who apparently visited Greenland and points westward around A.D. 1360,[8] and the *Icelandic Annals.* Larchwood chests found at the Norse settlement of Herjolfness in southern Greenland are further proof that the Norse Greenlanders had been to America; larchwood is common in Newfoundland and Labrador but unknown in Greenland, Iceland, or Scandinavia.[9] No one knows the extent to which these sagas are true in every detail. Occasionally they conflict on details, and some of them contain superstitious matters such as dead men talking, but much of their content correlates with known history and geographical data.

Vikings are commonly associated with the old Norse pagan religion which emphasized the warrior virtues of courage and valor in battle. In keeping with their harsh climate and rugged terrain, the early Norse believed in a universe inhabited by frost giants and evil spirits which threatened to engulf the world. Their chief god was Odin, the All-Father, strong but not all-powerful, wise but not all-knowing. Other gods (children of Odin) personified forces of nature, such as Thor, the god of thunder; Balder, the god of springtime and beauty; Tyr, the god of iron and battle; Heimdal, the watchman of the gods; Freya, the goddess of fertility, and others. Powerful though these gods may be, their future is as grim as a harsh northern winter; for Ragnarok is coming, the Twilight of the Gods, when the frost giants will overpower the gods and bring on the never-ending winter.

But there is hope. When a warrior dies bravely in battle, the daughters of Odin, winged warrior-maidens called valkyries, bear his spirit to Valhalla, the great hall of Odin. There they fight all day and feast all night, the true Viking heaven — all in training for the Great Day of Ragnarok, when they will fight alongside Odin, Thor, Tyr and Heimdal against the frost giants in the Twilight of the Gods.[10]

This stern religion undoubtedly inspired the early Vikings in their warlike ways. But the discovery and colonization of Vinland took place just at the time Norway was being converted to Christianity. This conversion was a struggle and was led by two kings, Olaf Tryggvason (A.D. 995-1000) and his grandson, Olaf Haraldson, known as St. Olaf (A.D. 1016-1030).

In his younger days, Olaf Tryggvason was a swashbuckling Viking adventurer. The great-grandson of King Harold Harfagre (Fairhair), Olaf's father was killed during civil strife in Norway and as a child Olaf was sold as a slave in Russia. Later ransomed by an uncle named Sigurth Eiriksson, Olaf became a Viking warrior and campaigned in Russia, Greece, England, Germany, and elsewhere.

In Breman, Germany, Olaf met a warrior-priest named Thangbrand. Thangbrand carried a shield with a crucifix on it. When Olaf asked the meaning of the symbol, Thangbrand explained the gospel to him, and Olaf was converted. Thangbrand gave him the shield, which Olaf always carried and credited with saving his life on many occasions. Olaf again met Thangbrand in England, and in A.D. 995 the two set out to convert Norway to the "white Christ."

When he landed at Trondheim, Olaf laid claim to the throne of Norway as great-grandson of King Harold Harfagre. Tired of civil war, the people of Trondheim received him as king, and he soon consolidated the country under his rule.

He strove to win his people for Christ, sometimes by preaching, sometimes by force. As the saga relates,

> Now when Olaf Tryggvason had become king in Norway, he resided a long time in Vik during the summer. There, many of his kinsmen and relatives by marriage came to him. Many had been great friends of his father and welcomed him heartily. Then Olaf called his maternal uncles, Lothin, his stepfather, and his relatives Thorgeir and Hyrning, to a conference with him, and with the greatest earnestness laid before them the matter they themselves should take hold of, together with him, and then further with all their strength; which was, to preach the gospel throughout the kingdom. And he said he would succeed in christening all of Norway or else die. "I shall make you all great and powerful men, because I put most trust in you because of our kinship or other affinity." They all agreed to this and to do what they could and follow him in all that he proposed, together with all those who would follow their counsel.
>
> Very soon King Olaf made it clear to all the people that he would proclaim Christianity in all his realm. And the first to agree to this order were they

who before had accepted the faith. They were also the most powerful of those who were present at the time, and all others followed their example. Then all who dwelled in the eastern part of Vik were baptized, whereupon the king proceeded north in Vik and commanded all to accept Christianity; but those who spoke against it he punished severely, killing some, maiming others or driving them out of the country. As a result, all the dominions which King Tryggvi, his father, had ruled as well as those which had been subject to Harald of Grenland, his kinsman, now accepted Christianity as Olaf ordered; so that during the summer and following winter everyone in Vik was baptized.[11]

His missionary efforts were a mixed success; while most people outwardly accepted Christianity under some duress, some probably remained pagans in their hearts. Nevertheless, Olaf preached Christ to his people with all the fervor, and sometimes the folly, of a new convert. When he came to Rogalind he called for an assembly of the people:

... King Olaf arose and at first spoke gently to the farmers. Still, it was plain from his speech that he meant them to become Christians. He asked them with fair words to agree to that; but in the end he added that those who opposed him and would not comply with his demands would feel his wrath and suffer punishment and stern conditions wherever he could reach them.[12]

In the autumn of that same year (A.D. 997) he summoned an assembly of the western districts of Norway:

In the end the king offered them two alternatives: either to accept Christianity and be baptized, or else to fight it out with him. But since the farmers saw no chance to fight the king they decided on having all the people christened.[13]

The next year, at an assembly in Tunsberg, King Olaf ordered the expulsion of all magicians, sorcerers, and warlocks from Norway. He burned some of them and later executed others by the common Norse method of binding them to ocean skerries so they would drown when the tide came in. Later that year, at Maerin, he entered the pagan temple, where "he found [an image of] Thor sitting there as the most honored of all the gods, adorned with gold and silver. King Olaf lifted up the gold-adorned rod he held in his hand and struck Thor, so he fell from his pedestal. Then the king's men ran up and shoved all the gods from their pedestals."[14]

And so it went. Some accepted the gospel, some pretended to, some refused at their peril. Slowly the old pagan rites faded away, and along with them went the pagan practices of exposing infants and old people to die. Gradually the Norse gave up their Viking ways and settled down to a more peaceful way of life. Lest we judge Olaf too harshly for his methods of "evangelism," let us remember that this was an age of force, that religious liberty as we understand it today was an unknown concept, and that the pagans would have used force against King Olaf given the opportunity.

Meanwhile Olaf sent his old friend and mentor Thangbrand to convert the Icelanders. According to the Saga his motive was mixed:

[Thangbrand] was a man of great overbearing and much inclined to violence, but otherwise a good cleric and a brave fellow. However, because of his turbulent ways the king did not want to have him about him and entrusted him with the mission to journey to Iceland and convert that land to Christianity. He was given a merchantman, and it is told of his journey that he made land in Iceland in the South of Alptafjord in the Eastfjord District and stayed with Hall of Sitha during the winter following. Thangbrand preached Christianity in Iceland, and owing to his eloquence Hall let himself be baptized, together with his household and many other chieftains; but there were far more who opposed him. Thorvald Veili and the skald Vetrlithi composed scurrilous verses about Thangbrand, and he killed both. Thangbrand stayed two years in Iceland and had slain three persons before leaving.[15]

When Thangbrand returned to King Olaf's court, he told the king about the Icelanders' stubbornness and said he considered it unlikely that that land would ever be Christian.

The king became so furiously angry that he had the trumpets sounded to summon all Icelanders in the town, and said that all were to be killed. But Kjartan, Gizur, and Hjalti, as well as the others who at that time had been baptized, went before the king and said, "You will not want to go back on your word, sir king, because you have been saying that there is no man, however much he has done to provoke your wrath, who will not be pardoned by you if he will let himself be baptized and will give up heathenish ways. Now all Icelanders here are willing to let themselves be baptized; and we shall find ways and means to bring it about that Christianity is accepted in Iceland. There are here many influential men's sons from Iceland, and their fathers are likely to afford us great help in this matter. But Thangbrand proceeded there, as he did here with you, with overbearing, and committed manslaughter, and people there would not stand for that." Then the king began to listen to what they had to say. And then all Icelanders who were there were baptized.[16]

Later King Olaf sent Gizur the White and Hjalti Skeggjason to proclaim Christianity in Iceland, and the Icelandic Althing (Parliament) accepted Christianity as the official religion of the land in the year A.D. 1000.

But Eric the Red lived in Iceland during pagan times and followed the old gods. Around A.D. 982 Eric killed a man in a quarrel. The Althing found him guilty of manslaughter but, not having the power to impose punishment, sentenced him to three years "outlawry," meaning he was outside the protection of the law and the victim's relatives could legally kill him. Eric had to leave Iceland, and hearing that sailors off the west coast of Iceland had sighted land to the west, he decided to travel to that land.

Three years later he returned to Iceland, told the people about the land he had discovered, and called it Greenland. Some who have not seen Greenland have suggested that this was the tactic of a slick real estate promoter; but there is no greener, richer pasture anywhere than on the western coast of Greenland in summer, and the ice has a distinctive greenish hue. Eric persuaded twenty-five shiploads of colonists to come to Greenland, but due to storms at sea only fourteen of the ships arrived safely. The colonists established two settlements on the west coast of Greenland, Austerbygd (Eastern Settlement) near modern Juliannehaab, and the smaller Vesterbygd (Western Settlement) farther north near Godthaab.

At this time the Greenlanders were pagans. As Helge Ingstad says in *Land Under the Pole Star,*

> In general we are struck by the space given to superstition in old stories of Greenland — more than in Iceland and Norway. It was a wild, stern country where dangers abounded and where there was much to stimulate the imagination: endless inland ice, black mountains, blue-green glaciers with bottomless crevasses, Eskimoes, strange beasts, drift-ice that swept the coasts and, in the west, unknown shores beyond the horizon. Mighty and mysterious forces were at work and, as among the Eskimoes, thoughts took wing into a world of superstition.
>
> We hear much of dreams and omens, and particularly of ghosts, which people feared to an extent that we can scarcely imagine. In Eirik the Red's saga there is an account unique of its kind, dating from the early eleventh century, about a witch named Torbjorg.[17]

But the gospel came to Greenland in the person of Eric's son, Leif Ericson. As a young man and son of the "jarl" or chief of the Greenland colony, Leif decided to visit Norway around A.D. 999.

King Olaf received him in his court, and Leif stayed with King Olaf throughout the following winter. While there are a few factual discrepencies between the *Saga of Eirik the Red* and the *Saga of Olaf Trygvasson*, both agree that King Olaf preached the Christian faith to Leif, that Leif received the Christian faith and was baptized willingly, and that King Olaf then commissioned Leif to preach Christianity to the Greenlanders. As *Eirik's Saga* relates,

> On one occasion the king had a talk with Leif and said, "Are you intending to sail to Greenland this summer?"
>
> "Yes," replied Leif, "if you approve."
>
> "I think it would be a good idea," said the king. "You are to go there with a mission from me, to preach Christianity in Greenland."
>
> Leif said that it was for the king to command, but added that in his opinion the mission would be difficult to accomplish in Greenland. The king replied that he could think of no one better fitted for it than him—"and your good luck will see you through."
>
> "That will only be," replied Leif, "if I have the benefit of yours too."
>
> Leif set sail when he was ready; he ran into prolonged difficulties at sea, and finally came upon lands whose existence he had never suspected. There were fields of wild wheat growing there, and vines, and among the trees there were maples. They took some samples of all these things. Leif came across some shipwrecked seamen and brought them home with him and gave them all hospitality throughout the winter. He showed his great magnanimity and goodness by bringing Christianity to the country and by rescuing these men; he was known as Leif the Lucky.
>
> He made land at Eiriksfjord [in southern

Greenland] and went home to Brattahlid, where he
was given a good welcome. He at once began preaching Christianity and the Catholic faith throughout
the country; he revealed to the people King Olaf
Tryggvason's message, telling them what excellence
and what glory there was in this religion.

Eirik was reluctant to abandon his old religion;
but his wife, Thjodhild, was converted at once, and
she had a church built not too close to the farmstead.
This building was called Thjodhild's Church, and
there she and many others who had accepted Christianity would offer up their prayers. Thjodhild refused to live with Eirik after she was converted, and
this annoyed him greatly.[18]

Eirik's saga gives no indication that Eric ever accepted
Christianity. The *Saga of Olaf Tryggvason,* on the other
hand, relates that Eric reacted negatively to the priest who
accompanied Leif on the journey. He praised his son for
rescuing the shipwrecked seamen, but criticized him for
bringing the "shyster" priest, saying the two actions can-
celled each other out. Nevertheless, according to Olaf's
Saga, Eric finally did allow himself to be baptized.[19] (One
might debate whether Thjodhild's methods of "evangelism"
were more biblical or more effective than King Olaf's!)

Undoubtedly Eric was not the only holdout, but as a
whole the Greenlanders accepted Christianity. As the colony
grew, sixteen churches were established, twelve in the
Eastern Settlement and four in the smaller Western Settlement. Greenland was at first placed under the arch-diocese
of Hamburg-Bremen, later under that of Lund, Sweden,
and finally, under the new archbishopric established in
Trondheim, Norway. Eventually two monasteries were
established: one dedicated to St. Augustine and one to St.
Olaf, and also a Benedictine nunnery. Around A.D. 1113
Eirik Gnupsson became the first Bishop of Greenland,
probably residing at Sandness in the Western Settlement.
But Bishop Gnupsson sailed westward to Vinland in A.D.
1121, bringing "both emigrants and the faith," and was not
heard from again.

Two years later a jarl named Einar Sokkeson sailed to Norway to plead the Greenlanders' case for the appointment of a new bishop. During the deliberations, Einar produced a live polar bear as a gift for King Sigurd Magnusson, also known as Sigurd Jorsalfare (Jerusalemfarer) or Sigurd the Crusader. His mission was successful. As Ingstad says, "A polar bear in exchange for a bishop!"[20] The bishopric was established in Gardar, in the Eastern Settlement, where the ruins of the bishop's residence may still be seen today.

The Greenland settlements are most valuable to archeologists and historians because their frozen graves contain some of the best-preserved skeletons and clothing in the world for that period of time. Vadmal clothing of the type worn in Scandinavia in the 1400s has been found largely intact in the graves. The graves also contain many religious artifacts including crosses, crucifixes, bishop's staffs, signet rings, etc. Runic inscriptions on graves frequently give testimony to the faith of the people: "God Almighty protect Gudleiv well." "Torleiv made this Cross in praise and adoration of God Almighty." "Jesus Christ help." "Christ was born for us."[21]

The harsh climate and limited population of Greenland presented some unique problems for the Church. The Pope's prohibition of marriage within seven degrees of consanguinity was a hardship for the Greenlanders, so the Archbishop of Trondheim asked Pope Alexander to give the Greenlanders permission to marry within four degrees. The Pope refused, but gave the archbishop authority to give special dispensation for marriages within five, six, or seven degrees.

Because of the lack of grapes in Greenland, Pope Gregory wrote to Archbishop Sigurd in A.D. 1237 authorizing the Greenlanders to use a substitute (probably beer) for wine at Communion. Medieval letters reflect that the Greenlanders paid the special Crusade taxes and Peter's Pence in local commodities including walrus tusks, skins, fish, and wool. The amount collected for the Peter's Pence tax indicates that the Greenland population in the late 1200s was around 4,200.

Since Greenland is in the Western Hemisphere, the colony may be the first permanent European settlement in the West. But Norse Greenlanders went westward from Greenland and explored and colonized the North American continent.

When Leif returned to his father's house from his journey to Norway in A.D. 1000, he told his kinsmen of the lands he had seen while blown off course. There in Eric's Hall that winter, plans were laid for an expedition to those lands the following summer.

The *Graenlendinga Saga* describes Leif's expedition in the fullest detail. Leif purchased a ship from Bjarni Herjolfson, who had previously sighted lands to the west while blown off course during a storm, and sailed with a crew of thirty-four Norse Greenlanders and one "Southerner named Tyrkir" (probably a German). As they sailed, they discovered three lands. The first they called Helluland, which literally means "flat rock land." As the Saga describes the land, "There was no grass to be seen, and the hinterland was covered with great glaciers, and between glaciers and shore the land was like one great slab of rock."[22] This seems to correspond in description and geographical location to Baffin Island, just west of Greenland.

They sailed on and sighted a second land: "This country was flat and wooded, with white sandy beaches wherever they went; and the land sloped gently down to the sea."[23] They called this land Markland, meaning "forest-land," and it seems to correspond to Labrador, on the Canadian coast south of Baffin Island.

They sailed two days further and came to an island located in a sound with a headland jutting out to the north. They entered the sound and followed a river upstream to a lake, where they went ashore and decided to stay for the winter. They built shelters, and they discovered grapes in this land, so they named it Vinland, meaning vine-land or wine-land.

The location of Vinland is more difficult to pinpoint as a number of sites fit the description. The Saga says the days and nights were more even than those of Greenland and Iceland; on the shortest day of the year the sun rose by 9:00

a.m. and set not earlier than 3:00 p.m. This would place Vinland somewhere between New Jersey and the Gulf of St. Lawrence. The Saga also says salmon were large and plentiful in the river and lake; salmon usually are not found on the east coast farther south than the Hudson River. While various writers have identified Vinland as far north as Ungava Bay at the northern tip of Labrador[24] and as far south as Florida, Newfoundland and New England are the most common and most likely conclusions.

Leif and his men spent an uneventful winter in Vinland and returned to Greenland in the spring, taking with them a load of timber and grapes.

The following year Leif's brother, Thorvald Ericson, set sail to explore Vinland more fully. He and his thirty men spent two winters in Leif's shelters, exploring the area during the summers. During the second summer Thorvald discovered a beautiful promontary that jutted out between two fjords and said he would like to settle there for awhile.

Shortly thereafter they had two encounters with "Skraelings," an apparent reference to American Indians. In the first encounter they killed all but one. The cause of the fight is not stated. Then they were attacked by a large number of Skraelings in skin-boats, and while they successfully repelled the attack, Thorvald was mortally wounded by an arrow. He told his men,

> This will lead to my death. I advise you now to go back as soon as you can. But first I want you to take me to the headland I thought so suitable for a home. I seem to have hit on the truth when I said that I would settle there for awhile. Bury me there and put crosses at my head and feet, and let the place be called Korsness [Place of Crosses] for ever afterwards.[25]

His men did as he had asked, and they then returned without him to Eiriksfjord in Greenland.

The location of Korsness has been the subject of much conjecture. In 1831, in Fall River, Massachusetts, in a location that could correspond to the description of Korsness, a skeleton in medieval armor was unearthed. The Danish archeologist Carl Christian Rafn concluded that the body was that of Thorvald Ericson, and in his poem "The Skeleton in Armor" Henry Wadsworth Longfellow wove a love story of a Viking warrior and maiden and tied the skeleton with the enigmatic stone tower in Newport, Rhode Island. Unfortunately, the skeleton was destroyed in an 1843 fire. The armor was dispersed to several museums, and scholars disagree on whether it is Norse or English. The same dispute exists concerning the origin of the Newport Tower. Many insist it is colonial but its structure is more medieval and historical evidence indicates it precedes the colonial period.[26]

The third brother, Thorstein Ericson, made plans to sail to Vinland to recover his brother's body and return it to Greenland. Such a voyage may sound far-flung, but it was consistent with the belief and custom of the Norse Greenlanders. For the early Norse Christians, being buried in a churchyard was of vital importance ("grave" importance might be more appropriate); if not essential for salvation, it provided some assurance thereof. In Greenland, when a priest was unavailable to assist at a burial, a stake was often driven into the ground and upon the dead person's breast; when the priest arrived, the stake was removed and holy water was poured into the hole onto the corpse. The Sagas tell of a man known as Lik-Lodin (Lik means corpse) whose life mission was to traverse the barren coasts of northern and eastern Greenland to retrieve the bodies of shipwrecked Norsemen and bring them to the churchyard for burial.[27]

However, Thorstein died before he could sail to Vinland. His widow Gudrid then married a nobleman from Norway named Thorfinn Karlsefni. Karlsefni made plans to establish a colony in Vinland, using Leif's shelters, and sailed around A.D. 1010. The *Graenlendinga Saga* says he had sixty-five colonists with him, plus livestock; *Eirik's Saga* says one-hundred-sixty. They passed Helluland (Baffin Island) and Markland (Labrador) and settled in the area of Vinland, though again the exact site is uncertain.

Thorfinn and his colonists were mostly Christians, but

apparently at least two pagans were among them: Eric's illegitimate daughter Freydis Ericsdottir and Thorhall the Hunter. The following account from *Eirik's Saga* shows the perpetual conflict between Christianity and paganism. During the first severe winter the colonists were short of provisions:

> Then they prayed to God to send them something to eat, but the response was not as prompt as they would have liked . . . A little later a whale was washed up and they rushed to cut it up. No one recognized what kind of a whale it was, not even Karlsefni, who was an expert on whales. The cooks boiled the meat, but when it was eaten it made them all ill.
>
> Then Thorhall the Hunter walked over and said, "Has not Redbeard [Thor] turned out to be more successful than your Christ? This was my reward for the poem I composed in honour of my patron, Thor; he has seldom failed me."
>
> When the others realized this they refused to use the whalemeat and threw it over a cliff, and committed themselves to God's mercy. Then a break came in the weather to allow them to go out fishing, and after that there was no scarcity of provisions.[28]

In their hour of need the colonists as a group turned to God. When one of the pagans claimed the whale was actually a gift from Thor, the majority threw the meat away rather than eat meat that was supplied by a pagan god. They then threw themselves on God's mercy, and God answered their prayer and supplied their needs.

These colonists stayed in Vinland for about three years. During this time a child was born to Thorfinn and Gudrid Karlsefni. They named him Snorri Karlsefnisson, and he may have been the first European born on the North American continent. Toward the end they had several violent confrontations with Scraelings. Though they successfully repelled the attacks, they soon realized they could not withstand the Indians indefinitely, so they returned to

Greenland. A year later the family moved to Iceland, where the "all-American" child Snorri became the ancestor of many prominent Icelandic families.[29]

Eric's illegitimate daughter Freydis was an unprincipled pagan woman, but she also appears to have possessed strength, determination and resourcefulness. Around A.D. 1014 she set sail for Vinland with about sixty-five men and some women, and they spent the winter near Leif's shelters. The brief history of this colony is filled with deceit and bloodshed, mostly on the part of Freydis, and the following spring the survivors returned to Greenland.[30]

Except possibly for the obscure reference to Bishop Eric Gnupsson in A.D. 1121, there are no more confirmed Norse attempts to colonize the North American continent. After the Freydis fiasco, Vinland fades into mystery. There are accounts of further voyages to America, and possibly even colonization, but their authenticity is unconfirmed. But the Greenland colonies flourished as Christian communities throughout the 1100s and 1200s. During the 1300s they declined, and sometime in the 1400s or 1500s they apparently ceased to exist.

What caused their demise? That's a question for "Unsolved Mysteries!" Many theories have been advanced.

One factor may be neglect by the Scandinavian powers. In A.D. 1319 Norway came under the domination of Sweden, and in A.D. 1380 Norway came under the sovereignty of Denmark. The Swedes and the Danes were more interested in Germany, England, Russia, and nations of the Hanseatic League to the south and the east, rather than to tiny colonies in the distant Atlantic.

In 1349 the Black Plague hit Norway. Beset with internal problems, the Norse became even less interested in places like Greenland. It is possible the plague hit Greenland, too.

During the tenth century (the 900s A.D.) the climate of the North Atlantic became somewhat warmer, making navigation easier. But during the 1300s the climate grew colder again. Not only did this make navigation between Scandinavia, Iceland, and Greenland more difficult but it also made it more difficult to live off the land and sea. Most of us do not realize that a drop of just one or two degrees in the average ocean temperature can cause fish to move hundreds of miles southward.

The Dorset Eskimo culture began moving northward as the climate warmed during the 900s. The sagas relate very few contacts between Vikings and Eskimoes; occasionally Eskimoes are referred to as "trolls!"[31] They generally stayed in northern Greenland during the period of Norse colonization. But as the climate cooled in the 1300s, the Thule Eskimoes began moving south. This may have led to conflict, intermarriage, or both.

The Western Settlement, considerably smaller and 300 miles farther north, was the first to decline. In A.D. 1342 Father Ivar Bardson, an Icelandic priest, visited the Western Settlement and found it abandoned. He reported that the large Sandness Church was still standing and that there were many horses, goats, cows and sheep, but no people, either Christian or heathen. The Icelandic Annals contain this entry for that year:

> 1342. The inhabitants of Greenland fell voluntarily away from the true faith and the Christian religion, and after having given up all good manners and true virtues, turned to the people of America. Some say that Greenland lies very near the western lands of the world.[32]

The reference to the "inhabitants of Greenland" clearly refers only to the Western Settlement, since it is known that the Eastern Settlement continued to exist thereafter. The anachronistic reference to "America" occurs because part of the Annals were destroyed in a church fire around A.D. 1630 and were reconstructed by Bishop Gisle Oddson.

The statement that the colonists of the Western Settlement "turned to the people of America" suggests that they abandoned their settlement and sailed westward to the North American continent. But it appears that the statement is conjecture and that the author had no certain knowledge of what had happened to them.

In A.D. 1354 King Magnus Erickson commissioned an

Icelandic Lawspeaker (judge) named Paul Knudsen to conduct an expedition to Greenland to find out what had happened to the Norse Greenlanders and, if necessary, restore them to the Christian faith. The decree read as follows:

> Magnus, by the grace of God, King of Norway, Sweden and Skaane, sends to all men who see or hear this letter good health and happiness.
>
> We desire to make known to you that you [Paul Knudsen] are to take the men who shall go in the knarr [the royal trading vessell] whether they be named or not named . . . from my bodyguard and also from among the retainers of other men whom you may wish to take on the voyage who are best qualified to accompany him, whether as officers or men. We ask that you accept this our command with a right good will for the cause, inasmuch as *we do it for the honor of God, and for the sake of our soul, and for the sake of our predecessors who in Greenland established Christianity and have maintained it until this time, and we will not let it perish in our days* [emphasis added]. Know this for truth, that whoever defies this our command shall meet with our serious displeasure and receive full punishment.
>
> Executed in Bergen, Monday after Simon and Judah's Day in the six and thirtieth year of our rule [1354]. By Orm Ostenson, our regent, sealed.[33]

It is not known whether the expedition ever sailed. If it did, what would Knudsen have done upon reaching the Western Settlement and finding it abandoned? Given the 1347 entry in the Annals stating that the colonists went westward, Knudsen might have sailed to the North American continent, possibly exploring the Atlantic coast or possibly exploring Hudson Bay and inland rivers. The controversial Kensington Runestone, found near Alexandria, Minnesota, in 1898, bears the date 1362 and tells the story of a Norse expedition and an encounter with Indians, closing with "Ave Maria, save us from evil." If genuine, the runestone might have been left by the Knudsen expedition; but scholars are divided on its authenticity.[34]

The Western Settlement, then, was abandoned sometime prior to A.D. 1347. Possibly its inhabitants moved westward to America, where they may have intermarried with Indians.

The Eastern Settlement continued at least into the following century. The Icelandic Annals record that a ship from Markland (Labrador) was blown off-course in 1406, and its crew remained in Greenland four years. The following incident from the Annals of 1407 reveals that witchcraft and immorality were present among the Greenlanders, but also that they were officially disapproved and severely punished:

> A man in Greenland named Kollgrim was burned for lying with another man's wife who was called Steinunn and was a daughter of the lawman Rafn who perished in the landslide at Langelid. She married Torgrim Solvesson. Kollgrim enticed her with the black arts, and was later burned in accordance with the law. The wife was never afterwards in her right mind and died within a short time.[35]

The Annals also relate that one of the crewmen of this ship, Torstein Olavsson, married a Greenland girl named Sigrid Bjornsdattir on Holy Cross Day (September 16), 1408. The wedding took place at the Hvalsey Church, best-preserved of the Norse ruins in Greenland, and many were present at the wedding. The couple went to live in Iceland, and their descendents became a leading family.[36]

From that point on the fate of the Greenlanders is shrouded in mystery. A letter by Pope Nicholas V dated A.D.1448 describes a pirate attack upon Greenland:

> Thirty years ago, from the adjacent coasts of the heathen, the barbarians came with a fleet, attacked the inhabitants of Greenland most cruelly, and so devastated the mother-country and the holy buildings with fire and sword that there remained on that

island no more than nine parish churches which are said to lie farthest away and which they [the pirates] could not attain because of the steep mountains. The pitiable inhabitants of both sexes, and especially those whom they deemed strong and fit for continual burdens of slavery such as their tyranny imposed, they carried away prisoner to their own country. But, as is added to the same complaint, because the greater number have since returned from this captivity to their own homes and have here and there repaired the ruins of their dwellings, they most earnestly desire to restore and extend divine service.[37]

The letter is puzzling. Who were these "barbarians" from the "adjacent coasts of the heathen?" Eskimoes seem unlikely; they did not practice slavery, and their legends of the Norse Greenlanders reflect generally friendly relationships. Their legends also record pirate attacks and claim that they and the Norse fought side by side against the pirates.[38] More likely the pirates were European, or possibly Arabian or Berber. A 1432 treaty between King Erik of Norway and King Henry VI of England provided that the victims of English pirate attacks upon Norway and Iceland were to be returned to their homes.

Even more puzzling is the fact that, despite the Greenlanders' expressed desire to "restore and extend divine service," the Church apparently did not send any more priests or bishops to Greenland.

Problems of communication were part of the reason. When Bishop Olaf died in 1280, he was not replaced until eight years later. Bishop Thord died in 1314, and the Church continuously received erroneous reports about his successor, Bishop Arni. First it was thought that Arni died in 1325; then, in 1340, the Church was informed that Arni had in fact survived until 1328. So in 1340 the Archbishop of Trondheim consecrated Jon Erikson Skalle as Bishop of Greenland; however, Bishop Skalle apparently never arrived in Greenland. In fact Bishop Arni was still alive, and he functioned as bishop until his death in 1349; however, the Church in Norway was not informed of his death until 1364.

The last bishop known to have resided in Greenland was Bishop Alf, who served from 1368 until his death in 1377. Thereafter, other clerics were given the title of Bishop of Greenland but did not reside in or visit Greenland, with the exception of Bishop Anders who probably resided in Greenland around 1406.[39] The last titular Bishop of Greenland was Vincenz Kampe in A.D.1537; but he probably never visited Greenland, and in fact the Greenland colonies had probably ceased to exist before that time.

In 1492 Pope Alexander VI wrote an interesting letter:

> It is said that Greenland is an island near the edge of the world and that its inhabitants have neither bread, wine, nor oils and live on dried fish and milk. Because of the ice that surrounds the island, sailings there are rare, for land can only be made there in August when the ice has receded. For that reason it is thought that no ship has sailed there for at least eighty years, and no bishop or priest has been there. As a consequence, most of the inhabitants have abandoned their Christian faith, and the only remembrance they still preserve of it is that once a year they exhibit the corporal [cloth altar covering upon which Communion was served] that was used by their last bishop about a hundred years ago.[40]

What was Pope Alexander's source of information? What caused him to think the Greenlanders had abandoned Christianity? Could he or one of his priests have mistaken the report in the *Icelandic Annals* concerning the Western Settlement for all of Greenland?

Helge Ingstad flatly rejects the suggestion that the Eastern Greenlanders had left the faith:

> It appears that the Norse Greenlanders held fast to Christianity to the last — even after the link with Norway was broken. Archeological finds all point to

this; not one suggests that the people reverted to heathendom. Bodies from as late as about 1500 or so have been uncovered in Herjolfnes churchyard, clad in their strange woollen garments, with hands folded and often a little wooden cross at their breast.[41]

And then comes the troubling question: Knowing the plight of the Norse colonies, why didn't Pope Alexander send a bishop priest to Greenland? Ingstad addresses this problem:

> One can understand that the German Danish-Norwegian kings in Copenhagen should have left the Norse Greenlanders in the lurch; for the Danes, Greenland was something quite alien and outside their traditions. But for the Catholic Church it was another matter: throughout several hundred years it has assumed obligations toward the people in that far country. And now it failed them. This is a dark page in the history of the Church.[42]

The *Catholic Encyclopedia* records that in A.D. 1516 Bishop Erik Valkendorf of Trondheim tried to launch an expedition to Greenland "to assist the lost Norse brethren," but for unknown reasons the expedition either did not take place or failed.[43] In 1530 Christian III, Norway's first Lutheran king, encouraged his countrymen to homestead in Greenland but found no takers; according to the *Catholic Encyclopedia* "the perils of the sea journey deterred his subjects."[44]

The embers of curiosity about the Norse colonies continued to smolder and occasionally were fanned into flame. In 1721 a Norwegian missionary named Hans Egede set out with his family for Greenland to rediscover the Norse colonies and convert them to the Lutheran faith. He didn't find them, though he did see an occasional Eskimo with blue eyes or blond hair, suggesting possible strains of intermarriage. He devoted the rest of his life to preaching the gospel to the Eskimoes, eventually winning their trust and converting many. Even today, a monument in

Juliannehaab fondly remembers Egede as "the Apostle of Greenland."[45] Greenland remains mostly Lutheran to this day.

Nevertheless, Egede clung fast to his original dream. Not long before he died in 1758 he declared,

> Concerning the old Austerbygd [Eastern Settlement] of Greenland, I believe beyond a doubt that it survives and is inhabited by people of pure Norwegian Extraction, which by God's help in due time and when Occasion offers, may be discovered.[46]

And so, Viking Greenland and Viking America faded into the mists of time. The jarls continued to tell their sagas in halls of Iceland and Norway, but throughout the rest of Europe their exploits were largely forgotten.

Had Christopher Columbus heard of Leif Ericson? His writings give no evidence that he had. But Columbus did visit Iceland around 1477. Morison doubts that Columbus heard the Vinland saga since there is no evidence he understood Icelandic,[47] but Ingstad believes it is only reasonable to assume he had.[48]

In any event, the Viking ruins still stand today. Amid the windswept mountains of Greenland, they are a monument to a brave and rugged colony of Christian pioneers in a harsh and foreign land.

ENDNOTES

[1]Barry Fell, *America B.C.* (New York: Pocket Books, 1976, 1989).

[2]Charles Michael Boland, *They All Discovered America* (New York: Doubleday, 1963).

[3]Helge Ingstad, *Westward to Vinland* (New York: St. Martins Press, 1969).

[4]Snorri Sturluson, *Heimskringla: History of the Kings of Norway*, 13th century work trans. by Lee M. Hollander (Austin: University of Texas Press, 1964, 1967). The most complete discussion of the L'Anse aux Meadows sites is found in Helge Ingstad, *Westward to Vinland* (New York: St. Martin's Press, 1969).

[5]*The Vinland Sagas: The Norse Discovery of America*, trans. & intro. by Magnus Magnusson and Hermann Palsson (Baltimore: Penguin Books, 1965), p. 29.

[6]Ingstad, *Vinland*, pp. 25-27.

[7]Id., pp. 24-25.

[8]Ingstad, *Vinland*, p. 95.

[9]Magnusson, p. 28.

[10]For old Norse mythology and religion generally, Paul B. Du Chaillu, *The Viking*

Age Vols. I & II (New York: Scribner, 1889); Harald Hveberg, *Of Gods and Giants* (Dreyer, 1982); H.R. Ellis Davidson, *Gods and Myths of the Viking Age* (New York: Bell, 1981).

[11]Sturluson, Ch. 53, pp. 195-96.

[12]Id., Ch. 55, p. 197.

[13]Id., Ch. 59, p. 199.

[14]Id., Chs. 62-69, pp. 201-208.

[15]Id., Ch. 73, p. 209.

[16]Id., Ch. 84, pp. 217-18.

[17]Helge Ingstad, *Land Under the Pole Star* (New York: St. Martin's Press, 1966), p. 193.

[18]Magnusson, pp. 85-6.

[19]Sturluson, Ch. 96, p. 228.

[20]Ingstad, *Pole Star*, p. 196.

[21]Id., *Pole Star*, pp. 219, 220.

[22]Magnusson, p 55.

[23]Id.

[24]James Robert Enterline, *Viking America: The Norse Crossings and Their Legacy* (New York: Doubleday, 1972). Enterline argues that the word "vin" means pasture rather than vines or grapes and thus believes Vinland was farther north than others have placed it.

[25]Magnusson, p. 61.

[26]Boland, pp. 236-42. Longfellow's poem "The Skeleton in Armor" may reflect more nineteenth century American romanticism than sound Norse scholarship but is nevertheless reprinted below:

THE SKELETON IN ARMOR

Speak! speak! thou fearful guest!
Who, with thy hollow breast
Still in rude armor drest,
    Comest to daunt me!
Wrapt not in Eastern balms,
But with thy fleshless palms
Stretched, as if asking alms,
    Why dost thou haunt me?

Then, from those cavernous eyes
Pale flashes seemed to rise,
As when the Northern skies
    Gleam in December;
And, like the water's flow
Under December's snow,
Came a dull voice of woe
    From the heart's chamber.

I was a Viking old!
My deeds, though manifold,
No Skald in song has told,
    No Saga taught thee!
Take heed, that in thy verse
Thou dost the tale rehearse,
Else dread a dead man's curse;
    For this I sought thee.

Far in the Northern Land,
By the wild Baltic's strand,
I, with my childish hand,
    Tamed the gerfalcon;
And, with my skates fast-found,
Skimmed the half-frozen Sound,
That the poor whimpering hound
    Trembled to walk on.

Oft to his frozen lair
Tracked I the grisly bear,
While from my path the hare
    Fled like a shadow;
Oft through the forest dark
Followed the were-wolf's bark,
Until the soaring lark
    Sang from the meadow.

But when I older grew,
Joining a corsair's crew,
O'er the dark sea I flew
    With the marauders.
Wild was the life we led;
Many the souls that sped,
Many the hearts that bled,
    By our stern orders.

Many a wassail-bout
Wore the long Winter out;
Often our midnight shout
    Set the cocks crowing,
As we the Berserk's tale
Measured in cups of ale,
Draining the oaken pail,
    Filled to o'erflowing.

Once as I told in glee
Tales of the stormy sea,
Soft eyes did gaze on me,
    Burning yet tender;
And as the white stars shine
On the dark Norway pine
On that dark heart of mine
    Fell their soft spendor.

I wooed the blue-eyed maid,
Yielding, yet half afraid,
And in the forest's shade
    Our vows were plighted.
Under its loosened vest
Fluttered her little breast
Like birds within their nest
    By the hawk frighted.

Bright in her father's hall
Shields gleamed upon the wall,
Loud sang the minstrels all,
    Chanting his glory;
When of old Hildebrand
I asked his daughter's hand,
Mute did the minstrels stand
    To hear my story.

While the brown ale he quaffed,
Loud then the champion laughed,
And as the wind-gusts waft
    The sea-foam brightly,
So the loud laugh of scorn,
Out of those lips unshorn,
From the deep drinking-horn
    Blew the foam lightly.

She was a Prince's child,
I but a Viking wild,
And though she blushed & smiled,
    I was discarded!
Should not the dove so white
Follow the sea-mew's flight,
Why did they leave that night
    Her nest unguarded?

Scarce had I put to sea,
Bearing the maid with me,
Fairest of all was she
    Among the Norsemen!
When on the white sea-strand,
Waving his armed hand,
Saw we old Hildebrand,
    With twenty horsemen.

Then launched they to the blast,
Bent like a reed each mast,
Yet we were gaining fast,
    When the wind failed us;
And with a sudden flaw
Came round the gusty Skaw,
So that our foe we saw
    Laugh as he hailed us.

And as to catch the gale
Round veered the flapping sail,
'Death!' was the helmsman's hail,
    'Death without quarter!'
Mid-ships with iron keel
Struck we her ribs of steel;
Down her black hulk did reel
    Through the black water!

As with his wings aslant,
Sails the fierce cormorant,
Seeking some rocky haunt
    With his prey laden,
So toward the open main,
Beating to sea again,
Through the wild hurricane,
    Bore I the maiden.

Three weeks we westward bore,
And when the storm was o'er,
Cloud-like we saw the shore
    Stretching to leeward;
There for my lady's bower
Built I the lofty tower,
Which, to this very hour,
    Stands looking seaward.

There lived we many years;
Time dried the maiden's tears;
She had forgot her fears,
    She was a mother;
Death closed her mild blue eyes,
Under that tower she lies;
Ne'er shall the sun arise
    On such another!

Still grew my bosom then,
Still as a stagnant fen!
Hateful to me were men,
  The sunlight hateful!
In the vast forest here,
Clad in my warlike gear,
Fell I upon my spear,
  Oh, death was grateful!

Thus, seamed with many scars,
Bursting these prison bars,
Up to its native stars
  My soul ascended!
There from the flowing bowl
Deep drinks the warrior's soul,
Skoal! to the Northland! skoal!"
  Thus the tale ended.

[27]Ingstad, *Pole Star*, pp. 98-9, 123, 218, 237.

[28]Magnusson, pp. 70-72, 96.

[29]Id.

[30]Id., pp. 67-70.

[31]Ingstad, *Pole Star*, pp. 106, 212.

[32]*Icelandic Annals*, 1342.

[33]Hjalmar R. Holand, *A Pre-Columbian Crusade to America* (New York: Twayne Publishers, 1962), p. 24; cf. Ingstad, *Pole Star*, p. 167.

[34]Many books have been written on the Kensington Runestone and other possible Norse findings in inland North America. Those defending the authenticity of the Runestone include Hjalmar Holand, *A Pre-Columbian Crusade to America*, op., cit.; Holand, *Explorations in America Before Columbus* (New York: Twayne, 1956); Robert A. Hall, Jr., Professor Emeritus, Cornell U., *The Kensington Runestone Is Genuine* (Columbia, SC: Hornbeam Press, 1982; Alf Monge and O. G. Landsverk, *Norse Medieval Cryptography in Runic Carvings* (Glendale, California: Norseman Press, 1967); Orval Friedrich, *Early Vikings and the Ice Age* (Elma, Iowa: Friedrich, 1984); Barry Fell, *America B.C.*, op. cit.; and others. Among those doubting the Runestone are Erik Wahlgren, *The Kensington Runestone: A Mystery Solved* (Madison: U of Wisconsin Press, 1958; and Theodore C. Blegen, *The Kensington Rune Stone: New Light on an Old Riddle* (St. Paul: Minnesota Historical Society, 1968). Twenty years ago the Runestone was rejected by most scholars but accepted by many amateur historians, but in recent years the tide of opinion among scholars seems to have shifted somewhat in its favor, particularly with the works of Hall and Landsverk. In 1984 Orval Friedrich tied the runestone issue into the creation-evolution controversy. Noting that the runestone as translated refers to "this island," Rev. Friedrich says the knoll upon which the runestone was found was much more likely to be an island surrounded by water is A.D. 1362 if one accepts the creation and flood models of origins rather than the evolution model which postulates a much older ice age and much older Earth. His self-published book *Early Vikings and the Ice Age* may be obtained through Rev. Friedrich, Elma, IA 50628.

[35]Ingstad, *Pole Star*, pp. 178, 179.

[36]Ingstad, *Pole Star*, pp. 178, 180, 288.

[37]Letter of Pope Nicholas V, A.D. 1448, Catholic Encyclopedia, 1907 ed, "Greenland."

[38]Knud J. Krogh, *Viking Greenland* (Copenhagen, Denmark: National Museum, 1967), pp. 122-24.

[39]Holand, *Explorations in America Before Columbus*, pp. 120-21; Ingstad, *Pole Star*, pp. 200-01.

[40]Letter of Pope Alexander VI, 1492, *Catholic Encyclopedia*, 1907, "Greenland;" Ingstad, *Pole Star*, p. 288.

[41]Ingstad, *Pole Star*, p. 208.

[42]Ingstad, *Pole Star*, pp. 208-09.

[43]*Catholic Encyclopedia*, 1907, "Greenland."

[44]Id.

[45]Erling Nicolai Rolfsrud, *White Angakok: Hans Egede and the Greenlanders* (Rock Island, Illinois: Augustana Book Concern, 1952). I personnaly observed and read the monument to Egede as the "Apostle of Greenland" on a backpacking trip to Greenland, Juliannehaab, August 1976.

[46]Rolfsrud, id.; Ingstad, *Pole Star*, pp. 296, 297.

[47]Samuel Eliot Morison, *Admiral of the Ocean Sea* (Boston:

Little, Brown & Co., 1942), pp. 24-26.

[48]Ingstad, *Pole Star*, p. 169.

CHAPTER THREE

THE EUROPEAN MINDSET 1492: THE CRESCENT OR THE CROSS?

Just as American adults in the year 1992 have grown up under the threat of Communism, so European adults in the year 1492 had grown up under the threat of Islam.

Particularly during the 1950s, Americans were concerned that the forces of Communism threatened to engulf the world. Marx and Engels had promised exactly that. The Communists had seized power in the Soviet Union in 1917, in China in 1948, and together with Eastern Europe, Southeast Asia, and Cuba, controlled nearly one third of the world's land mass and nearly one half of the world's population. Americans took seriously Nikita Khrushchev's boast "We will bury you!" and despite the remarkable events of 1989-91, I am not yet convinced that Communism has collapsed and the threat is over.

Remembering how Americans felt about Communism in 1950 helps us understand how Europeans feared Islam in 1492.

Humanly speaking, Islam threatened medieval and renaissance Europe much as Communism threatens, or threatened, the Free World of the twentieth century. Like Communism, Islam was an ideology that transcended national boundaries. Like Communism, Islam engaged in rapid expansion. Like Communism, Muslims openly declared their goal of conquering the world for their cause. And like Communism, Islam posed a spiritual threat to Christianity — instead of atheism vs. Christ, the challenge was Allah vs. the Triune God of the Bible.

And just as American foreign policy throughout the second half of the twentieth century centered upon opposition to and containment of Communism — too much so in the eyes of some, not enough in the eyes of others, including me — so foreign policy in medieval and renaissance European nations focused upon opposition to and containment of Islam.

Why this discussion of Islam? Because unless one understands the threat Islam posed to European Christians during the medieval period and beyond, it is impossible to understand the mindset and motivations of the explorers. To Columbus, the voyage westward was a way of reaching the Orient, and, after Christianizing the Orient, joining forces with Asia to turn back the threat of Islam. To Cortez, the Aztecs were a heathen nation to be converted or conquered, just like the Muslim Moors and Turks.

Let us briefly trace world events leading up to 1492, for we need to appreciate this age-old conflict to understand the minds and motives of the explorers.

For the first three centuries after the birth of Christ, Christians were the subjects of frequent persecution by the Roman government. Then, around A.D. 312, the Emperor Constantine became a Christian and made Christianity the official religion of the Roman Empire. One result was that Christianity became identified with possession of certain territory, and lands under Christian rule came to be called "Christendom." Properly understood, this did not mean — or at least should not have meant — that one was a Christian simply because one lived in a "Christian" land. Rather it meant, or should have meant, that people in such lands were free to worship Christ and practice Christianity, and that the civilization and culture of such lands reflected biblical values.

For political reasons, Constantine also divided the Empire in A.D. 330. The eastern half of the Roman Empire was to be ruled from Byzantium, which was renamed Constantinople, and the western half was to be ruled from Rome.

The Roman Empire of the West declined. embattled by barbarians from outside its borders and weakened by moral and military decay within. Most historians date the end of the Western Empire at A.D. 476, when Germanic tribes took control of the city of Rome and placed their chieftain Odoacer on the throne as emperor. The Roman Empire of the East continued for another thousand years, until A.D. 1453, under Christian rulers and a Church that gradually became what is now known as the Eastern Orthodox Church.

Around A.D. 610 an Arabian businessman named Mohammed (sometimes transliterated from the Arabic as Muhammed or Mahomet) claimed to have special revelations from the one true God, whom he called Allah, and began preaching a new faith. Mohammed's teachings are found in the Koran, the holy book of Islam, and are usually summarized as the five dogmas of Islam:

(1) There is one and only one God, Allah. For this reason Muslims have objected to the Christian view of the Trinity, regarding trinitarianism as another form of polytheism.

(2) Mohammed was Allah's greatest messenger. Muslims believe Allah also spoke through Abraham, Moses and Jesus, and possibly to some extent through other Old Testament prophets, but Mohammed was the greatest of these. However, Mohammed was only a man, and he died like other men. For this reason, I am told, followers of this faith prefer to call themselves Moslems or Muslims rather than Mohammedans and prefer to call their religion Islam rather than Mohammedanism, because they do not worship Mohammed the way Christians worship Christ.

(3) The Koran is the Word of God, dictated to Mohammed by the angel Gabriel. Muslims also accept the Old Testament and the Gospels as divine revelation to the extent that they are consistent with the Koran. Where they contradict the Koran, Muslims believe, they have been corrupted from the original manuscripts. During the early centuries of

Islam a dispute arose among Muslims as to whether the Koran was co-eternal with Allah and therefore infallibly true and universally applicable, or whether the Koran was created by Allah in time and therefore is infallibly true but subject to different interpretations and applications over time. Eventually the first position won out.

(4) Gabriel heads a hierarchy of angels who serve Allah and intervene for man. Muslims also believe in "jinns," evil spirits created out of fire. Jinns are much like demons, but Muslims do not regard them as fallen angels.

(5) After death man faces Allah's judgment, reward in paradise or punishment in hell. This judgment is based upon works, although Muslims also emphasize that Allah is compassionate and merciful. His mercy is generally contingent upon man's repentance.

The Koran describes paradise as a place of luxury and sensuality: "Reclining upon couches lined with silk brocade, the fruit of both gardens near to hand. Therein are those of modest gaze, whom neither man nor jinni will have touched before them, [in beauty] like the jacynth and the coral-stone . . . And beside them are two other gardens, dark green with foliage, wherein are two abundant springs, wherein is fruit, the date-palm and pomegranite, wherein [are found] the good and beautiful — fair ones, close-guarded in pavilions — whom neither man nor jinni will have touched before them — reclining on green cushions and fair carpets." (Chapter 55).

How does one achieve these rewards in paradise? The Muslim answer is the obligatory duties known as the Five Pillars of Islam:

(1) Verbal profession that "There is one God, Allah, and Mohammed is his prophet."

(2) Prayer, which is to take place at five set times each day and according to prescribed positions and rituals.

(3) Almsgiving to the poor.

(4) Fasting, complete abstinence from food and drink during the hours of daylight during the month of Ramadan, the ninth month of the Islamic year,

plus additional fasting as penitence for certain sins.

(5) Pilgrimage to a holy shrine, Mecca being the favored site.

Muslims frequently speak of jihad or holy war, "fighting in the way of Allah" as a sixth pillar. I dwell upon jihad below not because of its importance in the life of the average Muslim believer, but because it has played a major role in the relations of Islamic powers with other nations, and because many Muslims do not like to admit that it is part of their religion. But jihad occupies a central place in the Koran:

Ch 2, v. 190: Fight in the way of Allah against those who fight against you, but begin not hostilities. Lo! Allah loveth not aggression.

191. And slay them wherever you find them, and drive them out of the holy places whence they drove you out, for persecution is worse than slaughter. And fight not with them at the Inviolable Place of Worship until they first attack you (there) then slay them. Such is the reward of disbelievers.

192. But if they desist, then lo! Allah is Forgiving, Merciful.

193. And fight them until persecution is no more, and religion is for Allah. But if they desist, then let there be no hostility except against wrongdoers.

216: Warfare is ordained for you, though it is hateful unto you; but it may happen that ye hate a thing which is good for you, and it may happen that ye love a thing which is bad for you. Allah knoweth, ye know not.

217: . . . And they will not cease from fighting against you till they have made you renegades from your religion, if they can.

246: Bethink thee of the leaders of the Children of Israel after Moses, how they said unto a Prophet whom they had: Set up for us a King and we will fight in Allah's way. He said: Would ye then refrain from fighting if fighting were prescribed for you? They said: Why should we not fight in Allah's way when we have been driven from our dwellings with our children? Yet, when fighting was prescribed for them, they turned away, all save a few of them. Allah is aware of evil-doers.

Ch 4, v. 74: Let those fight in the way of Allah who sell the life of this world for the other. Whoso fighteth in the way of Allah be he slain or be he victorious, on him We shall bestow a vast reward.

75: How should ye not fight for the cause of Allah and the feeble among men and women and the children who are crying: Our Lord! Bring us forth from out this town of which the people are oppressors! Oh, give us from Thy presence some protecting friend! Oh, give us from Thy presence some defender!

76: Those who believe do battle for the cause of Allah; and those who disbelieve do battle for the cause of idols. So fight the minions of the devil. Lo! the devil's strategy is ever weak.

78: Wheresoever ye may be, death will overtake you, even though ye were in lofty towers.

91: ... If they keep not aloof from you nor offer you peace nor hold their hands, then take them and kill them wherever you find them. Against such We have given you clear warrant.

104: Relent not in pursuit of the enemy. If ye are suffering, lo! they suffer even as ye suffer, and ye hope from Allah that for which they cannot hope. Allah is ever Knower, Wise.

Ch 9, v. 5: Then, when the sacred months have passed, slay the idolators wherever ye find them, and take them (captive), and besiege them, and prepare for them each ambush. But if they repent and establish worship and pay the poor-due, then leave their way free. Lo! Allah is Forgiving, Merciful.

29: Fight against such of those who have been

given the Scripture as believe not in Allah nor the Last Day, and forbid not that which Allah hath forbidden by His messenger, and follow not the religion of truth, until they pay the tribute readily, being brought low.

36: . . . And wage war on all the idolators as they are waging war on all of you. And know that Allah is with those who keep their duty (unto Him).

41: Go forth, light-armed and heavy-armed, and strive with your wealth and your lives in the way of Allah! That is best for you if ye but knew.

84: And never pray for one of them who dieth, nor stand by his grave. Lo! they disbelieved in Allah and His messenger, and they died while they were evil-doers.

123: O ye who believe! Fight those of the disbelievers who are near to you, and let them find harshness in you, and know that Allah is with those who keep their duty (unto Him).

Ch 47, v. 4: Now when ye meet in battle those who disbelieve, then it is smiting of the necks until, when ye have routed them, then making fast of bonds; and afterward either grace or ransom till the war lay down its burdens. (That is the ordinance). And if Allah willed He could have punished them (without you) but (thus it is ordained) that He may try some of you by means of others. And those who are slain in the way of Allah, he rendereth not their actions vain.

v. 5: He will guide them and improve their state,

v. 6: And bring them in unto the Garden which He hath made known to them.

Apologists for Islam are quick to point out that Ch 2 v.190 commands defensive warfare but forbids aggression. Note, however, that this distinction is missing in the other passages of the Koran commanding jihad or holy war.

Preaching this message, Mohammed won some converts and achieved some success, especially among the tribes-

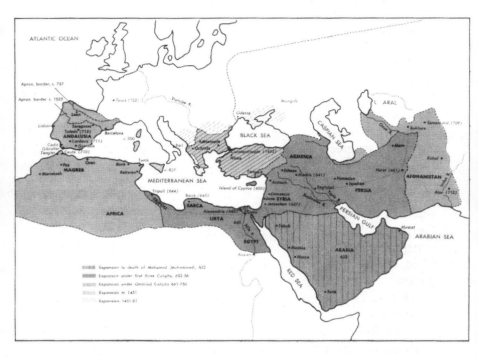

men of southern Arabia whose religious views were more compatible with Islam than those of northern Arabia. Following the commands of jihad as contained in the Koran, Mohammed and his followers sought to spread their message by force of arms. By the time Mohammed died in A.D. 632, nearly all of Arabia was under Muslim control.

After the death of Mohammed, Muslims established theocratic rule under a series of caliphs, beginning with Mohammed's disciple Abu Bekr who ruled from A.D. 632-634. Under his successor, Caliph Omar (A.D. 634-644), Muslims conquered Syria, Palestine, Persia, Mesopotamia, Egypt, Cyrene, and Tripoli. Under Caliph Othman (A.D. 644-656), they took the islands of Cyprus and Rhodes and began the conquest of Afghanistan.

The next Caliph, Ali (A.D. 656-661), was occupied with putting down revolts in Muslim territories, but under Caliph Mu'awiya (A.D. 661-680) they pressed eastward and conquered part of India. Then, under Caliph Yazid I (680-683), they expanded the western front to Morocco. No new conquests took place during the rule of Caliph Marwan (A.D. 684-685), and under Caliph Abd ul-Malik (A.D. 685-705) their westward expansion continued to Tunisia.

The following Caliph, Al-Walid (A.D. 705-715) completed the conquest of North Africa by taking Algeria. On the eastern front his armies pushed forward into Asia Minor, Turkestan, and India to the Ganges River.

The Muslims looked upon Europe as a prize to be secured in the name of Allah. Their strategy seems to have been a two-fold pincer action, attacking from the west across the Strait of Gibraltar into Spain and France, and from the east across the Strait of Bosporus into Central Europe by way of Greece and the Balkan Peninsula.

On the eastern front the Muslims were stopped cold by the Roman Empire of the East, the Byzantine Empire. Though not aggressive, the Byzantines had the best-disciplined and best-equipped military force in the world. Calif Sulaiman (A.D. 715-717) and Calif Omar II (A.D. 717-720) both laid siege to Constantinople, but the Byzantine army repelled them without much difficulty. For centuries thereafter, the Byzantine Empire stood as a shield protecting

Europe from Islam.

The Muslims then shifted their strategy: They would concentrate their attack upon western Europe, then proceed down the Danube River and strike the Byzantine Empire from the northwest, all the while continuing their pressure from the southeast.

So the focus shifted westward as Olive Beaupre Miller says in *A Picturesque Tale of Progress*:

> Clear across Northern Africa swept their victorious hosts till they reached the Atlantic Ocean. There, their impulsive leader spurred his horse chest-deep into the surging, crested waves. "Almighty Lord," he cried; "but for this sea I would have gone into still remoter regions, spreading the glory of thy name and smiting thine enemies!"
>
> But the sea did not check the Arabs. From the Pillars of Hercules, they looked with covetous eyes over fourteen miles of sea to where the Visigoths dwelt on the rocky coast of Spain.[1]

The assault upon western Europe began in A.D. 711, as a Muslim general named Tarik led a fleet of vessels across the Strait and landed under the shadow of the great rock that bears his name ("Gebel-Tarik" has been contracted to "Gibraltar"). Spain would one day become a mighty nation, but at this time it was a decaying society of rival kings more obsessed with fighting one another than with facing their common enemy. Tarik used that dissension to his advantage, obtaining the support of a rival ruler named Count Julian, two sons of a former king whom Roderick had deposed, Spanish Jews who felt Spanish Christians had persecuted them, and possibly the remnants of Arian Christianity. (Arianism was a school of Christian thought founded by Arius, who taught that Jesus Christ, though divine, was not equal with God the Father and was created by God the Father instead of existing co-eternally with Him. The Church condemned Arianism as heresy at the Council of Nicea and subsequent church councils.)

Roderick, last of the Visigoth kings of Spain, was fight-

ing in the North when the Moslems landed, but he gathered
his forces and pressed southward to meet the foe at Cadiz
in the mountains of southern Spain. Roderick and his forces
fought well, but with dissidents defecting to the banner of
Islam at key moments of the battle, Tarik and the Muslims
gained the victory. By some accounts Roderick was killed in
the battle; by others he drowned trying to escape. But
according to one of Spain's best-loved legends, Roderick
still lives, and when Spanish Christians are hard beset by
their enemies, they can call upon Roderick and he will come
to their aid.[2]

After the defeat of Roderick, the conquest of Spain was
relatively easy. As Colonel Dupuy says in *The Encyclopedia
of Military History,* "The suddenness and completeness of
the collapse in the face of the Moslem invasion (711, 712)
was less a measure of the military capability of the Saracens
than proof of the utter incompetence of a regime on the
verge of collapse."[3]

After completing the conquest of Spain, Tarik was recalled to Arabia. His successor, Abdalrahman, became the
governor of Spain and leader of the Muslim forces; Arab
writers describe him as a very able and renowned military
commander as well as a model of integrity and justice.
Abdalrahman continued the advance of Islam across the
Pyrenees Mountains into France according to *The Encyclopedia of Military History*:

> The major cause of the meteoric expansion of
> Islam was the fanaticism engineered by the charis-
> matic leadership of Mohammed, and by specific
> tenets of his teachings which promised everlasting
> pleasure in heaven to those who died in holy war
> against the infidel. No other religion has ever been
> able to inspire so many men, so consistently and so
> enthusiastically, to be completely heedless of death
> and of personal danger in battle.
>
> Thus it was energy more than skill, religious fa-
> naticism rather than a superior military system, and
> missionary zeal instead of an organized scheme of
> recruitment which accounted for Moslem victories. . .

Once their initial headlong rush had run its course, the Moslems began to realize that even their own religious fervor could not afford the appalling loss of life resulting from heedless light-cavalry charges — almost entirely by unarmoured men wielding sword and lance — against the skilled bowmen of China and Byzantium, or the solid masses of the Franks. Having by this time come into contact with practically every important military system in the world, the Mohammedans sensibly adopted many Byzantine military practices.[4]

Muslims began raiding southern France around A.D. 717. They captured Narbonne, but Duke Eudo of Aquitaine held them back from further advancement for many years. Finally, in A.D. 732, Abdalrahman defeated Duke Eudo at the Battle of Bordeaux and proceeded north to the plain between Tours and Poitiers. Miller has this to say about Abdalrahman:

[He] led the Moslems down through the rocky, difficult gorges into the rich lands of Gaul. The ruins of many a monastery smoked dismally in his wake, while saddle-bags grew heavy with the weight of jeweled crucifixes and ornaments of gold. It seemed as if nothing could stop the army of the Prophet. But at last, in the heart of Gaul, the Moslems came face to face with a strong Germanic race, the Franks.[5]

The Franks were a German tribe who had migrated into what is now France. They were ruled by a series of kings beginning with Meroveus known as the Merovingian dynasty and had embraced Christianity under the leadership of Clovis, grandson of Meroveus. Miller describes their conversion:

Worshipers of Thor and Woden, the Franks in these new-conquered lands, first came in contact with God as the Christians understood him, a God who desired humility and mercy, instead of bloodshed. Laughing at this God in scorn, they shook their battle-axes in salute to their bloody Thor, and fell like wolves on the spoils of monasteries and churches. But it chances at this time that in Burgundy there dwelt a beautiful Christian princess who was called by the name of Clotilda. Her uncle, Gundobald, had killed her father and mother in order to seize the throne, and he would have killed Clotilda, had she not fled for her life. When Clovis heard of her beauty, he sent messengers to Gundobald, demanding Clotilda's hand. Gundobald dared not refuse; he had no wish to bring the Franks like ravening wolves on his land. So Clotilda was sent to Soissons, and Clovis found her so gentle, that he loved her with all his heart.

Most of Clotilda's kinsfolk had been converted by Arian missionaries, but Clotilda was an Orthodox Christian; and from the first she determined to lead her husband, Clovis, away from his heathen gods. When a son was born to Clotilda, her husband rejoiced so exceedingly that he let the child be baptized. But the baby fell sick and died, and in his angry sorrow, Clovis turned on his wife. "You took our son and caused him to be baptized a Christian," he cried; "and behold he is dead! My gods are angry with me, and yours are not able to help us!" And he rushed off to further fighting to give his spirit relief. But when a second son was born, Clovis again in his joy, allowed the babe to be baptized, and Clotilda's heart was glad. But before many weeks had passed, little Chlodomer too, fell sick, and seemed about to die. And now, like a mad thing, Clovis called down curses on his wife's God. But Clotilda calmed her husband and besought him to be patient. As she prayed, the babe recovered, and in his great relief, Clovis began to think more kindly of her God.

When he was next at war with the stubborn Alemanni, and facing certain defeat, he remembered Clotilda's God. Having called in vain on his own gods, he determined to try her God and bargain for aid. "If thou wilt grant me victory over these foes," he cried, "I will believe in Thee, and will be baptized in Thy name; for I have called on my gods, but they are far from helping me." Lo, while the King thus prayed, the tide of battle turned. The Alemanni lost heart and fled before the Franks; and Clovis decided that God must be more powerful than Thor!

Great was the joy of the Queen when Clovis returned and told her of his promise to her God, and many were the preparations for the baptism of the King. On Christmas Day of the year A.D. 496, Franks and Gauls gathered in thousands at the Christian church in Rheims. White hangings, tapestried canopies, and a hundred gleaming candles lent splendor to the scene, while incense sweetened the air, and the chanting of monks rose and fell. It was a setting well calculated to inspire tremendous awe in the hearts of the simple Franks. Behind the candle-bearers, and the sacred symbol of the cross, Clovis himself, clad in white, and followed by three thousand warriors, likewise clad in white, approached the old Bishop Remi, who forthwith baptized the King and all his men.

Following their leader's example, most of the Franks became Christians.[6]

Throughout this conflict, as the Moslem armies advanced across North Africa and into Europe, God had been preparing the hearts, bodies, and spirits of the Franks to defend European Christendom. Through many military campaigns throughout Europe against the Frisians, Saxons, Swabians, Bavarians and others, the Franks had become the most powerful military force in western Europe. The generations that followed Clovis were strengthened in their Christian faith as well.

In A.D. 732, as Abdalrahman advanced toward Tours, the Merovingian king of the Franks was a juvenile; but the real power in the kingdom was a very capable chief of staff or palace mayor called Charles the Hammer, founder of the Carolingian dynasty of Frankish kings and grandfather of

Charlemagne. Charles was a strong Christian who encouraged missionaries to bring Christianity to the lands he conquered; one of these was St. Boniface. He was also a seasoned military commander who appointed as bishops and abbots, warriors who kept their own armor and would not wear clerical dress.[7]

The Battle of Tours was perhaps the most decisive battle in world history. Consider what the result would have been had the Moslems won that battle! Humanly speaking, there was no earthly power that could have kept them from dominating all of Europe. The historian Ridpath observes the following:

> The progress of the Mohammedans northward had now continued unchecked a distance of more than a thousand miles from Gibraltar. Another similar span would have carried the Crescent [symbol of Islam] to the borders of Poland and the Scottish Highlands; and in that event the conjecture of the sedate Gibbon that the Koran would today be used as the principal textbook in the University of Oxford, would appear to be justified.*
>
> Destiny, however, had contrived another end. The battle-axe of Charles, the bastard son of the elder Pepin, still showed its terrible edge between Abdalrahman and the goal. The Frankish warrior was already hardened in the conflicts of twenty-four years of service. In the emergency which was now upon the kingdom, it was the policy of Charles to let the Arabian torrent diffuse itself before attempting to stem the tide.[8]

*Gibbon's conjecture may come true after all. In the year 1900 there were two Moslem mosques in London. Today there are over 2,000! In these closing decades of the twentieth century, the threat of Islam is greater than it has been for centuries. The battle is being waged simultaneously on the military, political, economic, ideological, cultural, and religious fronts.

An early writer, Isodorus Pacensis, gives the classic description of the battle:

> The men of the north stood as motionless as a wall; they were like a belt of ice frozen together, and not to be dissolved, as they slew the Arabs with the sword. The Austrasians, vast of limb, and iron of hand, hewed on bravely in the thick of the fight; it was they who found and cut down the Saracen king.[9]

Miller offers a more detailed description:

> For seven days the two armies stood facing one another, the Arabs beating their drums and clashing their harsh, strident cymbals, working up their emotions into feverish enthusiasm, while the Franks grimly waited in silence. In the misty dawn of the eighth day, the Arabs attacked on their horses. With whirling scimitars, trumpet-blasts, and harsh cries of "Allah Akbar!" ["God is great!"] the desert tribes charged home! But it was as if they had charged against a wall of ice. The Frankish infantry locked their shields and laughed at the showers of spears. With their terrible battle-axes they hewed down both horse and rider at a single mighty blow. Wave after wave of the Arabs surged against that iron wall, to fall back in plunging disorder.[10]

It appears that on the decisive day of the battle, Charles observed that Abdalrahman was preparing a major cavalry assault. He therefore dismounted his cavalry and formed his army into a solid phalanx formation. As the Franks repulsed the Muslim cavalry charges, Charles at first fought on interior lines but later began to press his advantage without totally abandoning the phalanx formation. Ridpath describes the battle in vivid, decisive terms:

> Europe was arrayed against Asia and Africa; the Cross against the Crescent; Christ against

Mohammed. For six days of desultory fighting, in which each party, apparently conscious of the crisis in the affairs of men, seemed wary of the other, and forebore to close in the grapple of death, the victory inclined to the banner of Islam; but, on the seventh day of the fight, the terrible Germans arose with their battle-axes upon the lighter soldiery of the South and hewed them down by the thousands. Night closed upon victorious Europe. Charles had won his surname of the Hammer; for he had beaten the followers of the Prophet into the earth.[11]

With their general Abdalrahman slain in the battle, the Muslims retreated across the Pyrenees, where they continued to occupy parts of Spain until the 1400s. But on this fateful day in A.D. 732 — precisely a century after the death of Mohammed — the security of European Christendom was guaranteed for centuries to come.

Following the Battle of Tours, the flames of conflict between the Christian and Islamic worlds dwindled into an unfriendly but relatively stable truce. As Will Durant says,

For five centuries, from 700 to 1200, Islam led the world in power, order, and extent of government, in refinement of manners, in standards of living, in humane legislation and religious toleration, in literature, scholarship, science, medicine, and philosophy.[12]

During this period the Christian and Islamic cultures influenced each other more than either would care to admit according to Durant:

The influence of Islam upon Christendom was varied and immense. From Islam Christian Europe received foods, drinks, drugs, medicaments, armor, heraldry, art motives and tastes, industrial and commercial articles and techniques, maritime codes and ways, and often the words for these things — orange, lemon, sugar, syrup, sherbet, julep, elixir,

jar, asure, arabesque, mattress, sofa, muslin, satin,
frustian, bazaar, caravan, check, tariff, traffic,
douane, magazine, risk, sloop, barge, cable, admiral. The game of chess came to Europe from India via
Islam, and picked up Persian terms on the way;
checkmate is from the Persian sha mat — "the king
is dead." Some of our musical instruments bear in
their names evidence of their Semitic origin — lute,
rebeck, guitar, tambourine. The poetry and music of
the troubadors came from Moslem Spain into
Provence, and from Moslem Sicily into Italy; and
Arabic descriptions of trips to heaven and hell may
have shared in forming The Divine Comedy. Hindu
fables and numerals entered Europe in Arabic dress
or form. Moslem science preserved and developed
Greek mathematics, physics, chemistry, astronomy,
and medicine, and transmitted this Greek heritage,
considerably enriched, to Europe; and Arabic scientific terms — algebra, zero, cipher, azimuth, alembic,
zenith, almanac — still lie embedded in European
speech. Moslem medicine led the world for half a
millennium. Moslem philosophy preserved and corrupted Aristotle for Christian Europe. Avicenna
and Averroes were lights from the East for the
Schoolmen, who cited them as next to the Greeks in
authority.[13]

But the bloodshed at Tours and the calls for jihad were
never forgotten by either side. To each culture, the other
was of Satan; and Christians and Muslims alike knew the
day was coming when the coals of hostility would burst into
flames of war. Durant continues:

Behind this borrowing smoldered an undying
hate. Nothing, save bread, is so precious to mankind
as its religious beliefs; for man lives not by bread
alone, but also by the faith that lets him hope.
Therefore his deepest hatred greets those who challenge his sustenance or his creed. For three centuries Christianity saw Islam advance, saw it capture

and absorb one Christian land and people after another, felt its constricting hand upon Christian trade, and heard it call Christians infidels. At last the potential conflict became actual: the rival civilizations clashed in the Crusades; and the best of the East or West slew the best of the West or East. Back of all medieval history lay this mutual hostility, with a third faith, the Jewish, caught between the main combatants, and cut by both swords. The West lost the Crusades, but won the war of creeds. Every Christian warrior was expelled from the Holy Land of Judaism and Christianity; but Islam, bled by its tardy victory, and ravaged by Mongols, fell in turn into a Dark Age of obscurantism and poverty; while the beaten West, matured by its effort and forgetting its defeat, learned avidly from its enemy, lifted cathedrals into the sky, wandered out on the high seas of reason, transformed its crude languages into Dante, Chaucer, and Villon, and moved with high spirit into the Renaissance.[14]

The term "crusade" comes from the Latin word *crux*, meaning cross. Crusaders wore the cross on their tunics and shields, and one who embarked on a crusade was said to "take the Cross." As they set forth on these religious wars, on foot or on horseback across the expanses of Europe and into foreign and dangerous territory, they joined in hymns of praise to God. Knights and noblemen, priests and peasants alike joined in this religious mission. And as with any religious cause, they were also joined by some whose motives were, at best, mixed.

The Crusades had many causes; medieval Europeans legitimized them under just warfare doctrine because Muslims were threatening the safety of Christian pilgrims to Jerusalem.[15] But as Roland Bainton points out,

The purpose was not to recover stolen goods nor to repel an invasion, but to vindicate a right of religion under foreign jurisdiction. This was after all a war of faith.[16]

At the inauguration of the First Crusade in A.D. 1095, Pope Urban II exhorted the Christians of Europe and Africa:

> . . . And now that you have promised to maintain the peace among yourselves you are obligated to succour your brethren in the East, menaced by an accursed race, utterly alienated from God. The Holy Sepulchre of our Lord is polluted by the filthiness of an unclean nation. Recall the greatness of Charlemagne! O most valiant soldiers, descendants of invincible ancestors, be not degenerate. Let all hatred depart from you, all quarrels end, all wars cease. Start upon the road to the Holy Sepulchre to wrest that land from the wicked race and subject it to yourselves.[17]

St. Bernard of Clairvaux, author of such hymns as "Jesus, the Very Thought of Thee," echoed the Pope's call to arms in terms reminiscent of Islamic jihad: "Therefore, ye knights, attack with confidence and courage the enemies of the cross of Christ, assured that neither life nor death can separate you from the love of God which is in Christ Jesus our Lord."[18]

Initially the Crusaders enjoyed limited success. The First Crusade (A.D. 1096-1099), resulted in the capture of Antioch and, finally, Jerusalem after six weeks of fighting. But after the conquest most Crusaders were eager to return home. Too few of them remained to defend the captured lands, and within fifty years most of them were back in Muslim hands.

The Second Crusade (A.D. 1147-1149) was a failure. Not only were the Crusaders repulsed by the Turks in Asia Minor; the Turks were encouraged by their victory to renew their attacks upon Christian strongholds.

The Third Crusade (A.D. 1189-1192) pitted King Richard the Lion-Hearted of England against the Muslim leader Saladin. Defeating Saladin in several battles, Richard succeeded in capturing the City of Acre. He was unable to retake Jerusalem, but he did persuade the Muslims to let

Christian pilgrims enter the city freely.

The Fourth Crusade (A.D. 1201-1204) was a disaster. Merchants of Venice agreed to transport the crusaders to the Holy Land if, in return, the crusaders would help them attack the Byzantine Empire to help open up new trade opportunities. They did so, and the resultant weakening of the Byzantine Empire exposed Europe to a new Muslim peril several centuries later.

The Fifth Crusade (A.D. 1217-1221) was of little consequence. Christians captured the town of Damietta in Egypt but gave it up in exchange for a truce with the Muslims.

The Sixth Crusade (A.D. 1228, 1229) resulted in the return of Jerusalem to Christian rule, due to the skilled negotiations of Emperor Frederick II of the Holy Roman Empire (Germany), but the Muslims retook Jerusalem in A.D. 1244. In efforts to retake Jerusalem King Louis IX of France (St. Louis) led the Seventh and Eighth Crusades, both of which were unsuccessful. The fourteenth, fifteenth, and even sixteenth centuries saw papal attempts to organize new crusades, but they never got underway. Jerusalem remained under Muslim control until modern Israel received part of it in 1948.

The Crusades involved sinful men on holy missions, committing acts of nobility and courage, treachery, and savagery. One crusader, Raymond of Agiles, described the capture of Jerusalem in graphic terms:

> Some of our men (and this was more merciful) cut off the heads of their enemies; others shot them with arrows, so that they fell from the towers; others tortured them longer by casting them into the flames. Piles of heads, hands and feet were to be seen in the streets of the city. It was necessary to pick one's way over the bodies of men and horses. But these were small matters compared to what happened at the temple of Solomon, a place where religious services were ordinarily chanted. What happened there? If I tell the truth, it will exceed your powers of belief. So let it suffice to say this much at least, that in the temple and portico of Solomon, men rode in blood up

to their knees and the bridle reins. [Note Rev. 14:20.]
. . . Indeed, it was a just and splendid judgment of
God, that this place should be filled with the blood of
the unbelievers, when it had suffered so long from
their blasphemies.

Now that the city was taken it was worth all our
previous labors and hardships to see the devotion of
the pilgrims at the Holy Sepulcher. How they rejoiced and exulted and sang the ninth chant to the
Lord. It was the ninth day, the ninth joy and exaltation, and of perpetual happiness. The ninth sermon,
the ninth chant was demanded by all. This day, I
say, will be famous in all future ages, for it turned
our labors and sorrows into joy and exaltation; this
day, I say, marks the justification of Christianity
and the humiliation of paganism; our faith was
renewed. "The Lord made this day, and we rejoiced
and exulted in it," for on this day the Lord revealed
Himself to His people and blessed them.[19]

We must candidly acknowledge that many excesses
were committed by both sides. This was a violent age, and
as recent wars have reminded us, when men are at war,
emperiled, disoriented, far from home, and perhaps in ill
health, atrocities do take place even among men whose
basic motives are noble. And yet, there is something to be
said for a people whose faith is so strong and whose world
view is so God-centered, that they are willing to leave
everything behind and travel to a distant land to fight for
the cross of Christ. Even today Americans are inspired by
the ideal of the crusader, which in secular terms refers to a
person who commits himself to a cause greater than himself.

And as the *Catholic Encyclopedia* notes, "At a still later
date, it was the spirit of the true crusader that animated
Christopher Columbus when he undertook his perilous
voyage to the then unknown America, and Vasco da Gama
when he set out in quest of India. If, indeed, the Christian
civilization of Europe has become universal culture, in the
highest sense, the glory redounds, in no small measure, to

the Crusades."[20]

One reason the Crusades were less successful than they could have been is the fighting that took place among Christians. (Infighting is an art which Christians have honed to perfection. It has been said with some truth that the Christian army is the only army in the world that shoots its wounded and leaves its fallen leaders to die on the battlefield.) For example, during the Third Crusade Richard the Lionhearted of England and Philip of France quarreled, and Philip returned home leaving Richard to face Saladin and the Turks alone. A similar quarrel occurred on the Second Crusade between King Louis VII of France and Emperor Conrad III of Germany, and infighting also disrupted the First Crusade.

Even more destructive was the fighting between Western and Eastern Christians. The Catholic Church of Rome and the Orthodox Church of Constantinople had been more or less split since the fourth century, and in later centuries the Pope of Rome and the Metropolitan of Constantinople repeatedly excommunicated each other over such issues as the doctrine of procession, whether the Holy Spirit proceeds from both the Father and the Son (the Western view) or from the Father alone (the Eastern view). Because of these doctrinal disputes, plus differences in culture, ceremony, and language, the courts of Constantinople seemed almost as foreign as Arabia and Egypt, and Crusaders of the West seemed unsure whether their Eastern cousins were allies or enemies. For their part the knights of Byzantium, having held off the menace of Islam for many centuries without help from the West, perhaps regarded the Western crusaders as reckless fanatics and gave the Crusades rather lukewarm support.

The Crusaders' assault upon Constantinople during the Fourth Crusade was a travesty that had far-reaching results, for it greatly weakened the Byzantine Empire and opened the way to Muslim advances. In the 1300s a new world power arose, the Ottoman Turks. More aggressive and militant than the Seljuk Turks of the days of Saladin, the Ottoman Turks established the Ottoman Empire that was perhaps the number one world power during the 1500s and 1600s and that survived until 1922. In A.D. 1402 Bajazet, the Turkish sultan, vowed that he would sit on the throne of Constantine, feed his horses on the altar of St. Peter's, and abolish the worship of Christ throughout the world.[21] He did not live to fulfill these vows, but his successors would come close to making them come true.

By A.D. 1453 the Ottoman Turks, under the able and energetic leadership of Sultan Mohammed II, had conquered all of the Byzantine Empire except the city of Constantinople. According to ancient Islamic prophecies, Constantinople would fall only to a leader who bore the name Mohammed, and the new Sultan had been convinced from childhood that he was the destined man. And the aged and decaying Byzantine Empire rested on the shoulders of a courageous young emperor, Constantine XII. It was perhaps fitting that in these closing days of the Byzantine Empire, two brave and able leaders with the names of Constantine and Mohammed would face one another in a fifty-three-day siege. Miller describes the final days of Constantinople:

> The smouldering spark of enmity between these two young Kings needed only an ill-worded message from Constantine to Mohammed to set the fire ablaze. Mohammed came with a mighty force and laid siege to Constantinople. Constantine did what he could; but there was no heart for defense in a city so pitifully weakened. Too many people saw signs and omens of disaster. Sacred pictures perspired, or spoke solemn words of warning; and images of the Virgin fell down and refused to be lifted up. In April, 1453, the first great gun boomed out; for both sides made use of a very crude cannon, and the recently invented gunpowder, as well as of older weapons. Day after day, the great walls trembled and rocked with the shock.
>
> Mohammed, impatient to end the siege, worked out a clever plan. Going up the Bosphorus, he commanded eighty of his ships to be floated on wooden platforms. Then he had these dragged ashore to a

road made of well greased logs which led over hill and dale to the shadow of the Golden Horn. Teams of powerful oxen and a thousand jubilant Turks drew each ship inch by inch, while the sailors spread their sails and pretended with merry jesting to row through the empty air. Thus the eighty ships were borne to the Golden Horn, inside the protecting chain that guarded the harbor-mouth, and the Byzantines suddenly beheld a Turkish fleet sailing down their harbor and pointing its guns and catapults against the harbor walls.

The end of the struggle had come. A messenger came to the city-gates with terms of peace from Mohammed, but Constantine's only answer was an emphatic "No surrender!"

At the first faint glimmer of dawn on May 29, 1453, the Turks began the attack. From the sea, from the harbor, from the land they came; and there was no end to their coming! Hour after hour the cannon roared, and under cover of smoke, the besiegers swarmed up the walls. The defenders grew so wearied that they could hardly move; and then Mohammed ordered his Janissaries to charge. The final defeat of the Christians should be by their own sons; for the Janissaries were Christian children taken by the Turks and trained as Moslem warriors! As they advanced through a breach in the walls, the Christians turned to flee, and the Janissaries dashed forward. Then Constantine spurring his horse into the thick of the fight, fell trampled under-foot in the onrush of the victors. Over his bleeding body, the victorious Turks poured into Constantinople.

At Mohammed's bidding an imaum climbed to the pulpit and over the heaps of the slain who had fled to Sancta Sophia, sounded the long wail of Islam: "There is no God but Allah, and Mohammed is his Prophet! Come to prayer!" So fell Constantinople, queen of cities.[22]

Imagine the shock waves that reverberated across Europe. The two-thousand-year-old Byzantine Empire, which had stood for over eight centuries as a barrier protecting Christendom from the forces of Islam, had collapsed!

And in Genoa, Italy, the parents of two-year-old Christopher Columbus heard the news and shuddered. For the date was 1453 — just thirty-nine years before Columbus sailed!

The threat grew ever more imminent as the Turks attacked the Kingdom of Naples in A.D. 1480, coming within about one hundred miles of Rome and murdering an archbishop and many priests. The Ottoman army took Hungary and much of eastern Europe, and in A.D. 1527 they even laid siege to Vienna though they never captured the city. Luther's writings are filled with references to "the Turk" and prayers for divine deliverance.

Meanwhile, thoughtful men of Europe had begun to lay plans to combat Muslim expansion. Most notable of these was Prince Henry of Portugal, known as Henry the Navigator, who laid plans for a new, universal Christian order that would unite the nations of Europe, Africa and Asia against the forces of Islam.

Born in 1394 and educated by his mother Queen Philippa, Henry determined before reaching the age of twenty that his mission in life should be the expansion of Christianity and Christian civilization throughout the world. With this mission in mind, as Grand Master of the Military Order of Christ he led many battles against the Muslims. He was realistic enough, however, to recognize that economics plays a major role in world affairs; and it disturbed him greatly that the Muslim nations, located strategically between Europe and Asia, controlled trade between the two continents and frequently caused the cost of imported goods to rise as much as four thousand percent. Henry perceived that if a direct route to Asia could be developed, the Muslim deadlock on East-West trade could be eliminated. Furthermore, by bringing the nations of Asia and Africa to Christ, Christians could engulf the Ottoman Turks in a pincer action and close off their power. Legends abounded of a Christian priest known as Prester John [John the Preacher] who had established a Christian kingdom somewhere in

Africa (though others looked for him in Asia or even somewhere across the Atlantic). While there is no firm evidence Prester John ever existed, there were cities in Africa, larger and more advanced than most Westerners supposed, that held various forms of Christianity. It is easy to forget that for the first several centuries of the Christian era, North Africa was the center of Christendom.

To form this worldwide Christian order and check the Turkish advance, Henry believed, it was necessary to establish a battlefront on the northwest coast of Africa and also to block the entrance to the Mediterranean by taking control of both sides of the Strait of Gibraltar — Gibraltar on the Spanish side, Ceuta on the Moroccan side, both of which ports were controlled by the Ottoman Turks.

Furthermore, Henry said, the West needed to develop the economic and technological resources that would make ocean travel around Africa to Asia possible. He therefore established a scientific academy which brought together the finest experts in the world — navigators, shipbuilders, astronomers, geographers, cartographers, and mathematicians. Captains sailing at Henry's discretion discovered the Madiera islands, the Azores, and the Cape Verde islands, and also engaged in much exploration of Africa. The design of the caravel, the type of ship Columbus used, is another of Henry's developments. Without this technology it is questionable whether Columbus's voyage could have taken place. In a September 1453 papal bull *Romanus Pontifex* giving the Portuguese monarch dominion over Cape Bojador unto the southernmost parts of Africa, Pope Nicholas V commended Henry and described him as

> . . . burning with zeal for the salvation of souls and for the order of the faith as Catholic and true soldier of Christ, protector of all and fearless and undaunted defender of the faith and intrepid warrior, [who] made manifest, exalted and venerated, the most glorious name of the Creator himself throughout the entire world, even in those places most remote and unknown . . .[23]

Christopher Columbus shared this crusader's concern over Islamic expansion and burned with desire to reach the lands of the East with the gospel of Jesus Christ and the creation of a worldwide Christian order to combat Islam. He added a unique twist to the plans to evangelize the Orient: The best way to reach the East, he insisted, was to sail *west* across the Atlantic.

Alarm over renewed Muslim expansion was nowhere more fevered than in Spain. For the Spanish Christians, the Muslim powers were more than a distant threat; they were a present reality. The Muslim armies under Tarik, you will recall, conquered Spain in the early 700s and advanced northward. After Charles the Hammer and the Franks defeated them at the Battle of Tours in A.D. 732, they retreated south across the Pyrenees but remained in Spain. For hundreds of years thereafter they continued to govern parts of Spain, particularly the southern part of Spain known as Granada.

Muslim apologists insist that the Islamic rulers of Spain practiced religious toleration there and elsewhere. It is true that in many areas controlled by Islam non-Muslims were allowed to keep their old religions — provided they paid heavy tribute to followers of the Prophet. It appears the early Muslims learned from their Persian subjects that conquered peoples can be better governed if they are allowed to retain some degree of autonomy — a policy followed by the Persians as far back as Cyrus the Great.

Even where tribute was paid, non-Muslims were often restricted. Durant, who was hardly an apologist for Christianity, acknowledges Muslim toleration but adds the following:

> But there was another side to the picture, and it darkened with time. Though Christians were free, the Church was not. Most of her landed property had been confiscated by a decree affecting all active resisters to the conquest; many churches had been destroyed, and new ones were prohibited. The Moslem emirs inherited from the Visigoth kings the right to appoint and depose bishops, even to sum-

mon ecclesiastical councils. The emirs sold bishop-
rics to the highest bidder, though he might be a
skeptic or a libertine. Christian priests were liable
to abuse by Moslems in the streets. Moslem theologians commented freely on what seemed to them
absurdities in Christian theology, but it was dangerous for Christians to reply in kind.

Under such tense relations a minor incident
could lead to a major tragedy. A pretty girl of
Cordova, known to us only as Flora, was the child of
a mixed marriage. When her Mohammedan father
died she resolved to become a Christian. She fled
from her brother's guardianship to a Christian home,
was caught and beaten by him, persisted in apos-
tasy, and was turned over to a Moslem court. The
qadi, who might have condemned her to death, had
her flogged. She escaped again to a Christian home,
and there met a young priest, Eulogius, who con-
ceived for her a passionate spiritual attachment.
While she hid in a convent another priest, Perfectus,
achieved martyrdom by telling some Moslems what
he thought of Mohammed; they had promised not to
betray him, but the vigor of his expression so shocked
them that they denounced him to the authorities.
Perfectus might have saved himself by a retraction;
instead, he repeated to the judge his conviction that
Mohammed was "the servant of Satan." The judge
remanded him to jail for some months, hoping for a
change of mood; none came, and Perfectus was
condemned to death. He marched to the scaffold
cursing the Prophet as "an imposter, an adulterer, a
child of hell." The Moslems gloated over his decapitation; the Christians of Cordova buried him with
pomp as a saint (A.D. 850).

His death inflamed the theological hatred of both
sides. A group of Christian "Zealots" formed, led by
Eulogius; they were determined to denounce
Mohammed publicly, and to accept martyrdom joy-
fully as a promise of paradise. Isaac, a Cordovan
monk, went to the qada and professed a desire for

conversion; but when the judge, well pleased, began to expound Mohammedanism, the monk interrupted him: "Your Prophet," he said, "has lied and deceived you. May he be accursed, who has dragged so many wretches with him down to hell!" The qadi reproved him, and asked had he been drinking; the monk replied: "I am in my right mind. Condemn me to death." The qadi had him imprisoned, but asked permission of Abd-er-Rahman II to dismiss him as insane; the Caliph, incensed by the splendor of Perfectus' funeral, ordered the monk to be executed. Two days later Sancho, a Frank soldier of the palace guard, publicly denounced Mohammed; he was beheaded. On the following Sunday six monks appeared before the qadi, cursed Mohammed, and asked for not death only, but "your sharpest tortures;" they were beheaded. A priest, a deacon, and a monk followed their example. The Zealots rejoiced, but many Christians — priests as well as laymen — condemned this lust for martyrdom. "The Sultan," they said to the Zealots, "allows us to exercise our religion, and does not oppress us; why, then, this fanatical zeal?" A council of Christian bishops, summoned by Abd-er-Rahman, reproved the Zealots, and threatened action against them if they continued the agitation. Eulogius denounced the council as cowards.

Meanwhile Flora, her ardor raised by the Zealot movement, left her convent, and with another girl, Mary, went before the qadi; they both assured him that Mohammed was "an adulterer, an imposter, and a villain," and that Mohammedanism was "an invention of the Devil." The qadi committed them to jail. The entreaties of their friends had inclined them to retract when Eulogius prevailed upon them to accept martyrdom. They were beheaded (A.D. 851), and Eulogius, much encouraged, called for new martyrs. Priests, monks, and women marched to the court, denounced Mohammed, and obtained decapitation (A.D. 852). Eulogius himself earned martyrdom seven years later. After his death the movement subsided.[24]

Shortly thereafter Islamic fervor waned in Spain but was rekindled late in the eleventh century. For the next four centuries Christian-Muslim relations in Spain were marked by constant warfare. Romanticized by Washington Irving in *The Alhambra* and *The Conquest of Granada* and by the 1950s movie *El Cid*, these religious wars drove Spanish Christians into a religious fervor that some have called fanaticism,[25] and increasingly to the conviction that all of Spain must be under Christian rule. And we must candidly acknowledge that the zeal of the Spanish Christians sometimes overflowed into abuses, such as the excesses of the Inquisition and the expulsion of the Jews.

At first the various Spanish kingdoms were too divided to fight effectively against the Moors. Then in A.D. 1469 Queen Isabella of Castile married King Ferdinand of Aragon, and together they united Christian Spain.

Through a series of battles the Spanish Christians took city after city, freeing Christian captives from the dungeons but at the same time imprisoning Muslims.[26] Eventually they won control of all of Moorish Spain except for the city of Granada. Located amid snow-capped mountains in southern Spain and protected by the Alhambra, possibly the most magnificent fortress ever built in a Muslim land, Granada was a formidable city indeed. The armies of Ferdinand and Isabella besieged Granada for six months and then offered terms of peace: If the city surrendered, those who chose to leave would be sent free of charge to Africa. Those who chose to remain had to acknowledge Ferdinand and Isabella as king and queen, but would be allowed freedom of worship and the right to be governed by their own laws, administered by Moorish rule. The Moors accepted, and the Emir of Granada emerged from the walls and presented the keys to the city to Ferdinand and Isabella.[27]

In a triumphal procession, "the Spanish army marched into Granada. Cardinal Mendoza raised a great silver cross over the Alhambra, and Ferdinand and Isabella knelt in the city square to give thanks to the God who after 781 years had evicted Islam from Spain."[28]

One of those who marched into Granada with Ferdinand and Isabella was Christopher Columbus.[29]

And the date was January 2, 1492.

ENDNOTES

[1]Olive Beaupre Miller, *A Picturesque Tale of Progress* (Chicago: Book House for Children, 1931, 1953), Nine Vols., V: 138.

[2]Id., V: 140.

[3]R. Ernest Dupuy, Colonel, USA (Ret.), and Trevor N. Dupuy, Colonel, USA (Ret.), *The Encyclopedia of Military History* (New York: Harper & Row, 1970), p. 201.

[4]Id., pp. 199-200.

[5]Miller, V: 141.

[6]Id., V: 144-47.

[7]Id., V: 152.

[8]John Clark Ridpath, *History of the World* (Cincinnati: Jones, 1914), pp. 510-12.

[9]Isodorus Pacensis, quoted by Dupuy, p. 205.

[10]Miller, V: 153.

[11]Ridpath, pp. 510-12.

[12]Will Durant, *The Story of Civilization* (New York: Simon & Schuster, 1944). Ten Vols., IV: 341.

[13]Id., p. 342.

[14]Id., p. 343.

[15]Roland H. Bainton, *Christian Attitudes Toward War and Peace: A Historical Study and Critical Re-Evaluation* (Nashville: Abington, 1950), p. 114.

[16]Id.

[17]Pope Urban II, A.D. 1095, quoted by Bainton, pp. 111-12.

[18]Bernard of Clairvaux, quoted by Bainton, p. 114.

[19]Raymond of Agiles, quoted by Bainton, pp. 112-13.

[20]*Catholic Encyclopedia*, 1913, "Crusades."

[21]Miller, VI: 89.

[22]Id., VI: 89-92.

[23]Pope Nicholas V., Papal Bull, September 1453; see generally *Catholic Encyclopedia*, 1913, "Henry the Navigator."

[24]Durant, IV: 300-01.

[25]Miller, VI: 116.

[26]Jean Plaidy, *The Spanish Inquisition* (New York: Citadel, 1967) p. 177.

[27]Miller, VI: 115.

[28]Durant, VI: 204.

[29]Samuel Eliot Morison, *Admiral of the Ocean Sea* (Boston: Little, Brown & Co., 1942), p. 101.

CHAPTER FOUR

CHRISTOPHER COLUMBUS: CONQUISTADOR OR CHRIST-BEARER?

A cherished Catholic tradition tells of a third-century pagan prince named Offerus. Being of great size and physical strength himself, he resolved to serve only the strongest and bravest king, but found none worthy of his allegiance. One day, while he was carrying people across a raging river, he carried on his shoulder a child who continually grew heavier, so that Offerus seemed to have the weight of the whole world on his shoulders. Asked who He was, the Child identified himself as the Creator and Redeemer of the world, Jesus Christ. Offerus pledged his allegiance to Christ, became known as St. Christopher (meaning the Christ-bearer), and eventually became a martyr for the Christian faith.

Christopher Columbus took the tradition of his namesake seriously and applied St. Christopher's role to himself. His son Ferdinand Columbus wrote this of him,

> . . . So the surname of Colon [Italian form of Columbus] which he revived was a fitting one, because in Greek it means "member," and by his proper name Christopher, men might know that he

was a member of Christ, by Whom he was sent for the salvation of those people. And if we give his name its Latin form, which is Christophorus Colonus, we may say that just as St. Christopher is reported to have gotten that name because he carried Christ over deep waters with great danger to himself, and just as he conveyed over people whom no other could have carried, so the Admiral Christophorus Colonus, asking Christ's aid and protection in that perilous pass, crossed over with his company that the Indian nations might become dwellers in the triumphant Church of Heaven. There is reason to believe that many souls that Satan expected to catch because they had not passed through the waters of baptism were by the Admiral made dwellers in the eternal glory of Paradise.[1]

And in the year 1500 Juan de la Cosa, pilot of the Nina (one of the three ships made famous by Columbus's first voyage), made a map of the known world. At the top of the map is a drawing of St. Christopher wading ashore bearing the Christ child on his shoulders. And the figure of St. Christopher appears to be modeled after Columbus himself, the man who bore the good news of Jesus Christ to the New World.[2]

Columbus was controversial in his own time, and he has been controversial ever since. In 1554 the historian Lopez de Gomara called Columbus's achievement "the greatest thing since the creation of the world (excluding the incarnation and death of Him who created it)."[3] But in 1768 an anti-slavery writer from Massachusetts, Cornelius de Pauw, declared that "the discovery of the New World has been the most disastrous event in the history of mankind."[4] In the Western Hemisphere more cities, parks, rivers, and landmarks are named for Columbus than any other person. In the United States Columbus Day is a national holiday in October; and in 1992, the five hundredth anniversary of Columbus's first voyage, great celebrations are planned. But various Native American groups celebrated Columbus Day 1991 as the five hundredth anniversary of the last year of independence for Native Americans.[5]

Who was this man? What were his true motivations? What did he accomplish and where did he fail?

Columbus's background is shrouded in mystery. His birth in Genoa, Italy, between 25 August and 31 October 1451 is conceded by nearly everyone, but his ethnic background is disputed. Many ethnic groups claim him as their own; those with the strongest evidence appear to be the claim that he was from a long line of Italian descent, that he came from a Norwegian family with business interests in Genoa, or that he was from a family of Spanish conversos (Jewish converts to Christianity) who had emigrated to Genoa.[6] While all of these claims are interesting, what he believed and what he did are of far greater importance than his background.

His father, Domenico Columbus, was a weaver who worked with woolen goods, as was his father Giovanni Columbus before him. Christopher may have learned his family trade; other than that he appears to have had little if any formal schooling.

As a young man he began his career as a sailor, hiring out to several ships, and may have engaged in sea-battles against Muslim Barbary pirates.[7] Then, in 1476 at the age of about twenty-five he was shipwrecked off the coast of Portugal. He stayed in Lisbon and established a business as a mapmaker and soon brought his younger brother Bartholomew to Lisbon as his partner.

Two of Christopher's brothers were faithful co-laborers in the field of discovery. While Christopher presented the case for an expedition to the West to the royal courts of Spain, Bartholomew was presenting the case to the authorities in England and France. Bartholomew was with Christopher during part of the second voyage, and Christopher appointed him adelantado or governor of the Indies; he also accompanied his brother on the fourth voyage. Another brother Diego (Giacomo) accompanied Christopher on the second voyage and with Christopher's help became a "Don" or lord and later entered the priesthood. The brothers shared Christopher's dreams, his glory, and also, as we shall see, his humiliation.

While attending Mass at the chapel of the Convento dos Santos in Lisbon, Christopher met Dona Felipa Perestrello e Moniz. As her title "Dona" suggests, she was the daughter of one of Portugal's leading families; their marriage in 1479 suggests that Columbus had been a successful businessman. Around 1480 she bore him one son, Diego, and she died in or before 1485.

Several years later Columbus fell in love with a young peasant woman of Cordova named Beatriz Enriquez de Harana. Their child Ferdinand was born in 1488. Some have questioned whether Columbus and Beatriz ever married, because no record of their marriage has ever been found. But marriage records were not carefully kept until after the Council of Trent, and Columbus' marital status was never questioned, even by his bitterest enemies, until 72 years after his death when his male heirs became extinct, and even then the legal challenges were unsuccessful.[8] Columbus treated the mother and son well, provided for them throughout his life and in his will, and made the brother and cousin of Beatriz responsible officers in his fleets.

Both of Columbus's sons became pages in the royal court and served with their father in the New World. Diego inherited his father's titles: Admiral of the Ocean Sea and viceroy of the Indies. While growing up he traveled with his father to the royal courts while his father sought approval for his voyage; he represented his father in the Spanish courts while his father was overseas; and he governed the island of Hispaniola after his father's death.

Ferdinand accompanied his father on his fourth voyage, and in 1509 accompanied his half-brother Diego to Hispaniola, where the Spanish Crown gave twenty-one-year-old Ferdinand the responsibility of setting up churches and monasteries on the island. After he returned to Spain he served on several royal commissions, including one appointed to resolve conflicting Spanish and Portuguese claims to the Molucca islands. But he was best known and respected as a classical scholar and author of a biography of his father's life. He showed an admirable loyalty to his half-brother Diego and fought ably and successfully before the royal courts to establish and preserve Diego's claims to their father's titles.

During his lifetime Columbus received many titles and honors, but that which he prized above all others was Admiral of the Ocean Seas. Accordingly, I will refer to him as "the Admiral."

Three major misconceptions exist about the Admiral of the Ocean Seas. The first is that he "discovered" America. He was not the first person to glimpse, explore, or colonize the Western Hemisphere. He wasn't even the first European. The Norse were here five centuries before Columbus, and other Europeans may have been here even earlier. But their explorations and colonizations lacked permanence and had little lasting effect upon the current of world history.

Unlike these earlier explorers and colonists, the Admiral of the Ocean Sea brought the two worlds together.

The second misconception is that Columbus proved that the world is round. With characteristic modern arrogance, we assume that everyone who lived before 1492 was an ignoramus who thought that sailors who ventured too far out to sea would drop off the edge of the earth, if the sea serpents didn't get them first.

In fact, throughout the Middle Ages all well-informed people, whether Christians, Jews, or Arabs, knew the world was round. The ancient Greeks and Romans had established that, and early church scholars like Augustine and Duns Scotus agreed. The Old Testament speaks of the "circle of the earth" (Isa. 40:22).

As we shall see, medieval debates centered not upon the shape of the earth — its roundness was conceded by all — but rather upon the size of the earth, the distance to the other side, the obstacles that may be confronted along the way, and the comparative advantage of alternate routes to the East such as sailing around the southern cape of Africa.

The third misconception is that Columbus sailed only for secular reasons. Nothing could be further from the truth! Throughout his lifetime Christopher Columbus repeatedly stressed his fervent Christian convictions and leaves no doubt that these convictions were his primary motive for sailing. He opens his journal for his first voyage across the Atlantic by addressing the king and queen with these words:

> In the Name of Our Lord Jesus Christ
>
> Because, most Christian and very Exalted, Excellent and mighty Princes, King and Queen of the Spains and of the Islands of the Sea, our Lord and Lady, in this present year 1492, after Your Highnesses had made an end to the war with the Moors who ruled in Europe, and had concluded the war in the very great City of Granada, where in the present year, on the second day of the month of January, I saw the Royal Standards of Your Highnesses placed by force of arms on the towers of the Alhambra (which is the citadel of the said city),
>
> And I saw the Moorish King come forth to the gates of the city and kiss the Royal Hands of Your Highnesses and of the Prince my Lord, and soon after in that same month, through the information that I had given to Your Highnesses concerning the lands of India, and of a Prince who is called Gran Can [Grand Khan], which is to say in our vernacular "King of Kings," how many times he and his predecessors had sent to Rome to seek doctors in our Holy Faith to instruct him therein, and that never had the Holy Father provided them, and thus so many people were lost through lapsing into idolatries and receiving doctrines of perdition;
>
> And Your Highnesses, as Catholic Christians and Princes devoted to the Holy Christian Faith and the propagators thereof, and enemies of the sect of Mahomet and of all idolatries and heresies, resolved to send me, Christopher Columbus, to the said regions of India, to see the said princes and peoples and lands and the disposition of them and of all, and the manner in which may be undertaken their conversion to our Holy Faith, and ordained that I should not go by land (the usual way) to the Orient, but by the route of the Occident, by which no one to this day knows for sure that anyone has gone . . .[9]

Throughout this journal Columbus repeatedly emphasizes his goal of converting people to Christ:

> 12 October 1492 . . . I, in order that they might develop a very friendly disposition towards us, because I knew that they were a people who could better be freed and converted to our Holy Faith by love than by force, gave to some of them red caps and to others glass beads, which they hung on their necks, and many other things of slight value, in which they took much pleasure. They remained so much our [friends] that it was a marvel . . . I believe that they would easily be made Christians, because it seemed to me that they belonged to no religion.[10]
>
> 16 October . . . I don't recognize in them any religion, and I believe that very promptly they would turn Christians, for they are of very good understanding.[11]
>
> 6 November . . . I maintain, Most Serene Princes, that if they had access to devout religious persons knowing the language, they would all turn Christian, and so I hope in Our Lord that Your Highnesses will do something about to with much care, in order to turn to the Church so numerous a folk, and to convert them as you have destroyed those who would not seek to confess the Father, Son and Holy Ghost. And after your days (for we are all mortal) you will leave your realms in a very tranquil state, and free from heresy and wickedness, and will be well received before the eternal Creator, to whom I pray to grant you long life and great increase of many realms and lordships, and both will and disposition to increase the holy Christian religion, as hitherto you have done.[12]
>
> 27 November . . . But now, please our Lord, I shall see the most that I may and little by little I shall come to understand and know, and I will have this language taught to people of my household, because I see that all so far have one language. And afterwards the benefits will be known, and it will be

endeavored to have all these folk Christians, for that will easily be done, since they have no religion; nor are they idolators . . . and I say that Your Highnesses ought not to consent that any foreigner does business or sets foot here, except Christian Catholics, since this was the end and the beginning of the enterprise, that it should be for the enhancement and glory of the Christian religion, nor should anyone who is not a good Christian come to these parts.[13]

12 December. [Columbus raised a great cross at the entrance of the harbor of Moustique Bay on the northwest coast of the island of Hispaniola] as a sign that Your Highnesses hold the country for yours, and principally for a sign of Jesus Christ Our Lord, and honor of Christianity.[14]

16 December . . . Because they are the best people in the world and above all the gentlest, I have much hope in Our Lord that Your Highnesses will make them all Christians, and they will be all yours, as for yours I hold them.[15]

24 December . . . Your Highnesses may believe that in all the world there can be no better or gentler people. Your Highnesses should feel great joy, because presently they will be Christians, and instructed in the good manners of your realms; for a better people there cannot be on earth, and both people and land are in such quantity that I don't know how to write it.[16]

As the Admiral returned from his first voyage, he composed a letter to King Ferdinand and Queen Isabella through one of their chief officials. In this letter he declared that he had forbidden his men from trading unfairly with the natives because he did not want to be a bad witness for Christ in their presence. He stressed their naivete but emphasized that this was not because of lack of intelligence:

. . . I forbade that they should be given things so worthless as pieces of broken crockery and broken glass, and lace points, although when they were able to get them, they thought they had the best jewel in the world; thus it was learned that a sailor for a lace point received gold to the weight of two and a half castellanos, and others much more for other things which were worth much less; yea, for new blancas, for them they would give all that they had, although it might be two or three castellanos' weight of gold or an arroba or two of spun cotton; they even took pieces of the broken hoops of the wine casks and, like animals, gave what they had, so that it seemed to me to be wrong and I forbade it, and I gave them a thousand good, pleasing things which I had bought, in order that they might be fond of us, and further-more might become Christians and be inclined to the love and service of Their Highnesses and of the whole Castilian nation [Spain], and try to help us and to give us of the things which they have in abundance and which are necessary to us. And they know neither sect nor idolatry, with the exception that all believe that the source of all power and goodness is the sky, and they believe very firmly that I, with these ships and people, came from the sky, and in this belief they everywhere received me, after they had overcome their fear. And this does not result from their being ignorant (for they are of a very keen intelligence and men who navigate all those seas, so that it is wondrous the good account they give of everything), but because they have never seen people clothed or ships like ours.[17]

He closes the letter by saying,

So, since our Redeemer has given this triumph to our most illustrious King and Queen, and to their renewed realms, in so great a matter, for this all Christendom ought to feel joyful and make great celebrations and give solemn thanks to the Holy Trinity with many solemn prayers for the great exaltation which it will have, in the turning of so many peoples to our holy faith, and afterwards for material benefits, since not only Spain but all Christians will hence have refreshment and profit.[18]

Columbus emphasized this goal of converting the world to Christ throughout his life. Around 1501, during those difficult days between his third and fourth voyages, the Admiral compiled the *Book of Prophecies*, which is in part a compilation of the various Old and New Testament prophecies that foretell the spreading of the Word of God to distant lands. The Admiral especially relied upon his favorite passages in Isaiah:

Surely the isles wait for me, and the ships of Tarshish first, to bring thy sons from far, their silver and their gold with them, unto the name of the Lord thy God, and to the Holy One of Israel, because he hath glorified thee (60:9).

Listen, O isles, unto me; and hearken, ye people, from far; The Lord hath called me from the womb; from the bowels of my mother hath he made mention of my name (49:1).

Also throughout the book was a special emphasis upon Columbus himself as an instrument chosen of God to bring the gospel to these unknown lands:

I will also give thee for a light to the Gentiles, that thou mayest be my salvation unto the end of the earth (49:6).

And the book contained another theme that was never far from the center of the Admiral's thought: the reconquest of Jerusalem and the liberation of the Holy Sepulchre from Muslim control:

And Jeremiah says again: At that time they shall call Jerusalem the throne of the Lord: and all the nations shall be gathered unto it, to the name of the

Lord, to Jerusalem; neither shall they walk any more after the imagination of their evil heart (Jer. 3:17).[19]

The spirit of the Crusaders was far from forgotten in Europe, especially after the fall of Constantinople in 1453. Repeatedly the Admiral declared his burning desire to see Jerusalem back in Christian hands and insisted that any gold discovered through his voyages must be earmarked for that Crusade. Perhaps the Admiral even hoped to lead the final Crusade himself: "The Abbot Joachim of Calabria said that he who was to rebuild the Sepulchre on Mt. Zion would come from Spain."[20]

The book also stresses Columbus's belief that his generation was living in the "Last Days" before the Lord's return: "For, behold, I create new heavens and a new earth: and the former shall not be remembered nor come into mind" (Isa. 65:17). He believed the world would come to an end 7,000 years after Creation. Since King Alfonso the Wise had calculated that the world was 5,343 years and 318 days old when Christ was born, and 1,501 years had subsequently passed, the earth had to be 6,845 years old and the end was only 155 years away.

Christ had promised that all prophecies would be fulfilled before the end time, and the signs showed that the Lord was hastening their fulfillment. Most significant of all proofs was the fact that the gospel was now being preached in lands across the ocean — due of course to the voyages of Columbus.

The book is in rough form, and probably incomplete; it is likely that Columbus intended to finish and revise it. He planned to present the book to King Ferdinand and Queen Isabella to persuade them to commit their full resources to these undertakings. But ill health, his fourth voyage, and his death in 1506 prevented him from doing so, and it is questionable whether the king and queen ever saw the book.

In this *Book of Prophecies* Columbus declared that the Word of God was his primary motivation to sail and his primary source of information:

I prayed to the most merciful Lord about my heart's great desire, and He gave me the spirit and the intelligence for the task . . . It was the Lord who put into my mind (I could feel His hand upon me) to sail to the Indies. All who heard of my project rejected it with laughter, ridiculing me. There is no question that the inspiration was from the Holy Spirit, because He comforted me with rays of marvelous illumination from the Holy Scriptures . . . encouraging me continually to press forward, and without ceasing for a moment they now encourage me to make haste.

Our Lord Jesus Christ desired to perform a very obvious miracle in the voyage to the Indies, to comfort me and the whole people of God. I spent seven years in the royal court . . . and in the end they concluded that it was all foolishness, so they gave it up. But since things generally came to pass that were predicted by our Savior Jesus Christ, we should also believe that this particular prophecy will come to pass. In support of this, I offer the gospel text Matthew 24:25, in which Jesus said that all things would pass away, but not his marvelous Word. He also affirmed that it was necessary that all things be fulfilled that were prophesied by himself and by the prophets.

I said that I would state my reasons: I hold alone to the sacred and Holy Scriptures, and to the interpretations of prophecy given by certain devout persons.

It is possible that those who see this book will accuse me of being unlearned in literature, of being a layman and a sailor. I reply with the words of Matthew 11:25: "Lord, because thou hast hid these things from the wise and prudent, and hast revealed them unto babes."

The Holy Scripture testifies in the Old Testament by the prophets and in the New Testament by our Redeemer Jesus Christ, that this world must come to an end. The signs of when this must happen are given by Matthew, Mark, and Luke. The prophets also predicted many things about it:

Our Redeemer Jesus Christ said that before the end of the world, all things must come to pass that had been written by the prophets. Isaiah goes into great detail in describing future events and in calling all people to our holy catholic faith ... For the execution of the journey to the Indies I did not make use of intelligence, mathematics, or maps. It is simply the fulfillment of what Isaiah prophesied ...

These are great and wonderful things for the earth, and the signs are that the Lord is hastening the end. The fact that [the] gospel must still be preached to so many lands in such a short time — this is what convinces me.[21]

Some have speculated that Columbus may have been influenced by Protestantism. While Madariaga says he was "already a protestant,"[22] he would not deny that the Admiral was a lifelong devoted Catholic who was loyal to the Church and who believed the basic doctrines of Roman Catholicism including the Catholic view of the Sacraments and veneration of Mary and the other saints. The Protestant Reformation did not really get underway until a quarter of a century after Columbus sailed; Luther posted his ninety-five theses in 1517.

Still, stirrings of the Reformation began well before Columbus, with men like John Wycliff and John Huss. And Columbus did reflect certain Protestant themes. His personal study of Scripture, made possible in part by Gutenburg's printing of the Bible, coupled with his belief that the simple and childish could instruct the wise and learned in the ways of God, fit well with the Protestant emphasis on the priesthood of all believers and the belief of Luther and Calvin that every plowboy should be able to read and interpret the Scriptures for himself. His consuming interest in Bible prophecy, millennialism (the belief that Christ will reign on earth for a literal one-thousand year period), and his belief that the last days before Christ's return were at hand were also characteristic of some (but not all) Protestants. At the same time, such beliefs were fairly common among the Franciscan order of the Roman Catholic Church, with whom Columbus maintained some ties.[23] In short, Columbus may be considered a devout Catholic with some Protestant leanings.

As forthrightly and fervently as Columbus sets forth his Christian beliefs and motivations, it is amazing that this side of the Admiral is routinely ignored today. A leading translator of Columbus's writings, August J. Kling, has said, "Columbus' use of the Bible is one of the best documented facts of his remarkable career, but it is one of the least known to the general public."[24]

School history texts frequently downplay or omit the Admiral's statements about religion, leading the reader to the erroneous conclusion that religion was not an important factor in Columbus's voyages. Especially pathetic is a 1991 children's book published by Sears-Roebuck titled *The Voyage of Columbus in His Own Words* which purports to speak for Columbus but censors out all reference to God or Christianity.

Devoting only a few pages to Columbus, it is possible for a textbook writer to gloss over the Admiral's religious beliefs. It is more difficult to write a detailed biography of the man without discussing his religion, for his references to Christianity are too numerous to ignore.

For some authors, this creates difficulty. One's world view affects one's interpretation of history, and many modern historians have a secular world view. Since religion is not very important to them, they reason that religion couldn't have been very important to Columbus either. But when virtually every page of the Admiral's own writings shout Christianity, what is a secular historian to do?

One approach is to assume that Columbus was faking it. He obviously didn't take Christianity seriously; what intelligent renaissance man could? So he must have inserted these references to impress someone. This assumes, first, that Columbus was insincere and phony; and second, that there was someone important who was worth impressing and who was impressed by Christianity, i.e., Queen Isabella and her advisors.

Another suggestion is that Columbus kept his journal with its Christian references only to impress the king and queen and maintained a secret journal that reflected his true feelings and therefore presumably left religion out of the picture. Needless to say, this secret journal has not been found!

The notion is preposterous. It is true that Columbus kept a private mileage log to record distances traveled each day. He openly states that he understated the distances covered because the crew might become alarmed if they knew how far from Europe they had sailed. (Ironically, the Admiral's official log turned out to be more accurate than the private log!)[25] But there is no reason to believe the private log contained anything more than mileage.

If Columbus was faking his Christianity when he wrote his journals, he was also faking it throughout his life; for his entire life and all his writings clearly show his devotion to the Christian religion.

I am far from suggesting that secret conspiracies do not exist. But one problem with an overly conspiratorial view of history is that it can lead anywhere the human mind is capable of traveling. Using the same evidence available to the secular historians, I could just as easily claim Columbus was a secret Satanist, a closet charismatic, a New Age Hindu, or a Communist agent who carefully concealed his true beliefs because they would not have been accepted at the time. When confronted with the total lack of evidence for such a conclusion, I could respond, "That's proof the conspiracy worked! See what a great job he did of covering up the evidence!"

Because such methodology can lead to irrefutable but absurd conclusions, the best method is to assume that historical figures said what they meant and meant what they said, without evidence to the contrary.

And so, due to the near-impossibility of ignoring the Admiral's professions of Christian faith and the difficulty of trying to claim that these Christian professions were insincere, some historians have taken another tack: to highlight the Spaniards' Christian professions and contrast them with Spanish crimes and misdeeds, thereby placing Christianity in a bad light. Milton Meltzer, in *Columbus and the World Around Him* (New York: Franklin Watts, 1990), does a particularly shoddy job of this. Amid poor documentation and factual errors, Meltzer delights in pointing out Spanish acts of brutality toward Native Americans and then adds a comment like, "That evening, he joined all the other Spaniards in singing a hymn to the Blessed Virgin."[26] When Columbus uses Scripture to justify his conclusions, Meltzer says, "Instead of grappling with the facts, Columbus's mind spun off in fantasy."[27] So much for objectivity!

By contrast, some writers either ignore or whitewash the sins and errors of Columbus. I intend to follow none of these approaches. I do not deny that Columbus made mistakes and committed sins. Everyone does. Few would define Christianity in terms of sinless perfection. I consider myself a Christian even though I know I am far from sinless. The slogan, "Christians aren't perfect — just forgiven," leaves me with mixed emotions. It correctly emphasizes that we are merely redeemed sinners, but we often use it to excuse ourselves for being less righteous than we should be with God's help.

Rather, I will argue that the sins of Christopher Columbus and the other explorers were sins that a dedicated Christian could have committed, given the times and circumstances. Some of their actions were wrong; but these do not disprove the basic thesis that the explorers were committed Christians whose basic motive was to bring Christianity to the lands across the ocean.

This is not to say that Columbus was interested in nothing but religion. Christianity was his major interest, his major purpose in life, and the yardstick by which he measured everything he did. But he was also keenly interested in science, as were many leading churchmen of his day. He had a brilliant mind, and while not well-educated in the sense of academic degrees, he was very well-read in many fields of science and skilled in astronomy, cartography (mapmaking), and navigation. He was a skilled debater, and he spoke with an air of authority and conviction that reflected his sense of divine mission and inspired respect and confidence. An engaging conversationalist, he had a unique ability to captivate people and make them his allies.

Madariaga has this to say about Columbus:

> . . . how can we dissect a living man born in the midst of biblical faiths and legends, bred in the midst of cosmographical truths and errors, grown in the midst of sailing yarns and marvels, and analyze the vigorous impulse which led him across a sea of errors to the shore of truth?
>
> He does not know Colon [Columbus] who does not realize this baffling complexity of his character. Ptolemy and Esdras have an equal value in his mind, a mind both medieval and modern, or better still, neither modern nor medieval. This immortal voyage, conceived with a prophetic imagination, is carried out with a seamanship and a spirit of observation admired by sailor and scientist alike.[28]

His son Ferdinand, a noted scholar whose biography of Christopher Columbus gives great insight into his life and character, offers the following description of his father:

> The Admiral was a well-built man of more than average statute, the face long, the cheeks somewhat high, his body neither fat nor lean. He had an aquiline nose and light-colored eyes; his complexion too was light and tending to bright red. In youth his hair was blonde, but when he reached the age of thirty, it all turned white. In eating and drinking, and in the adornment of his person, he was very moderate and modest. He was affable in conversation with strangers and very pleasant to the members of his household, though with a certain gravity. He was so strict in matters of religion that for fasting and saying prayers he might have been taken for a member of a religious order. He was so great an enemy of swearing and blasphemy that I give my word I never heard him utter any other oath than

"by St. Ferdinand!" and when he grew very angry
with someone, his rebuke was to say "God take you!"
for doing or saying that. If he had to write anything,
he always began by writing these words: IESUS
cum MARIA sit nobis in via. And so fine was his
hand that he might have earned his bread by that
skill alone.[29]

Bartolome de Las Casas, the priest who became a
champion of the rights of Native Americans and an outspo-
ken critic of Spanish policies in the New World, is still
known as the "Apostle to the Indies." He knew Columbus
personally; his father and uncle had been shipmates and
colonists under the Admiral. At times Las Casas was
critical of the Admiral's actions, although he blames most
of the problems on those who came after him. But he had a
high regard for Columbus as a man. His character sketch
begins very much like that of Ferdinand Columbus, and
then continues:

In matters of the Christian religion, without
doubt he was a Catholic and of great devotion, for in
everything he did and said or sought to begin, he
always interposed "In the name of the Holy Trinity
I will do this," or "launch this" or "this will come to
pass." In whatever letter or other thing he wrote, he
put at the head "Jesus and Mary be with us on the
way," and of these writings of his in his own hand I
have plenty now in my possession. His oath was
sometimes "I swear by San Fernando;" when he
sought to affirm something of great importance in
his letters on oath, especially in writing to the
Sovereigns, he said, "I swear that this is true."
He observed the fasts of the Church most faith-
fully, confessed and made communion often, read the
canonical offices like a churchman or member of a
religious order, hated blasphemy and profane swear-
ing, was most devoted to Our Lady and to the seraphic
father St. Francis; seemed very grateful to God for
benefits received from the divine hand, wherefore, as

in the proverb, he hourly admitted that God had conferred upon him great mercies, as upon David . . . He was extraordinarily zealous for the divine service; he desired and was eager for the conversion of these people [native Americans], and that in every region the faith of Jesus Christ be planted and enhanced. And he was especially affected and devoted to the idea that God should deem him worthy of aiding somewhat in recovering the Holy Sepulchre . . .

He was a gentleman of great force of spirit, of lofty thoughts, naturally inclined (from what we may gather of his life, deeds, writings and conversation) to undertake worthy deeds and signal enterprises; patient and long-suffering (as later shall appear), and a forgiver of injuries, and wished nothing more than that those who offended against him should recognize their errors, and that the delinquents be reconciled with him; most constant and endowed with forbearance in the hardships and adversities which were always occurring and which were incredible and infinite; ever holding great confidence in divine providence. And verily, from what I have heard from him and from my own father, who was with him when he returned to colonize Hispaniola in 1493, and from others who accompanied and served him, he held and always kept on terms of intimate fidelity and devotion to the Sovereigns.[30]

Along with the Admiral's sense of divine mission came a certain absorption in his own self-importance as the central instrument of God's plan, a determination that some might call stubbornness, a confidence that might border on arrogance, an absolute certainty of the correctness of his theological and scientific conclusions even in the face of overwhelming evidence (reminiscent of the North Dakota judge I used to know who was fond of saying "I'm often wrong, but I'm never in doubt"), and an incurable optimism but with it a tendency toward depression and self-pity when his dreams were not realized as quickly as he expected. He was a flawed, imperfect being, to be sure, as are we all; but he was also a man of greatness who was mightily used of God. A less bull-headed man would not have persevered against all the obstacles. Had Columbus looked at the evidence objectively and realized how far away Asia actually was, he would not have undertaken the journey.

Gianni Granzotto gives valuable insight into the books that influenced Columbus:

> We have fairly reliable indications in the books that Fernando [Columbus's son] preserved in his own library, which were later passed on to the Columbian archives in Seville, where one can still read the volumes annotated by Columbus himself. There were four or five books in particular, however, which he carried with him throughout his entire life, even when crossing the ocean; they are *Historia Rerum* by Cardinal Piccolomini, who later became Pope Pius II; the *Imago Mundi* of Pierre Cardinal d'Ailly, rector of the Sorbonne in the first part of the century; the *Book of Marco Polo*, also known under the title of *Il Milione*; Pliny's *Natural History*; and Zacuto's *Perpetual Almanac*.
>
> The most important of these for Columbus was Cardinal d'Ailly's text, which was actually a rather elementary compendium of ancient texts, but which for America's discoverer constituted an invaluable sampling of Greek and Latin thought on the world's geography, a kind of recapitulatory digest of things he had to know. Without having to resort to other texts, he thus gained some knowledge of Plato, Aristotle, Theophrastus, Cicero, Seneca, Pomponius Meland Macrobius, the authors most often commented on in the margins of the d'Ailly book, where the cardinal made reference to them.
>
> All this notwithstanding, Columbus's main source remained the Bible. A text that he certainly must have been familiar with was a much-consulted handbook of sorts put together by a fifteenth-century

Spanish luminary, which brought together all the Bible's various passages on cosmographical and astronomical matters, providing all the proper concordances. Over the centuries, the custodians of biblical truth for Christendom had been the church fathers. Among them Columbus seemed to favor St. Augustine. But in the end the most essential author, on whom all geographical knowledge was based, was Ptolemy. Ptolemy was Columbus's passion and his torment, a source of both knowledge and perplexity. If he had believed blindly in everything Ptolemy says, he never would have discovered America. Yet without Ptolemy he never would have been able to discover it.[31]

Ptolemy, an astronomer and geographer who lived around AD 100-165, taught that the earth is round, but also that the sun revolves around the earth. He helped to expand and clarify knowledge about the geography of the known world at the time, but he taught that the oceans beyond the known world were uninhabited and unnavigable. Granzotto has more to say about Columbus's knowledge of geography:

By this time all of Columbus's letters, notes, marginalia were centered around this dilemma — the limits of land and ocean, what lay or might lie beyond the ocean. He saw flashes of hope from time to time. Macrobius spoke of a "fourfold earth," presuming the existence of a "fourth" region of the world. Plato, in relating the legends of the Island of Atlantis, saw a "hidden land" larger than Asia and Africa. Pomponius Mela alluded to an "alter orbis," another world beyond the known ones. Cicero maintained there were two habitable zones on earth. These were glimmers in the dark. They would appear, then disappear. In the d'Ailly book, Columbus underlined Anchise's famous lines to his son Aeneas in the Aeneid: "There are lands beyond the signs of the zodiac, beyond the course of the years and the sun." Beyond. Even the great master Virgil believed in it.

Other notes that Columbus made in his copy of
Imago Mundi — and it really is exciting to sense the
life, the human presence, anxious and full of doubt
and hope, still perceptible in that yellowed parch-
ment in the Seville library — give an indication of
the progress of his thought in Lisbon. For example:
"Mare totum navigable," all seas are navigable. Or:
"all seas are peopled by lands;" "the Ocean Sea is no
emptier than any other;" "every country has its east
and west." Columbus was remarkably swift to intuit, in everything he read and heard, allusions to
the future events toward which his life was heading
with increasing momentum. He cast himself headlong in that direction, though unsure of the road.
Intuition guided him in applying inventiveness to
the stimuli that reality provided, yet remained suspended between marginalia — anxious and excited,
yet always written with an eye toward his hopes —
show his entire investigation to be imbued with a
nearly prophetic sense, under whose spell every
word, every argument rises up and becomes something very close to poetry. Invention, imagination,
prophecy and poetry, with an occasional mad leap
from reality: it all pointed toward his goal, like an
arrow already in flight and trembling in midair as it
shoots toward its target.[32]

Believing with Roman Catholics that the Apocrypha is
part of the Bible, Columbus seized upon the passage from
the Book of Esdras: "And on the third day Ye united the
waters and the earth's seventh part, and dried the six other
parts." Columbus gave this passage a very literal interpretation. "Esdras," he wrote, "asserts that the world is made
up of six parts earth and one part water."[33] Because of this
interpretation, Columbus underestimated the size of the
oceans. He accepted the work of ancient geographers who
had divided the globe into 360 degrees of latitude and
longitude. But where the ancient geographers had asserted
that a degree at the equator was 56 miles, Columbus
erroneously assumed that a Roman mile was the same as

an Arabic mile when in reality it is much shorter. This caused him to conclude that the earth's circumference is about 18,750 miles, about 25% less than it really is.

The error was complicated by overestimating the size of Europe and Asia, an overestimate caused partly by reliance on Esdras and partly on Marco Polo. Polo's mistake was easy to make. I love horses, but if I were to ride on horseback all the way from Italy to China, I'd probably overestimate the size of the Eurasian continent too!

Three errors came into conjunction: (1) The earth is 25% smaller than it really is; (2) The earth is 6/7 land and only 1/7 ocean; (3) The Eurasian continent is much larger than it really is. Put these calculations together, and you conclude that the Pacific Coast of China must be much closer to the Atlantic Coast of Spain than it really is. And so, as he wrote in the margin of a page of Cardinal d'Ailly's Imago Mundi, "Between the edge of Spain and the beginning of India the sea is short and can be crossed in a matter of a few days."[34]

And so, the thought began to grip him: The best way to sail from Spain to the Orient is westward across the ocean, not eastward around Africa. And because the Lord had implanted this revelation in his mind and had given him the scientific knowledge, navigational skills, and physical vigor for such an undertaking, and had placed within his heart the zeal to do divine work, the Lord had obviously chosen him, predestined him, Christopher Columbus, to lead this great voyage. Through Christopher Columbus souls would be saved for all eternity; the realm of Christendom would be vastly increased; and the resources would be obtained to mount a successful Crusade to free Jerusalem and the Holy Sepulchre from Muslim control. His heart and mind quickly warmed to the task.

Two other factors may have sparked this sense of divine mission in Christopher Columbus. In 1476, at the age of twenty-five, the ship on which Columbus was sailing caught fire in a sea battle, and he found himself in the open water. He found a floating oar and managed to swim; as Ferdinand says, "and so it pleased God, who was preserving him for greater things, to give him the strength to reach the shore.

However, he was so fatigued by his experience that it took him many days to recover."[35] Madariaga and others have suggested that this grapple with death was a religious experience in which Columbus began to suspect that God's preserving hand was upon him for future work.

Two other voyages may have shaped his thinking. In 1482-84 he made one or two voyages to Sao Jorge da Mina on the Gold Coast of Africa where he studied the climate at the equator. And in a fragment of a letter or diary preserved by his son Ferdinand he writes, "In the month of February, 1477, I sailed a hundred leagues beyond the island of Thule . . . When I was there the sea was not frozen."[36] Thule is an ancient word for Iceland; a league is normally about three miles. Sailing three hundred miles beyond Iceland to the northwest would have brought Columbus in the vicinity of Greenland, and he very likely would have encountered ice; sailing three hundred miles to the northeast would have brought him to the vicinity of Jan Mayen Island, where the seas frequently are free of ice in winter — especially likely in this instance since Icelandic records relate that the winter of 1476-77 was unusually mild. Why did the Admiral refer to Iceland by the old name of Thule? The Icelandic explorer Viljalmur Stefansson and others believe he was referring to Seneca, who in his tragedy *Medea* referred to Iceland as "ultima Thule." The medieval world believed the world south of the equator and north of Iceland was uninhabitable, as was the world west of the Atlantic. Columbus was saying he'd been south to the equator, and north of Iceland; both are inhabitable, both are navigable. Now let's find out about the West![37]

Burning with love for Scripture, science, and adventure, with his feet planted firmly in the Middle Ages but his mind soaring into the Renaissance and beyond, Christopher Columbus approached King John II of Portugal in 1483. Armed with the Bible, classical scientists, maps from Toscanelli, and his own keen intelligence, Columbus sought to persuade the king of Portugal that his proposal was a worthy undertaking. The king appointed a royal commission to study the proposal.

The commission was far from a collection of ignorant

bigots who believed the world was flat. Landstrom explains:

> The royal commission that studied Columbus' plan was composed entirely of learned men. The Bishop of Ceuta, like many of those in the service of the Church, was a scientist; Rodrigo was an astronomer and the king's physician; and Josepe was Jose Vicinho, the well-known cosmographer and astronomer, whom Columbus mentions in his notes as Yosepius. Columbus could not have asked for, or been granted, a more learned body of men in the whole of Europe, but their decision was inevitable: the route to Cipangu [Japan], if there really was any such island, was much too long. The earth was far larger and the ocean far wider than Colon [Columbus] imagined. Al Farghani was right, but his miles were Arabian and not Roman ones. The king was not encouraged to place any faith in the theories of this man Colon.[38]

Note that on each of their points of disagreement, the commission was right and Columbus was wrong. Columbus had confused Arabian miles with Roman miles. The circumference of the earth was much larger than Columbus thought. The distance to Asia was much farther than Columbus insisted. For these and other reasons this proposed voyage to the Orient by way of the West, even if possible, just did not make good economic or geographical sense.

But according to his son Ferdinand, the real reason Portugal rejected Columbus's proposal was divine providence: "God had reserved that prize for Castile" [Spain].[39]

When Queen Isabella of Castile married King Ferdinand of Aragon, Spanish Christians finally began to achieve some unity. And in these Sovereigns Columbus found a sympathetic audience and, particularly in Isabella, a kindred spirit. Isabella was a devout, some said fanatical, Christian, an intelligent and articulate person, generous and ceremonious, and very forthright in her convictions.

Ferdinand shared her Christian devotion but also was a practical politician and statesman, kind, pleasant, sympathetic, and a lover of justice.[40]

In 1486 Columbus presented his proposal to the Spanish Crown, who, like the Portuguese, appointed a commission to study the matter. Like the Portuguese, the Spanish commission was composed of leading men of science. And like the Portuguese, the Spanish commission rejected the Admiral's proposal for many of the same reasons: Columbus's views of the size of the earth simply were at odds with those of the leading scientists of the day and throughout history. In the third century B.C. Eratosthenes had calculated the earth's circumference at 27,750 miles. (It is currently thought to be around 25,000 miles.) He said according to Strabo, "If the Atlantic Ocean were not so extremely large, we could sail from Iberia [Spain] to India along the same latitude on the other side of the earth."[41] But Eratosthenes calculated the size of that ocean to be 14,400 miles and this distance was prohibitive.[42]

But Ferdinand and Isabella did not totally close the door. Isabella in particular seemed gripped by the vision of a mission to the Orient. However, at the time their energies and finances were consumed by the war against the Moors. Columbus was urged to return after Granada had been freed from Muslim control.

Again in 1489 Columbus tried to persuade the king and queen to accept his proposal; again it was referred to the commission, and again in 1490 the commission recommended against it. Then, in 1491, Columbus travelled to Granada in Southern Spain where King Ferdinand and Queen Isabella had the Muslim stronghold under siege. Landstrom suggests that Columbus may have participated in some of the skirmishes against the Moors.[43] And when Granada fell to the Christians on January 2, 1492, the Admiral joined the triumphal procession and thanksgiving services with the rest.

With the war over and Spain united under Christian rule, the king and queen were ready to consider a new crusade. They turned their attention to Columbus, indicated their willingness to accept his proposal, and asked him to state the terms on which he would sail. They listened in shock as he set forth his conditions: one-tenth of all the riches that might be found in the Indies, the title Don Cristobal Colon, and the rank of Admiral of the Ocean Sea and Viceroy and Governor of the Indies.

They had not expected such terms from a poor foreigner with so speculative a proposal and thought they were being generous to even approve the venture. Columbus's terms were refused, and he rode off in the direction of Cordova, intending to try next in the courts of France. But after he had traveled a short distance a horseman overtook him and said the queen had ordered his return. When he returned, he found that the king and queen had changed their minds and had acceded to his demands.

What happened to change their minds? According to Ferdinand Columbus, Luis de Santangel, the Crown's financial secretary, interceded on Columbus's behalf. Santangel told the queen:

> . . . he was surprised that her Highness, who had always shown a resolute spirit in matters of great weight and consequence, should lack it now for an enterprise that offered so little risk [of capital] yet could prove of so great service to God and the exaltation of His Church, not to speak of the very great increase and glory of her realms and kingdoms . . . As for the foolish argument that it would discredit the Queen to have contributed to the project in case the Admiral did not fulfill his promises, he [Santangel] was rather of the opinion that the Sovereigns would be regarded as generous and highminded princes for having tried to penetrate the secrets of the universe, as other princes and rulers had been praised for doing.[44]

Knowing that the king and queen were exhausted from the Granada campaign and that the treasury was depleted, Santangel offered to loan the money for the venture himself. Isabella then assented; Columbus was brought back to court; and an agreement was drafted giving Columbus what he had demanded.

The Admiral's demands may seem unreasonable, and the Crown's concessions generous, but Columbus was risking a great deal on the venture. He might lose his life or come back disgraced as a failure and laughing-stock. And the ten percent concerned only what was recovered in the Indies; ten percent of nothing is nothing. As Columbus saw it, the Crown was getting a good deal: ninety percent compared to his ten percent; and the Crown would get nothing if he didn't sail. Morison suggests the stiff terms reflect Columbus's resentment at the rejection and insults he had suffered for so long at the hands of the royal courts of Europe.[45]

Provisions and a crew of ninety men were assembled, along with three ships. Of these, the Santa Maria was the largest and best-known, being the ship the Admiral sailed on; but the Nina was probably the most sea-worthy vessel of the three.

On August 3, 1492, they were ready to sail. Every man and boy on the crew gave a last confession to a priest and received absolution and Holy Communion. Then, says Las Casas, Columbus "received the very holy sacrament of the Eucharist on the very day that he entered upon the sea; and in the name of Jesus ordered the sails to be set and left the harbor of Palos for the river of Saltes and the Ocean Sea with three equipped caravels, giving the commencement to the First Voyage and Discovery of the Indies."[46]

After a stop in the Canary Islands, the three ships resumed their course westward. Life aboard ship settled into a routine that was designed to impress upon the seaman his need for a right relationship with God. In this age of expressions like "drunk as a sailor" or "cuss like a sailor," we would do well to remember the words of Samuel Eliot Morison, dean of Columbus scholars:

> In the great days of sail, before man's inventions and gadgets had given him false confidence in his power to conquer the ocean, seamen were the most religious of all workers on land or sea. The mariner's philosophy he took from the 107th Psalm: "They that go down to the sea in ships and occupy their

business in great waters; these men see the works of the Lord, and his wonders in the deep. For at his word the stormy wind ariseth, which lifteth up the winds thereof . . ."[47]

As each day began, a young sailor sang out:

Blessed be the light of day
and the Holy Cross, we say;
and the Lord of Veritie
and the Holy Trinity.
Blessed be th' immortal soul
and the Lord who keeps it whole,
blessed be the light of day
and He who sends the night away.

In good Catholic fashion the young sailor then recited the "Pater Noster" (Lord's Prayer) and "Ave Maria" and then added,

God give us good days, good voyage, good passage to the ship, sir captain and master and good company, so let there be, let there be a good voyage; many good days may God grant your graces, gentlemen of the afterguard and gentlemen forward.

Time was measured by an hourglass that had to be turned every half hour. As the seaman turned the hourglass he sang out,

Blessed be the hour our Lord was born,
St. Mary who bore Him,
and St. John who baptized Him.

The day closed with the unison singing of the "Salve Regina," a hymn to the Virgin Mary, at sunset; and each sailor including Columbus had his own private devotions.[48] No one would guarantee that such a routine by itself would keep a sailor free from sin; but it can help to keep the mind and soul focused upon God and eternal values while sailing far from home.

Sometime around October 6 Columbus held a conference with the officers of the three ships as to whether they should continue westward or turn back. Accounts as to what happened at this conference conflict, but apparently some objected that because of the easterly winds prevailing on this voyage, they would have great difficulty getting back at all if they didn't turn back soon. Columbus is said to have replied that God who gave them these winds to sail would give them other winds to return. This did not satisfy the others, but they all agreed to sail westward for three more days. After three days they had still not sighted land, but no one objected to going farther because they had seen signs that land was near: land vegetation floating in the water, birds that normally do not travel far from land, a piece of driftwood that appeared to have been carved by human tools.

Then, early on the morning of October 12 (Columbus Day!), 1492, land was sighted. They went ashore on this island and then on to a second (October 15), third (October 16), and fourth (October 19). The names Columbus gave to these islands clearly reflect his priorities as he says in his letter to the king and queen:

> To the first island which I found I gave the name San Salvador [Holy Saviour], in recognition of His Heavenly Majesty, who marvelously hath given all this; the Indians call it Guanahani. To the second I gave the name Isla de Santa Maria de Concepcion [St. Mary]; to the third, Ferrandina; to the fourth, La Isla Bella; to the fifth, La Isla Juana; and so to each one I gave a new name.[49]

Columbus claimed these islands for Christendom and for Spain, erecting a cross thereon "as a token of Jesus Christ our Lord."[50]

Throughout the next three months the Admiral and his crew stayed in the Indies, visiting various islands, including Cuba and Hispaniola (on which Haiti and the Dominican Republic are located). As the journals reveal, they had substantial contact with Native Americans, mostly of the peaceful Arawak tribes, and they engaged in some trade and evangelization. The natives for the most part received them well, in some cases believing them to be "men from Heaven." They took some as interpreters, sometimes willingly, sometimes by the natives' request, and sometimes by force.

On December 24 the Santa Maria ran aground off the coast of Haiti and had to be abandoned. The local cacique (tribal chief), Guacanagari, came to their aid as Columbus says in his journal:

> Informed of our misfortune, the king shed tears and immediately sent all his people and many large canoes to the ship. So they and we began to unload, and in a short time we had cleared the whole deck, so helpful was the king in this affair. Afterwards, he in person, together with his brothers and relations, kept careful watch both aboard and ashore to see that all was done properly. And from time to time he sent me one of his relatives to tell me not to grieve, that he would give me whatever he had. I assure Your Highnesses that nowhere in Castile would better care have been taken of the goods, so that not a lace point was missing. He caused all our goods to be placed together near the palace, where they remained until two houses that he gave as storehouses had been emptied. He stationed two armed men to watch over those goods day and night; and he and all the other natives wept as if our misfortune were their own.[51]

It was Christmas eve, and not the best Christmas present. But Columbus decided to leave a garrison of forty men behind at that spot, and they called the fort and settlement La Navidad or "Nativity" or "Christmas." The fort was built largely with planks, timbers, and fastenings from the wrecked Santa Maria.

Relations with natives were not always that friendly. The peaceful Arawaks had told Columbus about another tribe that was menacing them from the south and west, known as the Caribs from whom the words "carob" and "Caribbean" are derived, or Canibs from when we get the word "cannibal." The Spaniards were told that the Caribs captured people and ate them; at first the Admiral did not believe them but he soon became convinced.

Their first contact with hostile natives, apparently Caribs, took place on January 13. At first they engaged in peaceful trade, but then the Caribs picked up ropes to bind the Spaniards. Las Casas abstracted the account in the Admiral's journal:

> Seeing them running towards them, the Christians, being prepared as always the Admiral advised them to be, fell upon them, and gave an Indian a great slash on the buttocks, and wounded another in the breast with an arrow. Seeing that they could gain little, although the Christians were not more than seven, they 50 and more, began to flee, until not one remained, one leaving his arrows here, and another his bows there. The Christians would have killed many of them, it is said, if the pilot who went with them as their captain had not prevented it. The Christians returned to the caravel with their boat, and when the Admiral knew of it he said that on the one hand he was sorry and on the other not, since they would have fear of the Christians, because without doubt, says he, the folk there are bad actors (as one says), and he believed that they were Caribs, and ate men . . .[52]

Two days later, on January 15, Columbus decided it was time to return to Spain, as the crew was becoming restless. They left the island of Hispaniola on January 16, and despite a storm at sea they arrived at the Azores on February 18, Columbus having steered a perfect course homeward that landed right on target. Having steered to the North Atlantic, the Admiral took advantage of westerly trade winds that would carry him to Europe. Many believe Columbus was the first person to understand the wind patterns of the Atlantic.[53]

On March 4 they landed at Lisbon, Portugal, where Columbus had an interview with King John II. With great relish, coupled with a dash of "I-told-you-so" and "Look-at-the-wonderful-opportunity-you-and-Portugal-missed-because-you-wouldn't-listen-to-me," Columbus told the Portuguese king about his discoveries. With the help of one of the Native Americans he had brought with him, Columbus used some beans to make a map showing the location of the various islands. The king, realizing the opportunity he had lost, declared, "O man of little comprehension!" and "Why did I let slip an enterprise of so great importance?"[54]

On March 15 they landed in Palos, the Spanish port from which they had departed six months earlier. They were summoned to appear before the king and queen in Barcelona, and the royal reception they received was probably the high point of the Admiral's career. He was addressed with the titles he had sought, and he was toasted as a hero and a discoverer. The natives he brought with him were baptized, signifying the many conversions that would follow as result of the "Christ-bearer's" work.

But the Admiral's spirit was restless for more adventure. He promptly laid plans for a second voyage, this time for colonization as well as discovery. Something more permanent was needed, it seemed, if voyages to the Indies were to become a profitable enterprise.

Perhaps Columbus's biggest disappointment from the first voyage was the lack of gold. The natives they traded with did have a little gold, gold nuggets and gold ornaments here and there, but nothing remotely approaching the vast wealth that Marco Polo had described in the Orient. And remember, Columbus believed he had reached the Orient, or islands close to it. Naturally he believed that if his calculations of the circumference of the earth and the size of the Eurasian continent were correct, that's exactly where he would have been!

When Columbus asked the natives about gold, they repeatedly told him that gold was to be found several days' journey westward. Possibly they were referring to the Aztecs, Incas, or remnants of Mayan civilization. That was all the proof the Admiral needed: This was indeed the Orient!

Columbus set forth his plans for this second voyage in a letter to the king and queen April 9, 1493. He suggested the importation of about two thousand colonists to be located in three or four towns, that each town and village have its own magistrate and notary according to the custom of Spain, and that "there be a church and abbots or friars to administer the sacraments, perform divine worship, and convert the natives."[55]

The king and queen responded on May 29, 1493, with instructions for the Admiral's second voyage:

> ... it hath pleased God, Our Lord, in His abundant mercy to reveal the said Islands and Mainland to the King and Queen, our Lords, by the diligence of the Don Christopher Columbus, their Admiral, Viceroy and Governor thereof, who hath reported it to Their Highnesses that he knew the people he found residing therein to be very ripe to be converted to our Holy Catholic Faith, since they have neither dogma nor doctrine; wherefore it hath pleased and greatly pleaseth Their Highnesses (since in all matters it is meet that their principal concern be for the service of God, Our Lord, and the enhancement of our Holy Catholic Faith); wherefore, desiring the augmentation and increase of our Holy Catholic Faith, Their Highnesses charge and direct the said Admiral, Viceroy and Governor that by all ways and means he strive and endeavor to win over the inhabitants of the said Islands and Mainland to be converted to our Holy Catholic Faith ... [56]

To aid Columbus in converting the natives, they announced they were sending priests and clerics with him. With their help the Admiral was "to see that they be carefully taught the principles of Our Holy Faith."[57] They further directed that Columbus was to

> ... force and compel all those who sail therein as well as all others who are to go out from here later on, that they treat the said Indians very well and

lovingly and abstain from doing them any injury,
arranging that both peoples hold much conversation
and intimacy, each serving the others to the best of
their ability. Moreover, the said Admiral shall gra-
ciously present them with things from the merchan-
dise of Their Highnesses which he is carrying for
barter, and honor them much; and if some person or
persons should maltreat the said Indians in any
manner whatsoever, the said Admiral, as Viceroy
and Governor of Their Highnesses, shall punish
them severely by the virtue of the authority vested
in him by Their Majesties for this purpose . . .[58]

With seventeen ships and twelve hundred colonists,
Columbus set sail from Cadiz, Spain, on September 25,
1493. After a short stopover in the Canary Islands, they
landed in the Indies November 3, briefly visiting several
islands which the Admiral named Dominica (possibly after
his father), Mariagalante, Todos los Santos (Feast of All
Saints), and St. Maria de Guadalupe. On the last of these
they found some natives, apparently Arawak youths who
had been captured by Caribs. Michele de Cuneo, a young
Italian nobleman who sailed on the voyage, described what
happened in a letter to a friend:

In that island we took twelve very beautiful and
very fat women from 15 to 16 years old, together
with two boys of the same age. These had the genital
organ cut to the belly; and this we thought had been
done in order to prevent them from meddling with
their wives or maybe to fatten them up and later eat
them. These boys and girls had been taken by the
above mentioned Caribs; and we sent them to Spain
to the King, as a sample.[59]

They traveled in a westerly direction, island-hopping for
several days, and were attacked by Caribs on the island of
Santa Cruz (Holy Cross). Seeing the fierceness of the
Caribs, Columbus became concerned for the garrison at
Navidad. His darkest fears were realized: all forty men

were dead. Talking through interpreters to their friend from the previous voyage, Guacanagari, they found the natives evasive but eventually pieced together the story. Shortly after Columbus left, the Spaniards began fighting among themselves. They then degenerated into chasing native women and trying to steal gold. A Carib cacique, Caonabo, then attacked the fort with a large body of warriors and killed them all. The Arawaks insisted that Guacanagari and his men had fought against Caonabo in defense of the Spaniards, but some of Columbus's party were skeptical. Some suspected Guacanagari of complicity in the destruction of La Navidad, and urged that he be put to death; but Columbus refused, saying there was doubt as to his guilt.[60] The remains of the Spaniards were given a Christian burial, and after some time Caonabo was captured. Again the men wanted to execute him, but Columbus refused, saying that a cacique of his rank should stand trial before the royal courts of Spain. Caonabo was placed on a ship and sent back to Spain, but he died en route.

Columbus and his colonists established two settlements, Isabella on the northern coast of Hispaniola and Santo Domingo on the southern coast. With the settlers safely ashore, the crews of the ships were no longer needed, so the Admiral sent twelve of the seventeen ships back to Spain along with a report to the king and queen and a request for provisions. Columbus then left the colony for five months of exploration, and came back in ill-health and semi-comatose. But to his pleasant surprise he found that his brother Bartholomew had arrived in Isabel! Columbus greeted him warmly and with questionable legal authority appointed Bartholomew adelantado (governor) of the colony. Their younger brother, Diego Columbus, arrived later.

Together the Admiral and the adelantado faced a host of problems. Quarrels were frequent, both among the Spaniards themselves and between the Spaniards and the natives. Supplies were short, as was food, disease was plentiful, and the colony was rife with discontent. When the next fleet sailed for Spain, two hundred colonists returned, many in bad health and most complaining about Columbus. In response, in October 1495 the Crown sent a royal inspector to investigate conditions in the colony. This infuriated Columbus, and in March 1496 the Admiral decided that he had to return to Spain to answer to the king and queen.

To Ferdinand and Isabella, Columbus had become something of a problem. I disagree with those who think the king and queen had come to dislike the Admiral and regret the enterprise. I believe they genuinely liked him, particularly Isabella, and were truly pleased and proud of what he had accomplished for Christendom and for Spain in opening new lands to the gospel. But his demands were becoming more strident, and the frequent complaints about his government of the Indies were an irritation and an embarrassment. They had made him viceroy and governor of the Indies, and they wanted to keep their commitment to him; but by this time they probably were beginning to wonder whether the appointment was truly in the long-term interests of all concerned.

Besides, at this time war with France was impending, and the crown simply could not spare the resources needed for Hispaniola.

Under the circumstances, Ferdinand and Isabella were most patient and generous with Columbus. They granted him an audience, questioned him, and were satisfied with his answers. They agreed to give him six ships for his third voyage, although he had to wait awhile because of affairs in Europe. They departed on May 30, 1498, three ships heading straight west to Hispaniola and three, including Columbus, heading along a southern route by way of the Cape Verde Islands.

Having announced that the first new land he discovered on this voyage would be named after the Trinity, Columbus considered it a sign from God when the first land he saw took the form of three peaks.[61] Lying off the coast of Venezuela, the island of the three peaks still bears the name Trinidad. Behind Trinidad he saw Venezuela and became the first European in recorded history to see the continent of South America. He called this land Gracia (the Isle of Grace), and he believed it might be near the Garden of Eden. When he arrived at Hispaniola, he wrote to the king and queen:

> Holy Scripture testifies that the Lord created the
> Earthly Paradise, and planted in it the Tree of Life,
> and that a fountain issued from it, which is the
> source of the four chief rivers of the world . . . I do not
> find, and have never found, any Latin or Greek work
> which gives the precise terrestrial position of the
> Earthly Paradise, nor have I seen it marked, by any
> reliable authority, on any map of the world . . . Some
> pagan writers tried to show by argument that it was
> in the Fortunate Islands, which are the Canaries,
> etc. St. Isadore, Bede, Strabo, the master of *Historia
> Scholastica*, St. Ambrose, Duns Scotus, and all the
> reliable theologians are agreed that the Earthly
> Paradise is in the East . . .
>
> I return to my discussion of the land of Gracia
> and of the river and lake I found there, which latter
> is so large that it could more correctly be called a sea
> than a lake, for a lake is a place where there is water,
> and if it is large it is called a sea, as we speak of the
> Sea of Galilee and the Dead Sea. I say that if this
> river does not come from the Earthly Paradise, then
> it must come from an immense land in the south,
> about which we as yet know nothing. But I am quite
> convinced in my own mind that the Earthly Para-
> dise is where I have said, and I rely on the argu-
> ments and authorities I have cited above.[62]

When he arrived at Hispaniola, his brother, the adelanto,
met him with bad news. Disease and privation had taken a
huge toll on the colony; many had died and many more were
sick. When Bartholomew had gone to the Southwest to
collect taxes from the Indians, leaving the youngest brother,
Don Diego, in charge, a revolt had occurred and Don Diego
was not forceful enough to crush it. The Admiral was in
such bad health that he was unable to deal effectively with
the rebels, so he negotiated an agreement with them by
which they were given two ships to return home. Amid this
chaos and despair Columbus turned to the Lord for help.

The day after Christmas Day, 1499, all having left me, I was attacked by the Indians and the bad Christians, and was placed in such extremity that fleeing death, I took to sea in a small caravel. Then Our Lord aided me, saying, "Man of little faith, do not fear, I am with thee." And he dispersed my enemies, and showed me how I might fulfill my vows. Unhappy sinner that I am, to have placed all my hopes in the things of this world![63]

But the worst was yet to come! The rebels and malcontents had returned to Spain with such condemnation of Columbus that the king and queen decided something had to be done. They appointed Francisco de Bobadilla, Comendador of the Order of Calatrava, as governor of the Indies with authority to dispense royal justice. By all accounts Bobadilla was an honorable aristocratic gentleman who was respected by all in Spain. But even he was totally unprepared for what he faced in Hispaniola.

When he arrived in Hispaniola, August 23, 1500, the first sight that greeted Bobadilla was gallows with two fresh Spanish corpses hanging on it. He recoiled in understandable horror, not knowing the full circumstances that had led to such drastic measures. When he learned that five more Spanish rebels were scheduled for execution, he demanded that they be handed over to him immediately.

At this time the Admiral and Bartholomew were in separate parts of the colony dealing with discontent, and Don Diego, the youngest brother, was in charge of the town. When Diego refused to hand over the five condemned prisoners without the Admiral's permission, Bobadilla had him arrested. The Admiral returned and disputed Bobadilla's authority, and Bobadilla arrested him as well, placing him in irons. Bartholomew planned to free his brothers by force; then the Admiral sent him a message ordering him to obey Bobadilla. Bartholomew returned to Santo Domingo, and Bobadilla placed him in irons. The brothers were then sent back to Spain in chains to stand trial.

Overnight, Christopher Columbus fell from Admiral of

the Ocean Sea and Viceroy and Governor of the Indies,
favorite of the king and queen and discoverer of the New
World, to a chained prisoner leaving the colony he had
founded and crossing the ocean he had navigated bound in
irons to stand trial as a criminal! It was his moment of
deepest humiliation, and yet it was also a moment of
triumph. For while Columbus felt the anguish of humiliation deeply, he also knew how to use it to his advantage. For
Columbus those chains became a badge of persecution and
a visible symbol by which he could demonstrate to the king
and queen how dreadfully he was misunderstood and
mistreated. As soon as the ship was out of Bobadilla's sight,
the captain offered to remove the chains. But Columbus
refused, saying those chains had been placed on him by
royal authority and would be removed only by royal authority.

The Admiral set the stage for his vindication by writing
to Dona Juana de Torres, a friend and confidante of Queen
Isabella, either on shipboard or shortly after disembarking.
As Madariaga says, Columbus "was ever ready to rely on
the Lord but never adverse to lending the Lord a helping
hand in all that concerned him personally. This time, the
very depth and infamy of his position was — he knew — his
best defense. Bobadilla had overshot the mark and enabled
[Columbus] to surpass himself in the art and craft of
humility, of which he was a past master."[64] In the letter he
declares his faithfulness to the Crown and despairs over his
wretched state. But he affirms his faith in Jesus:

> Hope in Him who created all men sustaineth me:
> His succor hath always been very near. At another
> time, not long ago, when I was in great distress, He
> helped me up with his right hand, saying, "O man of
> little faith, arise, for it is I; fear not."
> I came with such cordial affection to serve these
> princes, and I have served them with unheard of and
> unseen devotion. Of the New Heaven and Earth
> which Our Lord made, as St. John writes in the
> Apocalypse, after he had spoken it by the mouth of
> Isaiah, He made me the messenger thereof and

showed me where to go.
. . . I undertook a new voyage to the New Heaven
and World which hitherto had been hidden. And if,
like the rest of the Indies, this is not held in high
esteem over there; this is no wonder, since it came to
light through my exertions.
    The Holy Spirit inspired St. Peter and, with him,
the others of the Twelve, and they all struggled in
this world, and many were their labors and their
hardships; in the end they triumphed over all.[65]

As Columbus had hoped, when the king and queen
learned that the Admiral had been brought back to Spain
in chains, they were shocked. They ordered him set free,
and they sent him enough money so that he and his
brothers could come to the royal court dressed appropri-
ately for their rank.

The king and queen were holding court in Granada, and
the three brothers appeared before them on December 17,
1500. Madariaga describes the scene:

    . . . the Admiral stood speechless for a while,
    tongue-tied by his deep emotion; then he sank to his
    knees and burst into tears and sobs; the King and
    Queen made him stand up; he recovered on hearing
    the friendly tone of voice of Ferdinand and Isabel,
    and spoke at length to assure them of his loyalty and
    to explain that his errors had been committed in
    good faith.
    Don Bartolome would neither weep nor kneel. He
    reminded the King and Queen that he was abroad
    when the discovery was made, and that he had been
    asked by his brother to come and work in Castile
    because he would rise in honour and gain; which, on
    his arrival, their Highnesses had confirmed to him
    by their letters; that he had given to this conquest
    seven years, during five of which he could swear he
    had not slept in a bed nor undressed, always with
    death by his side, and now, the service done, he was
    put in irons and deprived of his honour; and he asked

to be paid his salary; he offered his services to the King and Queen if wanted, for otherwise he was in a position to provide for himself.

The contrast between the two men could not be clearer. Don Bartolome was an adventurer and nothing more. He had come to Spain from France because he thought there was money and honour in it. If he were wanted, he would stay; if he were not, he would go. He was not worried about his future. He was thirty-nine; he was able, strong and brave, and he knew enough of the Indies and of discovery in general to rise to the top wherever he went. His feet were on the ground, his head was on his shoulders, and he never allowed his dreams to rise higher than his straight, steely eyes. Don Cristobal was not of so metallic a composition. There was more of the ocean and of the sky in his fluid and stormy soul. His head was in the clouds and even his feet were more at home on the rolling decks of caravels than on the tracks of mother earth or on the polished floors of princely houses. He saw visions and he heard voices. In his tense heart, he felt the unbearable pull of the imaginative passions — ambition, envy, resentment, vindictiveness, but above all, power, power over the world. This King and this Queen were his friends, but his friends from above. He loved them with a passionate hatred. He bowed before them, he knelt before them with infinite pride. While his body bent and fell at their feet, his soul rose triumphant over their heads in dreams of victory. He wept and sobbed, not from grief or repentance, but from sheer helplessness before their might, and while he sank, weak and dejected at their feet, his intimate demon, deep down under storm, worked, dry-eyed and assiduous, to build his greatness anew on the solid foundations of the royal pity. Broken and insulted, the Admiral-Viceroy would rise again and conquer all his enemies.[66]

Ferdinand and Isabella were moved by the Admiral's

display of emotion — and the emotion was undoubtedly genuine even if the timing of it was controlled for effect. They restored his title and continued to refer to him as "Our Admiral of the Ocean." But they were realistic enough to know that Columbus could not continue to govern the Indies. To avoid affronting him, they deliberately did not give the title of Viceroy to anyone else, but they appointed another governor of the Indies. They restored the property Bobadilla had confiscated and removed Bobadilla as governor, but did not condemn Bobadilla's actions. They also restored the one-tenth of revenues to which Columbus was entitled by their original agreement of 1492.

About this time, Columbus began writing his *Book of Prophecies*, the collection of Bible prophecies from the Old and New Testaments concerning the bringing of the gospel to distant lands. We have already discussed this book. The Admiral's purpose in writing it was to persuade the king and queen that those were the last days before the end of the world, that the gospel must be preached across the world before the Second Coming, and that God had chosen Columbus as His instrument to open these new lands to the Word of God. The gold to be gained was to be used for a new crusade to free Jerusalem and the Holy Sepulchre from Muslim control.

But as the year 1501 drew to a close, even though he was in failing health, the Admiral began planning a fourth voyage. The purpose this time was to go beyond Hispaniola and find the continent of Asia. In February 1502 he asked for royal permission, which he promptly received; but the king and queen directed that he not go to Hispaniola, ostensibly because time would not permit, but actually because they knew his arrival in Hispaniola would stir up more trouble. They did say that he could visit Hispaniola on the way back if he chose.

In May 1502 the Admiral, his brother the Adelantade Bartholomew, and his son Don Ferdinand (age thirteen) prepared to sail. But just as they were ready to leave, the old crusader learned that the Moors had besieged the Portuguese fortress of Arzila in Morocco. He went to the defense of the Portuguese, but before he arrived the Moors had been driven away. So the four vessels set their course westward across the Atlantic. Contrary to instructions, the Admiral headed straight for Hispaniola, ostensibly because one of their ships was having problems and Columbus wanted to replace it.

On June 29 they dropped anchor in the harbor of Santo Domingo, in Hispaniola. The Admiral sent one of his captains ashore to try to buy another ship and to warn the governor that a hurricane was coming. The governor imperiously refused to let Columbus come ashore, said no ship was available, and dispatched a fleet of twenty-eight ships to Spain in disregard of the Admiral's hurricane warning.

Columbus and his four vessels then sailed to the mouth of a river and escaped the brunt of the hurricane, but the storm hit the larger fleet full force. Twenty-four of the twenty-eight ships were destroyed and over five hundred people drowned, including the Admiral's old nemesis Bobadilla. As Landstrom says, "We need not be surprised that the Admiral's enemies maintained that he had raised the hurricane by sorcery, while his friends spoke of Divine Justice."[67]

Sailing from Hispaniola to Cuba, the Admiral led his expedition to the mainland and followed the coast of Central America southward by Honduras, Nicaragua, Costa Rica, and Panama. His health was so bad that he probably never went ashore, and he had a special cabin built on deck so he could observe the ocean. Then, heading eastward, they were stranded on the coast of Jamaica for over a year, from June 25, 1503 to June 29, 1504.

Shipwrecked on the coast of Jamaica, his body racked by pain, Columbus wrote once again to the king and queen, not knowing whether anyone would ever see the letter. Again, in his anguish, he trusts in God:

> In January the mouth of the river became obstructed. In April, the vessels were all worm-eaten, and I could not keep them above water. At this time the river cut a channel, by which I brought out three empty ships with considerable difficulty. The boats went back into the river for salt and water. The sea

rose high and furious and would not let them out again. The Indians were many and united and attacked them and in the end killed them. My brother and all of the rest of the people were living on board a vessel which lay inside. I was outside very much alone, on this rude coast, with a high fever and very fatigued. There was no hope of escape. In this state, I climbed painfully to the highest part of the ship and cried out for help with a fearful voice, weeping, to Your Highnesses' war captains, in every direction; but none replied. At length, groaning with exhaustion, I fell asleep, and heard a compassionate voice saying, "O fool, and slow to believe and serve thy God, the God of every man! What more did He do for Moses or for David his servant than for thee? From thy birth He hath ever held thee in special charge. When He saw thee at man's estate, marvelously did He cause they name to resound over the earth. The Indies, so rich a portion of the world, He gave thee for thine own, and thou has divided them as it pleased thee. Of those barriers of the Ocean Sea, which were closed with such mighty chains, He hath given thee the keys. Thou was obeyed in so many lands, and thou hast won noble fame from Christendom. What more did He do for the people of Israel, when He carried them out of Egypt; or for David, whom from a shepherd He raised to be king over Judea? Turn thou to Him and acknowledge thy faults; His mercy is infinite; thine old age shall not hinder thee from performing mighty deeds, for many and vast heritages He holdeth. Abraham was past 100 when he begat Isaac, and Sarah was no young girl. Thou criest out for succor with a doubting heart. Reflect, who has afflicted thee so grievously and so often, God or the world? The privileges and promises which God bestows, he doth not revoke; nor doth He say, after having received service, that this was not His intention, and that it is to be understood differently. Nor doth He mete out suffering to make a show of His might. Whatever He promises He fulfills with interest; that is His way. Thus I have told thee what they Creator hath done for thee and what He doth for all men. He hath now revealed to me a portion of the rewards for so many toils and dangers thou hast borne in the service of others."[68]

Even while shipwrecked on the coast of Jamaica he had sharp words for his critics:

Let us hear now from those who are full of blaming and finding fault, while they sit safely ashore, "Why did you not do thus and so?" I wish they were on this voyage; I well believe that another voyage of a different kind awaits them, or our faith is naught.[69]

Morison interprets this passage: "In other words, to hell with them!"[70]

And despite his age and illness he remained ever the crusader for the Lord, eager to lift his sword or raise his sail to advance the Cross. His letter continues:

Jerusalem and the Mount of Zion are now to be rebuilt by Christian hands, and God through the mouth of the prophet in the fourteenth Psalm said so. The abbot Joachim said that this man was to come from Spain. St. Jerome showed the way thither to the Holy Lady. The Emperor of Cathay some time since sent for wise men to teach him the religion of Christ. Who shall offer himself for this mission? If Our Lord takes me back to Spain, I vow in God's name I will undertake to convey them thither.[71]

It was not to be. Columbus and his crew were rescued after two crewmen used native canoes to travel to Hispaniola for help. In the meantime they had to fend for themselves for a year and occasionally depend upon the natives for help; on one occasion Columbus concluded from his books that a solar eclipse was coming and used the threat of the eclipse to convince the natives that God would be angry at them if they didn't help the Spaniards. Fortunately for Columbus, the book was accurate!

The Admiral returned from his last voyage on November 7, 1504, only fifty-three years old but broken in health and suffering from arthritis, gout, and feverish deliriums. Nineteen days later, on November 26, his heart was saddened by the death of his ally and true believer, Queen Isabella.

In his last years he set his affairs in order, received a substantial income from his interest in the Indies (though much less than he was promised), labored to secure his titles and positions for himself and his descendants, and still spoke of a crusade to Jerusalem.

On May 20, 1506, his condition suddenly grew worse. Surrounded by some of his most loyal captains and by his brother Diego, and sons Diego and Ferdinand, he received the Lord's Supper and the Last Rites. Then he passed away, his last words being, "In manus tuas, Domine, commendo spiritum meum." ("Into thy hand, Lord, I commend my spirit.")

Christopher Columbus's death remains as much a mystery as his birth. He was buried in Seville, in Spain, and King Ferdinand had an epitaph placed on his tomb:

TO CASTILE AND LEON,
COLUMBUS GAVE A NEW WORLD[72]

And yet, three ironies exist here. First, Columbus never really knew that he had found a new world. To the end of his life he remained convinced that the Indies were off the coast of Asia.

Second, the remains of Columbus may not be in Seville. Around 1537 Columbus's daughter-in-law requested permission to transfer his remains to the Cathedral in Santo Domingo, on Columbus's island of Hispaniola, and supposedly this was done. Also buried in Santo Domingo were his son Diego, his brother Bartholomew the adelantande, and two grandsons.

But when the French overran Hispaniola in 1795, Spanish authorities hastily removed the body and reburied it in Havana. Then, when Cuba became independent from Spain

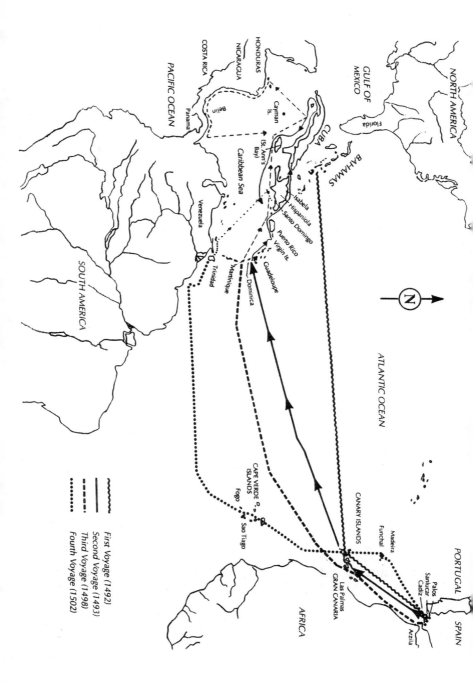

in 1899, the body of Columbus was moved again, this time back to Seville, in a marble tomb erected in his honor.

Or was it? Some researchers believe the body in the tomb in Seville is actually that of Diego Columbus. As of this writing the final resting place of Columbus's remains is still a mystery.[73]

The third irony is that Columbus remained as controversial in death as he was in life. In 1792, at the height of the French Revolution whose partisans claimed to be pro-American but really despised the true principles of liberty America stands for, the French Academy sponsored an essay contest on the subject, "Has the discovery of America been helpful or harmful to humankind?" One might ask, discovery by whom?

Columbus was greatly honored in Spain and parts of Latin America, but in colonial America he was given little attention; Americans of that day showed little interest in the things of Spain.

American interest in Columbus began after the war for independence. The famed novelist Washington Irving, who served as U.S. Ambassador to Spain, became fascinated with the life and deeds of Columbus, and in 1828 he wrote his famous and very readable work, *The Life and Voyages of Christopher Columbus*,[74] and Columbus became an American hero.

And now, as the five hundredth anniversary of the Admiral's voyage gets underway, Columbus-bashers are determined to make him into a villain.

What were the charges against Columbus, and how should we evaluate them? Let's look at them one by one:

1. Columbus was an inept, harsh, and unjust governor.

The charge has merit. The qualities that make a great sea-captain do not necessarily make a good governor. Columbus left the colony for voyages of discovery and trips to Spain when he was needed in Hispaniola. When things got out of hand, his attempts to restore order were seen as cruel and harsh. Columbus would undoubtedly have been happier, and his name in history far less blemished, if he had been Admiral of the Ocean Sea, but never viceroy and governor of the Indies. It is unfortunate that Ferdinand and Isabella didn't send him on further voyages of discovery and exploration instead of sending him back to Hispaniola with twelve hundred colonists. But that is the benefit of five hundred years of hindsight.

In fairness to the Viceroy of the Indies, it must be said that he took on a difficult situation. Many of those who came to Hispaniola were hidalgos, Spanish gentlemen who did not want to do physical work and looked down upon those who did, who came to the Indies to pick up their gold, get rich quick, and go back home to Spain. Others were convicted criminals, sometimes even sentenced to death, whose sentences were commuted on condition that they settle in Hispaniola. This is not the most promising material to begin with. And when we remember that they were thousands of miles from home, away from women of their own culture, dealing regularly with non-Christian natives, cut adrift from the civilizing influences of Spanish society, beset by disease and hunger and danger, and not finding the wealth they had been promised, we begin to understand why the situation got out of hand. Columbus had urged that only "good Christians" be allowed to come to the Indies. If his advice had been followed, the result might have been quite different.

While in chains awaiting his fate in Spain, Columbus said it well:

> They judge me there as a governor who had gone to Sicily or to a city or town under a regular government, where laws can be observed in toto without fear of losing all; and I am suffering grave injury. I should be judged as a captain who went from Spain to the Indies to conquer a people numerous and warlike, whose manners and religion are very different from ours, who live in sierras and mountains, without fixed settlements, and where by divine will I have placed under the sovereignty of the King and Queen our Lords, an Other World, whereby Spain, which was reckoned poor, is become the richest of

countries.

I ought to be judged as a captain, who for so long a time, up to the present day, hath borne arms without laying them down for an hour, and by knights of the sword and not by [men of] letters, unless they were Greeks or Romans or others of modern times, of whom there are so many and so noble in Spain; for otherwise I am greatly aggrieved, since in the Indies there is neither a town nor settlement.[75]

2. Columbus was obsessed with gold.

Certainly this motive existed. On island after island when Columbus visited he asked incessantly, "Where is the gold?" He found some, but much less than he had expected and hoped. The great gold discoveries came later, with Cortez in Mexico and Pizarro in Peru.

But let's get the issue in perspective. There's nothing wrong with wealth, so long as it is acquired honorably, used responsibly, and valued in its proper perspective. The Bible does not say money is the root of all evil; it says, "The love of money is the ['a' in the Greek] root of all evil" (1 Tim. 6:10).

Columbus's reasons for seeking gold went beyond simply acquiring wealth for himself. First, the costs of his enterprise were substantial: a fleet of ships, provisions, and a crew that needs to be paid, typically with six months' pay advanced. To advance these costs Columbus relied partly on private investors and partly on the Crown. He felt compelled to make the voyages profitable for his investors. With the royal treasury exhausted from the war in Granada, he was concerned that Ferdinand and Isabella might not be willing to support further voyages of discovery with more pressing local matters at hand unless the voyages carried the promise of profit. To "sell" the first voyage to the Royal Court he had spoken of the wealth of the Orient, and he felt compelled to deliver on that promise. Madariaga suggests that Columbus may have misjudged the king and queen; they may have been more willing to subsidize the spreading of the gospel than the Admiral thought;[76] but one can understand his concern.

Second, while Columbus undoubtedly wanted to be a rich man, wealth for him does not appear to have been an end in itself but rather a means to an end. He wanted to be a world-changer, an influential person who opens new worlds for the gospel and for western civilization. To Columbus, wealth meant influence.

And third, from the beginning to the end of his life, Columbus stressed his ultimate goal — bringing the Orient to Christ so that the Christian lands of the earth could repel the advance of the Ottoman Turks and mount a new crusade to free Jerusalem from Muslim control. Even more than voyages of discovery, wars and crusades cost money. Columbus repeatedly declared that the gold he discovered through his voyages was to be used to undertake this crusade.[77]

For those ivory-tower academics who are troubled by Columbus's desire for gold, let me offer a suggestion: Try thinking of it as a "research grant!"

However, the Admiral's attitude toward gold may have become obsessive as time went on. I have seen this happen with dedicated Christian leaders, and often with the best of motives. As I focus upon the special work of my own ministry, I come to equate my own ministry with the advancement of God's kingdom. Since God obviously wills the expansion of His kingdom, He therefore must will the expansion of my ministry. An ends-justifies-means mentality sets in, and without realizing it I begin to assume that that which advances my ministry must be the will of God. And when I analyze what is the main hindrance to the expansion of my ministry, I decide that it must be lack of funds. Therefore I conclude that that which brings in money for my ministry is the will of God, and that which doesn't, isn't.

This type of thinking is wrong and dangerous. But it is the kind of trap into which a dedicated Christian may easily fall.

3. Columbus had no right to claim the Americas for Spain.

Columbus, it is said, stole land from the natives and

gave it to the Crown. Did he?

It seems self-evident, but still bears repeating, that one cannot steal something unless it belongs to someone else. So if Columbus stole the Americas for Spain, whom did they belong to before?

The obvious and expected answer is the Native Americans.

But did they really own the land?

A basic principle of international law is that for a nation to acquire new and undiscovered territory, three elements must coalesce: (1) physical discovery of the territory; (2) occupation with a claim of ownership; and (3) actual, continuous, and peaceful display of the functions of government over the territory.[78]

Those we now call Native Americans were the first to physically discover America. They maintained a permanent presence in the Western Hemisphere for thousands of years, although many of the tribes and nations migrated a great deal. But did they exhibit an intent to claim ownership of the territory? And did they exercise an actual, continuous, and peaceful display of the functions of government over the territory?

Many authorities maintain that Native American nations, or at least many of them, did not believe in or practice real property rights in the sense that Europeans did.[79] Neither tribes nor individuals acquired permanent title to real estate. Rather, ownership was temporary and consisted of use. So long as you were using the land, it was yours; but when you ceased using it, anyone else was free to take it.

Again, who owned the land prior to 1492? Did the Caribs own the islands that bear their name? If so, how did they acquire those islands from the Arawaks? And who owned the islands before the Arawaks took them? In tracing titles and reverting to original ownership, how far back do we go?

The European view of property was different. Land ownership was a matter of permanent title. Columbus certainly was not the first person to set foot on the island of San Salvador. But he may well have been the first person to set foot on San Salvador with the intent of claiming title for his nation.

Another aspect of claiming title must be noted. In Columbus and the *Age of Discovery*, Zvi Dor Ner gives an account of Columbus's landing on San Salvador:

> He erected a cross "as a token of Jesus Christ Our Lord," and concluded his ceremony of taking possession by naming the island "San Salvador" — Holy Savior. Thus Columbus claimed his discovery not just for Ferdinand and Isabella, but for the faith to which they themselves were mere subjects. A Christian state had the absolute right to proclaim sovereignty over heathen and infidel domains. Earlier in that year of 1492, a similar prerogative had been exercised when the banners of Castile and Aragon went up over the Alhambra [the Muslim fortress of Granada in southern Spain].
>
> But more than simply declaring his nation's rights according to the rules of the day, Columbus in his ceremony on the beach was enacting a ritual that would be repeated hundreds of times as the great age of discovery unfolded. He was inventing the protocols of discovery — protocols that would be followed whenever banners and crosses were displayed in the names of distant sovereigns throughout the world. Cabot in Newfoundland, Cartier and Champlain in the St. Lawrence Valley, Henry Hudson in New York harbor, and Captain Cook in Polynesia would all act out some variation of Columbus's rite, setting the stage for a string of imperial struggles reaching down to the Falkland Islands war in our own day. And even when actual sovereignty is no longer sought, the outward forms still survive: on the moon today there is an American flag and a plaque signed by Richard Nixon. Such acts are potent symbols; they proclaim the power of a nation and the will of its people, and mark the accomplishments that power and will provide.[80]

Note the key point: Columbus claimed San Salvador, not

just for Spain, but for the Christian faith and the God to whom the Spanish rulers were subjects. Christianity teaches that civil rulers are established by God and act as His ministers or servants (Rom. 13:1-7). One may argue that God had already provided the local caciques or chiefs to rule over these people. But rightly or wrongly, the Spaniards believed they were extending the rule of God to lands that were hitherto outside His domain.

And King Ferdinand and Queen Isabella did not view the discovery of the Indies as a "land grab." In their view the Indies, its people and resources, were a new responsibility that God had placed in their hands as Madariaga verifies:

> For them, conquest was not a title of sovereignty when the spoliated sovereign was not a Christian. This was as good as gospel truth in those days for all Christendom. In later times, ethics have degenerated, since Christian princes spoliate other Christian princes without qualms of any kind. In the circumstances, Ferdinand and Isabella considered the Indians as their subjects ipso facto. They would not have taken the view which Las Casas was to take later — that the propagation of the gospel was the only ground on which a Christian conscience could countenance the intrusion of Spaniards into the Indies. Yet, though princes entitled to sovereignty by conquest over pagans, Ferdinand and Isabella were fully conscious of their responsibility as Christian princes, and they explicitly accepted as their first duty towards their new subjects the enlightenment of the Indians and their conversion to the law of Christ. No fair-minded person having had direct access to the royal documents can entertain any doubts whatever on the earnest and well-meaning eagerness with which the king and queen attended to the discharge of this duty.
>
> But, of course, the Indies belonged to them and not to the Indians! They were anxious to see the natives well-treated; to guard them against any spoliation or hardship; and to see that their liberty

and their property was respected; but, just as Castile and Aragon, though split into thousands of landowners, belonged to the king and queen, so the Indies, though the Indians were not to be deprived of their personal property, belonged to the king and queen. This was not even a claim on their part; it was an assumption which they had not stopped to analyse, owing to its sheer evidence.

What were they to do with their new territories? Obviously, to organize them first and then to develop them. So, they devise the best means for their government and defense, and they constantly urge [Columbus] to let them have the best possible information of the kind we would nowadays call scientific — geographical situation, climate, flora and fauna, minerals, fisheries, land produce.[81]

Certainly things did not always work out in practice as neatly as they sound on paper. But the intent of the Spaniards was good, and the question of land ownership is not as clear as some would suggest.

4. Columbus made slaves of a free people.

No question about it: slavery is wrong.

Anything I say in defense of the Spaniards on the slavery issue will be twisted and misquoted into a defense of slavery itself. But just so the record is clear, and so no honest reviewer will misinterpret me, let me say it again for the record: SLAVERY IS WRONG!

So let's get to the real issue: Does the existence of slavery prove that Columbus & Co. could not have been sincere Christians? I suggest it does not.

First, enslavement of the native population does not appear to have been the explorers' original intent. When they first crossed the Atlantic they expected to find not naked savages but Oriental empires with size, wealth, and might equal to or surpassing their own. The goal was to win these nations for Christ and make them allies against the Muslim Turks.

The thought of enslavement seems to have occurred

later, after the explorers saw the condition of the natives. Another possible reason Columbus considered slavery was his failure to find gold in substantial amounts and his desperate need to show the Crown how the Indies could be profitable.[82]

Second, slavery was widespread in the world of the fifteenth century. Again, this does not make slavery right, but it does explain why Christians might have accepted the practice. One is less likely to question a practice that has existed throughout the world from time immemorial. Timothy Foote elaborates on this issue in *Smithsonian*:

> Slavery existed everywhere — including the New World (though no one knew that yet) and Africa. The Turkish Sultan's whole army and many of his administrators were his personal slaves. William Phillips, author of the recent study *Slavery from Roman Times*, draws on data showing that Arab traders working West Africa brought back four million slaves for the Middle East alone.
>
> The cruelty and expansion of slavery in the New World seems more reprehensible, however, precisely because in 15th-century Europe slavery was relatively rare and getting rarer. This was partly because Christianity taught that manumission of slaves was pleasing to God, partly because peasants were more efficient than slaves in handling European agriculture.[83]

Third, by the ethics of the day Christians could not enslave other Christians, but it was considered proper to enslave non-Christians who were taken in battle. Muslims practiced a similar ethic, and during the Crusades and the fifteenth century Christian-Moor struggles in Spain, it was common for each side to enslave defeated captives from the other side. Foote offers more information on the subject:

> Christians were not allowed to enslave other Christians, but many city families in 15th-century Europe had a domestic slave or two. Mostly young,

white, and female, they lived with the family and found it relatively easy to marry or work their way to freedom. They were acquired as pagans, usually in Eastern Europe or Circassia, and baptized to save their souls only after they were in service. (As early as the 12th century, the word for "slave" in Italian, German, Spanish, French, and English derived from the word "slav.")[84]

Fourth, European Christians believed their right to enslave pagans applied only to those defeated in battle. Those who surrendered were usually allowed to keep their freedom if they paid tribute. The warlike Caribs were generally considered in the former category, the peaceable Arawaks in the latter.

And fifth, the Spaniards considered the practices of the Caribs to be savage. Dr. Diego Alvarez Chanca, chief physician on the Admiral's second voyage, describes with disgust an encounter with the Caribs on Guadeloupe Island:

> We inquired of the women who were prisoners of the inhabitants what sort of people these islanders were and they replied, "Caribs." As soon as they learned that we abhor such kind of people because of their evil practice of eating human flesh, they felt delighted . . . They told us that the Carib men use them with such cruelty as would scarcely be believed; and that they eat the children which they bear them, only bringing up those whom they have by their native wives. Such of their male enemies as they can take away alive they bring here to their homes to make a feast of them and those who are killed in battle they eat up after the fighting is over. They declare that the flesh of man is so good to eat that nothing can compare with it in the world; and this is quite evident, for of the human bones we found in the houses, everything that could be gnawed had already been gnawed so that nothing remained but what was too hard to eat; in one of the houses we found a man's neck cooking in a pot . . . In their wars

on the inhabitants of the neighboring islands these people capture as many of the women as they can, especially those who are young and handsome and keep them as body servants and concubines; and so great a number do they carry off that in fifty houses we entered no man was found but all were women. Of that large number of captive females more than twenty handsome women came away voluntarily with us. When the Caribs take away boys as prisoners of war they remove their organs, fatten them until they grow up and then, when they wish to make a great feast, they kill and eat them, for they say the flesh of women and youngsters is not good to eat. Three boys thus mutilated came fleeing to us when we visited the houses.[85]

Michele de Cuneo, who accompanied Columbus on the second voyage, made similar observations concerning Carib cannibalism and cruelty: "The Caribs whenever they catch these Indians eat them as we would eat kids [goats] and they say that a boy's flesh tastes better than that of a woman. Of this human flesh they are very greedy, so that to eat of that flesh they stay out of their country for six, eight, or even ten years before they repatriate; and they stay so long, whenever they go, that they depopulate the islands."[86] He says this concerning Carib religion:

We went to the temple of those Caribs, in which we found two wooden statues, arranged so that they look like a Pieta. We were told that whenever someone's father is sick, the son goes to the temple and tells the idol that his father is ill and the idol says whether he should live or not; and he stays there until the idol answers yes or no. If he says no, the son goes home, cuts his father's head off and then cooks it; I don't believe they eat it but truly when it is white they place it in the above-mentioned temple; and this they do only to the lords. That idol is called Seyti.[87]

He adds further that the Caribs, and to some extent the other natives, engaged in sodomy as well:

> According to what we have seen in all the islands where we have been, both the Indians and the Caribs are largely sodomites, not knowing (I believe) whether they are acting right or wrong. We have judged that this accursed vice may have come to the Indians from those Caribs; because these, as I said before, are wilder men and when conquering and eating those Indians, for spite they may also have committed that extreme offence, which proceeding thence may have been transmitted from one to the other.[88]

The Spaniards did not arrive at these conclusions lightly. As Ferdinand tells us, when the Admiral was first told about Carib cannibalism he didn't believe the reports. But they heard the same reports consistently from many sources; they spoke with Arawak prisoners of the Caribs; they personally observed mutilated prisoners; they saw the evidence of cannibalism in the Carib camps; they saw bodies of men with flesh eaten away from them; and they themselves felt firsthand the fury of Carib attacks. They soon became convinced.

They gradually concluded that not only would the Caribs never voluntarily submit to their sovereignty, but moreover, they could not rule an orderly realm with the Caribs at large. As sovereigns they had a duty to their Arawak subjects to protect them from Carib depredations.

Columbus therefore proposed that the Caribs be made temporary slaves. This would prevent them from enslaving the Arawaks and would protect the Arawaks and the Spaniards. It would also be a way — possibly the only way — of civilizing the Caribs and bringing them to the Christian faith. In the Spaniards' view, a brief period of servitude would be a minor imposition compared with the temporal and eternal benefits the Caribs and their posterity would receive.

And so, after Caribs had attacked his men, the Admiral

sent a punitive expedition against them. They returned with 1,600 Carib prisoners. Columbus selected 550 of these to be sent to Spain. Another 650 were given to the local settlers, and the remaining 400 were set free.[89]

Thus the slave trade began. It was to apply only to Caribs, since they were violent, unchristian, and a threat to civilized peoples, and were subject to enslavement under the laws of war as a conquered people. But as time went on, particularly in Columbus's absence, the distinction between Carib and Arawak was increasingly ignored, and unprincipled men began enslaving Arawaks as well.

A sixth factor should be noted about slavery in the Indies. Out of the same Spanish society that established slavery in the Indies, also came the critics of slavery. Ferdinand and particularly Isabella had misgivings about the idea from the beginning. When Columbus sent those 550 Caribs to Spain to be sold as slaves, she is reported to have said, "What right does My Admiral have to give My vassals to anyone?"[90] As subjects of the Spanish Crown and part of a Christian realm, they had a right to her protection. Ferdinand vacillated somewhat on the issue, but Isabella remained firmly against slavery. Interestingly, the royal instructions for Columbus's fourth voyage specifically prohibited him from taking slaves.[91]

And voices against slavery arose in the Indies, primarily among Church leaders. Father Anton Montecino, a Dominican friar preaching in 1510 in Santo Domingo, declared the following to his parishioners:

> You are in mortal sin. And you are heading for damnation . . . For you are destroying an innocent people.
>
> For they are God's people, these innocents, whom you destroyed. By what right do you make them die? Mining gold for you in your mines or working for you in your fields, by what right do you unleash enslaving wars upon them? They lived in peace in this land before you came, in peace in their own homes. They did nothing to harm you to cause you to slaughter them wholesale . . . Are you not under God's com-

mand to love them as you love yourselves? Yes. And that will bring you to damnation.[92]

When Father Montecino repeated his condemnation the following Sunday, the parishioners demanded that the governor (Columbus's son Diego) force the Dominicans to change their policy or leave the colony, but Diego refused to stop the Dominicans from preaching. Las Casas and others joined the battle for the rights of Native Americans.

Not all church authorities agreed with Father Montecino. With Vatican approval a document called "The Requirement" was drafted which Spanish authorities were to read to the various native tribes. In earnest language the Requerimiento stated that if the natives would acknowledge the Lordship of Christ they may remain free, but otherwise they would be made slaves. The intent was to treat the natives the same as people of the Old World, making slaves only of pagans who had been conquered in battle. In practice, however, Spanish officials sometimes read the document in Spanish or Latin, and the natives' blank stares were interpreted as rejection.[93]

By 1542 the Church had prevailed upon the Spanish government to prohibit the enslavement of Native Americans, though the African slave trade continued.

The point is that while slavery was wrong, under the circumstances it is understandable that well-meaning and sincere Christians might go along with it. Christians countenanced slavery, and in some instances Christians participated in slavery. But Christians also led the opposition to slavery, and in the end it was the Church that put a stop to it.

And unlike some totalitarian countries, the Spanish government gave the Church the freedom to do so.

6. Columbus forced Christianity and western culture on the Native Americans.

This is true — and millions of people are in heaven today as a result.

One who believes there is no absolute truth and that Jesus Christ is not the only way to the Father is likely to regard all religions and all value systems as equal. All Columbus did was replace one religion or value system with another.

If cannibalism is a legitimate lifestyle (or deathstyle, depending on which side of the fork you're on), if cutting off your father's head and cooking it is a matter of individual choice, if sodomy is just as good as monogamy, and if idolatry is just as good as worshipping the Triune God of the Bible, then the Caribs had every right to their preferences. But on the other hand, if there are no absolute rights and wrongs and anything goes, then what's wrong with forcing one's views on others? If my lifestyle consists of imposing my preferences on other people, why shouldn't I pursue that lifestyle? In this sense the liberal argument self-destructs by shooting itself in the back.

But if Jesus Christ is the Son of God who died for the sin of the world, if eternal salvation is available to those who trust in Him, and if God has established absolute standards of right and wrong that are found in His revealed Word and that apply to all societies, then we are remiss in our duties if we do not share Him with others.

Force isn't the way to do it. Columbus wanted to win the natives to Christ by love rather than by force, but the Spaniards didn't always follow his advice.

But as one who had himself found salvation through the Christian faith, Christopher Columbus had a duty to share the good news of Jesus Christ with the world — and I for one thank God that he did!

How, then, do we evaluate Christopher Columbus? As a man like other men, with flaws and imperfections, but a man with dreams and the iron determination to make his dreams come true, a man absolutely convinced of the truth of the Christian faith who resolved against all odds to bring that faith to the unknown world. The greatest navigator of his age, he brought two worlds together, the old and the new.

If Columbus were asked his greatest failing, he might echo the words he wrote while facing hardship in the Indies in 1500: "Unhappy sinner that I am, to have placed all my hopes in the things of this world!"[94] Perhaps Columbus depended too much upon himself and overestimated his personal importance in the plan of God. Perhaps he looked too much for recognition from men, and his failure to get the recognition that was due him prevented him from fully experiencing the joy that comes from being used of God in His plan.

But his heart was with God, and God used him mightily as Samuel Eliot Morison concludes:

> . . . Columbus had a deep conviction of the immanance, the sovereignty and the infinite wisdom of God, which transcended all his suffering, and enhanced all his triumphs. Waste no pity on the Admiral of the Ocean Sea! He enjoyed long stretches of pure delight such as only a seaman may know, and moments of high, proud exultation that only a discoverer can experience.
>
> One only wishes that the Admiral might have been afforded the sense of fulfillment that would have come from forseeing all that flowed from his discoveries; that would have turned all the sorrows of his last years to joy. The whole history of the Americas stems from the Four Voyages of Columbus; and as the Greek city-states looked back to the deathless gods as their founders, so today a score of independent nations and dominions unite in homage to Christopher the stout-hearted son of Genoa, who carried Christian civilization across the Ocean Sea.[95]

(This chapter is dedicated to our son, Justin Luther Eidsmoe, age two, whose eagerness to learn more about "Clundus and his boats" has been an inspiration to us all.)

ENDNOTES

[1]Ferdinand Columbus, *The Life of the Admiral Christopher Columbus* by his son Ferdinand, trans. Benjamin Keen (New Brunswick, NJ: Rutgers University Press, 1959), pp. 4,5. A brief note on sources is appropriate. Much as one would

like the actual journals of Christopher Columbus, they have been lost. However, two associates of Columbus, his son Ferdinand Columbus and Father Bartolome Las Casas, had copies of the journals and made abstracts thereof. In some places they quote the Admiral verbatim; in others they merely summarize. Both are considered quite accurate and are very helpful. Other original source documents are compiled in *Journals & Other Documents on the Life & Voyages of Christopher Columbus*, Samuel Eliot Morison (New York: Heritage Press, 1963).

For modern sources, Samuel Eliot Morison is considered the dean of Columbus scholars and his classic *Admiral of the Ocean Sea* (Boston: Little, Brown & Co.) set the standard in 1942 and remains unsurpassed. Other outstanding works include Salvador de Madariaga, *Christopher Columbus, Being the Life of the Very Magnificent Lord Don Cristobal Colon* (New York: Frederick Ungar, 1940, 1967), excellent for its detail and insight into the character of Columbus and his contemporaries; Gianni Granzotto, *Christopher Columbus: The Dream and the Obsession* (London: Collins, 1986); Felipe Fernandez-Armesto, *Columbus and the Conquest of the Impossible* (New York: Saturday Review Press, 1974); and Bjorn Landstrom, *Columbus* (New York: Macmillan, 1966). A new work by Zvi Dor-Ner, *Columbus and the Age of Discovery* (New York: Morrow & Co., 1991, published as the companion volume to the seven-hour Public Broadcasting Station documentary on Columbus that aired in October 1991), while not well-documented, is a very readable history, is beautifully illustrated, and addresses contemporary issues concerning Columbus in a reasonably even-handed manner.

[2]*American Heritage*, February-March 1981, p. 9.

[3]Lopez de Gomara, *History of the Indies*, 1554, quoted by Granzotto, p. 274.

[4]Cornelius DePauw, 1768, quoted by Granzotto, p. 279.

[5]Suzan Shown Harjo, "I Won't Be Celebrating Columbus Day," *Newsweek*, Special Columbus Issue 1991, p. 32.

[6]The claim that Columbus was of Italian descent is based on his Genoese birth, Genoese family ties, and references to himself as a Genoese. The Spanish Converso theory, advanced ably by Madariaga, is based on Columbus's sense of divine mission and fascination with Scripture as Jewish traits (note that these are also Christian traits), various linguistic details which indicate he identified himself as a new convert to Christianity, his use of Spanish rather than Italian, the fact that he apparently never returned to Genoa after settling in Lisbon at age 25, and his apparent reluctance to discuss his ethnic background, perhaps because of fear of anti-semitic persecution. The Scandinavian claim is based upon Columbus's physical traits (light reddish hair, light ruddy complexion, blue eyes, tall stature), the fact that Christopher (Kristoffer) is a common Scandinavian name, and the existence in the 15th century of a strong trade connection between Genoa and Bergen, Norway, with many Norwegian families having homes and businesses in Genoa.

[7]Morison, *Admiral*, pp. 21-4.

[8]"The Truth about Columbus' Mistress, *Verbum*, 1992, p. 2-3.

[9]Morison, *Journals*, pp. 47-8.

[10]Id., p. 65.

[11]Id., p. 72.

[12]Id., p. 91.

[13]Id., pp. 105-06.

[14]Id., p. 117.

[15]Id., p. 121.

[16]Id., p. 133.

[17]Christopher Columbus, Letter to Sovereigns, 1493, reprinted in Morison, *Journals*, pp. 183-84.

[18]Id., p. 186.

[19]Christopher Columbus, *Book of Prophecies*, quoted by Madariaga, p. 361.

[20]Christopher Columbus, *Book of Prophecies*, quoted by Landstrom, p. 155.

[21]Christopher Columbus, *Book of Prophecies*, quoted by Steve Wilkins, *America: The First 350 Years, Tape Album and Study Guide* (224 Auburn Avenue, Monroe, LA 71201, 1988), pp. 3-4. This an outstanding series on American history.

[22]Madariaga, p. 360.

[23]Arnesto, p. 199.

[24]August J. Kling, "The Christopher Columbus that Few People Know," *Moody Monthly*, October 1972; quoted by Robert Flood, *America: God Shed His Grace on Thee* (Chicago: Moody Monthly, 1988), p. 27.

[25]Morison, *Admiral*, p. 191.

[26]Milton Meltzer, *Columbus and the World Around Him* (New York: Franklin Watts, 1990), p. 127.

[27]Id., p. 153.

[28]Madariaga, p. 201.

[29]Ferdinand Columbus, p. 9.

[30]Bartolome de Las Casas, *Historie de las Indias*; quoted by Morison, *Admiral*, pp. 45-6.

[31]Granzotto, pp. 39-40.

[32]Id., pp. 40-41.

[33]Christopher Columbus, quoted by Granzotto, p. 56.

[34]Christopher Columbus, quoted by Granzotto, p. 54.

[35]Christopher Columbus, quoted by Ferdinand Columbus, p. 11.

[36]Vilhjalmur Stefansson, *Ultima Thule* (New York: Macmillan, 1943), p. 158.

[37]Stefansson, generally.

[38]Landstrom, p. 31.

[39]Ferdinand Columbus, p. 37.

[40]Madariaga, pp. 6, 9.

[41]Eratosthenes, cited by Landstrom, p. 9.

[42]Id.

[43]Landstrom, p. 41.

[44]Ferdinand Columbus, p. 43.

[45]Morison, *Admiral*, p. 101.

[46]Bartolome de Las Casas, quoted by Morison, *Admiral*, p. 149. Historians note that Columbus sailed on August 3, the day following the deadline by which Spanish Jews had to either accept Christian baptism or leave the country. This was a travesty, and an unnecessary one; unlike the Moors, the Jews were no threat to Christian Spain. Madariaga asks us to understand the motivations of King Ferdinand and Queen Isabella in ordering the expulsion of the Jews. They were not motivated by racial hostility, he says; many of the chief ministers of the royal court were Jews who had converted to Christianity. Rather, having just freed Granada from Moorish control, they believed a united Christian Spain was necessary. They sincerely wanted the Jews to convert and remain in Spain, and perhaps they were genuinely surprised when so many did not. As the Jews gathered at their ships to leave Spain, Christian friends gathered urging them to accept baptism and remain, while their rabbis urged them to remain true to faith and accept exile. The point is that while the exile was tragic, it was not motivated by hostility. See generally Madariaga, pp. 119-35.

[47]Morison, *Admiral*, p. 171.

[48]Morison, *Admiral*, p. 170-74. See also *Catholic Encyclopedia*, 1913, "Salve Regina."

[49]Christopher Columbus Letter to Sovereigns 1493, reprinted in Morison, *Journals*, p. 182.

[50]Dor-Ner, p. 150.

[51]Ferdinand Columbus, p. 82.

[52]Morison, *Journal*, p. 152. Las Casas says these were actually Arawaks who had adopted warlike Carib ways to defend themselves against the Caribs.

[53]Dor-Ner, p. 192.

[54]Morison, *Admiral*, p. 346.

[55]Christopher Columbus Letter to Sovereigns 9 April 1493, reprinted in Morison, *Journals*, p. 200.

[56]Ferdinand & Isabella Letter to Columbus 29 May 1493, reprinted in Morison, *Journals*, pp. 203-04.

[57]Id., p. 204.

[58]Id.

[59]Michele de Cuneo, Letter 1495, Reprinted in Morison, *Journals*, pp. 211-12.

[60]Granzotto, p. 206.

[61]Landstrom, p. 141.

[62]Christopher Columbus Letter to Sovereigns 1498, reprinted in Morison, *Journals*, 287.

[63]Christopher Columbus, quoted by Ferdinand Columbus, p. 219.

[64]Madariaga, p. 353.

[65]Christopher Columbus Letter to Dona Juana de Torres, 1500, reprinted in Morison, *Journals*, pp. 290-91.

[66]Madariaga, pp. 353-54.

[67]Landstrom, p. 163.

[68]Christopher Columbus, Letter Rarissima to Sovereigns, 1503; reprinted in Morison, *Journals*, p. 378.

[69]Id., p. 379.

[70]Morison, *Admiral*, p. 634.

[71]Christopher Columbus, Letter Rarissima to Sovereigns, 1503; reprinted in Morison, *Journals*, p. 383.

[72]Ferdinand Columbus, pp. 284-85.

[73]Granzotta, pp. 282-85; cf. Dor-Ner, pp. 326-28.

[74]Washington Irving, *The Life and Voyages of Christopher Columbus* (New York: Co-operative Publication Society, Inc., 1828). Unfortunately Irving (pp. 68-70) also gave us the myth that Columbus's detractors argued that the world was flat, which Morison labels "pure moonshine."(*Admiral*, p. 89). Irving also acknowledges that some of Columbus's detractors did admit the world was round (p. 69).

[75]Christopher Columbus, Letter to Dona Juana de Torres, 1500; reprinted in Morison, *Journals*, p. 296.

[76]Madariaga, pp. 299-301.

[77]See Endnotes 19, 20, 71.

[78]American Jurisprudence 2d, "International Law," Section 28; Johnson and Graham's Lessee v. William M'Intosh, 8 Wheaton 543 (1823).

[79]*The American Heritage Book of Indians*, Alvin M. Josephy, Jr., ed. (American Heritage Publishing Co., Inc., 1961), pp. 108, 203; Kirkpatrick Sale, *The Conquest of Paradise* (New York: Knopf, 1990), pp. 314, 315.

[80]Dor-Ner, pp. 150-51.

[81]Madariaga, pp. 300-01.

[82]Morison, *Admiral*, p. 486.

[83]Timothy Foote, "Where Columbus Was Coming From," *Smithsonian*, December 1991, p. 40.

[84]Id.

[85]Dr. Diego Alvarez Chanca, Letter, quoted by Arnesta, p. 118.

[86]Michele de Cuneo, Letter, 1495, reprinted in Morison, *Journals*, p. 219.

[87]Id., p. 220.

[88]Id.

[89]Morison, *Admiral*, pp. 486-87; Landstrom, pp. 130-31.

[90]Queen Isabella, quoted by Dor-Ner, pp. 218.

[91]King Ferdinand and Queen Isabella, Royal Instructions, Fourth Voyage, 1502, reprinted in Morison, *Journals*, p. 312.

[92]Father Anton Montecino, Sermon, 1510, quoted by Dor-Ner, pp. 220-21.

[93]Dor-Ner, pp. 220-24.

[94]Christopher Columbus, quoted by Ferdinand Columbus, p. 219.

[95]Morison, *Admiral*, pp. 670-71.

CHAPTER FIVE

HERNANDO CORTEZ: FOR GOD OR FOR GOLD?

The year is AD 1528. A distinguished-looking gentleman kneels in prayer at the Shrine of Our Lady of Guadalupe in Estremadura, Spain.

"Who is this man?" a pilgrim whispers. "He's been praying here for nine straight days."

"He's Hernando Cortez, the Conquistador of Mexico," a priest answers. "He's praying for forgiveness of his sins, and for the souls of his departed wife, father, and a fellow conquistador."[1]

"That's appropriate," the critics of Cortez might say. He had plenty of sins to seek forgiveness for.

But the incident, relatively late in Cortez's life, demonstrates an aspect of his character that is missed by many: He was a man of conscience.

Hernando Cortez, most magnificent and most capable of the conquistadors, was also the most controversial. To some he was the ideal Christian soldier who carried the cross into a strange land amid great danger and against overwhelming odds. To others he was a brutal butcher who slaughtered thousands of natives and enslaved others, robbing them of their land, their gold, and their gods. Thus Cortez's conquest of Mexico is enshrined in Jon Canning's book among the "100 Events that Changed the World," but Canning calls him "among the most ruthless and cruel military leaders the world has ever seen."[2]

Cortez's image problem in current opinion mirrors that of Spain itself. Historians — even European historians, or especially European historians — paint a negative picture of Spain, because through much of modern history Spain has been the enemy of the English, the French, the Dutch, the Germans, those who have the ear of North America. Religion added another factor; for Protestants of America and Northern Europe, Spain represents the epitome of dogmatic Roman Catholic authoritarianism Protestants (and secularists raised in a Protestant culture) love to hate.

And the prejudice against Spain also contains a twinge of racism. Even today it is said in France, "Africa begins at the Pyrenees" (the mountains on the border between France and Spain). After eight centuries of Moorish influence, Spain is looked upon as less "European," and therefore less civilized, than her northern neighbors.[3]

Certainly abuses and cruelties took place in Spain and in her colonies; the same can be said of every nation on Earth. But the evaluation of W.H. Prescott, who certainly entertained no pro-Spanish or pro-Catholic bias, concerning Spain in the year 1500 may be surprising to some who have grown up among anti-Spanish prejudices and have come to accept them as factual: "The nation at large could boast as great a degree of constitutional freedom as any other, at that time, in Christendom."[4] This freedom made it possible for church leaders like Bartolome Las Casas, Anton Montecino, Jeronimo de Mendieta, and others to speak out against these abuses and eventually eradicate most of them. In real totalitarian societies news is suppressed, and the free world knows nothing of the abuses.

Pizarro y Orellana claims Hernando Cortez was born on November 10, 1483 — the same day as the birth of Martin Luther.[5] The birthday coincidence is ironic, since Cortez led half the Western Hemisphere out of paganism into the Roman Catholic Church, while Luther led half of Europe out of Roman Catholicism into the Protestant Reformation. But while the exact date of Cortez's birth is uncertain, most historians believe Orellano is in error and that Cortez was actually born in 1485.

Unlike Columbus, Cortez was unquestionably of Spanish birth, though his distant ancestors may have been Lombard or Tuscany royalty. His own family was respectable but not wealthy. As a child Cortez did not seem like conquistador material; he was of frail health and frequently near death. His parents sent him to the University of Salamanca to study law, but he did not find scholarship to his liking, dropped out, and decided to seek his fortune in the Indies. Upon his arrival on the island of Hispaniola in 1504 at age nineteen, the governor (Christopher Columbus's son Diego) gave him a grant of land and a commission as a notary, and Cortez settled down to the life of a frontier hidalgo and became quite wealthy.

This life was comfortable, but not fully satisfying, and Cortez thirsted for more. In 1511 Cortez joined with Diego Velasquez in the conquest of Cuba, and while in Cuba he entered into an arranged marriage with Catalina Xuarez, daughter of an aristocratic Spanish family, and became a gentleman farmer and alcalde (town mayor) in Cuba.

Then, in 1518, Captain Pedro de Alvarado came to Cuba with tidings of an expedition to Yucatan, the southeastern peninsula of Mexico, where ruins of a great civilization had been sighted. Velasquez, now governor of Cuba, commissioned Cortez to lead an expedition to explore this area more fully.

At that point begins an adventure tale of blood and gore, courage and savagery, treasure and danger that make *Treasure Island*, the Indiana Jones movies, and *Lost Horizon* look like Sunday school picnics by comparison. As the story is commonly related, Cortex and his cruel conquistadors brutally deceived and conquered poor, simple, trusting Montezuma and his fellow Aztecs.

Now wait a minute. Is that really what happened? Does that explanation even make sense?

Think about it. Cortez left Cuba with a force of approximately five hundred men, ten cannons, and sixteen horses. By the time he reached Mexico City, the Aztec capital, his forces had dwindled to about four hundred. He faced the most powerful empire of the Western Hemisphere, an emperor named Montezuma who, in addition to his regular

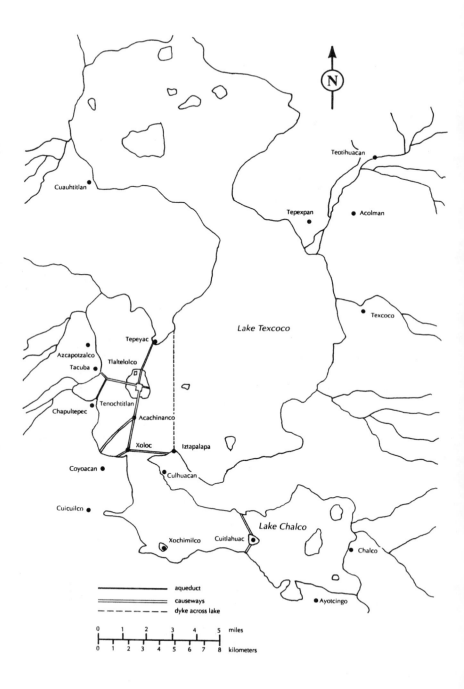

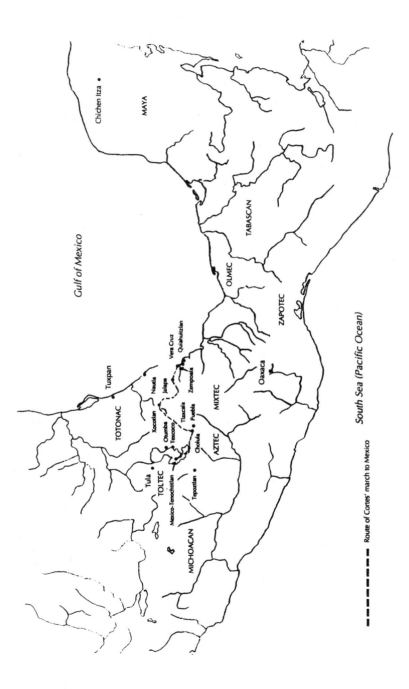

subjects and armies, had thirty vassals, each of whom was capable of producing one hundred thousand warriors at the emperor's command.[6]

Since various sources give differing figures for the size of Cortez's forces and those of the Aztecs, a word on sources would be appropriate at this point. During the conquest Cortez himself wrote several letters to the Emperor Charles V which provide much helpful detail but are not and were not intended to be a comprehensive account. But after Cortez died in 1547 his personal secretary and chaplain, Francisco Lopez y Gomara, wrote a detailed account of the conquistador's life and exploits, relying upon his intimate knowledge of Cortez and his life and other source documents apparently including narratives by some Native American chroniclers. Completed in 1552 and translated by Lesley Byrd Simpson, his work is titled *Cortez: The Life of the Conqueror by his Secretary* (Berkeley: U of California Press, 1964). Then, around 1568, Bernal Diaz del Castillo wrote an eye-witness account of the conquest. His exact rank is not clear, but he was in the thick of the conquest from start to finish and was given substantial responsibility. One of his announced purposes in writing was to correct certain inaccuracies in the Gomara account; most of these deal with precise figures such as size of armies, casualty losses, etc. These discrepancies do not indicate a lack of integrity by either man; when an army of Aztecs charges you, it is difficult to judge its size. The Gomara and Diaz accounts show remarkable agreement, and when they disagree on figures, those of Diaz, which are usually more conservative than those of Gomara, are generally considered more accurate. While more recent and condensed editions exist, I have relied upon the five-volume edition translated by Professor Alfred Percival Maudslay of the National Museum of Mexico and published in London in 1908 by the Hakluyt Society as *The True History of the Conquest of New Spain by Bernal Diaz del Castillo, One of Its Conquerors.*

A critical 16th-century account is that of the Catholic priest and champion of Native Americans, Bartolome de Las Casas. Las Casas's work, *A Brief Relation of the Destruction of the Indies* (reprinted in part by John Francis Bannon, *The Spanish Conquistadors: Men or Devils?*, New York: Holt, Rinehart & Winston, 1960), contains valuable insights and shocking details of Spanish cruelty. But it deals more with the Indies than with Mexico, and that which pertains to Mexico is more after the conquest than during the conquest.

In 1843 William Hickling Prescott published his two-volume work *The Conquest of Mexico* (London: Dent & Sons, 1908, 1965), Prescott's work draws upon those of Gomara, Diaz and others. As a North American Protestant, Prescott shows a certain bias against both Spanish Catholicism and Aztec paganism. Apparently these two prejudices cancel each other out, as Prescott's work is universally acclaimed as the outstanding work in the field, except by those who believe the way to make one's reputation in academia is by destroying the reputation of someone else, preferably someone who is dead and cannot respond.

Among 20th-century sources, Salvador de Madariaga provides valuable details and insights in *Hernan Cortes: Conqueror of Mexico* (Chicago: Regnery, 1955). Henry Morton Robinson's *Stout Cortez: A Biography of Spanish Conquest* (New York: The Century Co., 1931) is one of the most readable accounts. *The Conquistadors* by Hammond Innes (New York: Knopf, 1969) contains good background information including excellent maps, photographs and illustrations. Maurice Collis provides good insight into the personalities of these two great leaders in *Cortes and Montezuma* (London: Faber & Faber, 1954). Also helpful is *Cortes* by William Weber Johnson, former *Time* magazine bureau chief in Mexico City (Boston: Little, Brown, 1975).

And that was not an army of three million savages. The Aztecs were in many respects a very advanced culture — if we are to believe their apologists today, far more advanced than the European powers of the day. The capital city had, according to some accounts, sixty thousand households, or a population of several hundred thousand, much larger than any city in Spain at the time, and a central market-place in which one hundred thousand people could transact business. They had aqueducts, watercourses, and a sanitation system far ahead of anything in Europe. They had an advanced knowledge of astronomy, mathematics, and a very accurate 365-day calendar based on a 52 year cycle.

The Aztecs did not have iron, but they had developed a form of bronze made of an alloy of tin and copper. Their warriors used sword-like weapons made of wood with razor- sharp pieces of obsidian for blades; while they lacked the durability of castilian steel, they could be wielded with such force as to sever a horse's head with one blow. They used shields of wood and leather, and they had armor but normally chose to go without it to be more mobile. They used spears and arrows with stone or copper tips. Their longbows lacked the range and accuracy of European cross-bows but could be reloaded more quickly.

Moreover, Mexico City, or Teotlichan as the Aztec capital was then called, was an almost impregnable fortress. It was located on an island in a large highland lake (the lake was drained by the Spaniards in the 1600s) and could be reached only by crossing a series of crossways with gates and drawbridges. An invading army trying to cross on these causeways was subject to spear and arrow attacks from mobile Aztec war canoes on the lake. Many of the city streets were canals, and even the houses were capable of being turned into fortresses for defense. From the city walls Aztec warriors were ready to shower spears, arrows and rocks on an invading force.

The victory of Cortez cannot be credited simply to superior technology. The Aztecs had nothing comparable to European firearms, but even these were primitive and few in number. Only thirteen of Cortez's soldiers had muskets, only thirty-two had crossbows, and there were only ten cannons. The vast majority of the Spaniards fought with swords, spears, and lances. Instead of steel breastplates most of them wore quilted cotton as protection; only a few of the officers wore mail. And during the retreat from Mexico City the Spaniards had lost all of their cannons, muskets, and crossbows, and still managed to defeat a vastly superior Aztec force at Otombo.

Of greater significance were the sixteen horses. The Aztecs had never seen anything like a horse, and at first they thought the armored horse and rider were one creature, terrifying and possibly divine. Cortez capitalized on this belief, and at first he quickly buried horses that were killed in battle to prevent the Aztecs from learning their true nature. But very soon in the conflict the Aztecs managed to kill a horse, dismember it, and distribute its parts among their chiefs to assure them that this was indeed a mortal creature.

In addition to an advanced technology, the Aztecs had a well-organized government. The leader was an elected monarch, chosen to rule for life by a council of elders. Schools were established for the training of those who were to become priests, warriors, or government officials; and the training was rigorous indeed.

Aztec society was organized into clear strata, with several well-established classes of slaves. The empire was held together by an excellent communications system consisting of runners on well-built highways. A uniform system of taxation existed throughout the empire, including tribute from vassal states, and the legal system included clear prescriptions of right and wrong, with the death penalty for many offenses and a well-developed court system.

Two central features of Aztec society were religion and war — and these were closely bound together. Aztec religion was in some respects similar to New Age pantheism today. At the heart of Aztec religion was the belief in a fundamental spiritual unity of the entire cosmos.[7]

Our understanding of Aztec religion is hampered somewhat by the lack of original Aztec sources. The Aztecs themselves had a highly-developed system of writing. After the Spanish conquest, Catholic priests recorded the Aztec beliefs and practices in meticulous detail, for their own understanding and that of their countrymen. But several decades later Church officials decreed that the writings of the Aztecs and other natives of Central America were "lies and superstitions of Satan" and ordered them destroyed. Only a few native writings have survived. (It is easy for 20th-century Americans to look down upon such actions as bigoted book-burning fanaticism; but to 16th-century bishops these books were instrumentalities used by Satan for the destruction of human souls.) Fortunately, as Michael D. Coe, Professor of Anthropology at Yale and Curator of the Peabody Museum of Natural History, says in *The Maya* (New York: Thames & Hudson, 1966, 1987), ". . . it is our good fortune that the early Spanish missionaries were accomplished scholars, and that owing to their eagerness to understand the nations they wished to convert to the Cross they have left us with first-class anthropological accounts of native culture as it was just before they came."(p. 155).

Prescott relies upon some of these works in explaining Aztec culture and religion. Among 20th-century works, one that gives a good broad view of Aztec religion is *The Aztecs: People of the Sun* by Alfonso Caso, Director of Archeology of the National Museum of Mexico (Norman, Oklahoma: U of Oklahoma Press, 1958, 1988). Victor Wolfgang von Hagen's *The Ancient Sun Kingdoms of the Americas* (Cleveland: World Publishing Co., 1957, 1961) gives good information about the Aztecs, Mayas, Incas, and neighboring peoples. Another good source of information is *Man, Myth & Magic: An Illustrated Encyclopedia of the Supernatural* (New York: Marshall Cavendish, 1970).

Hunbatz Men, who claims to be a descendent of

the Mayas, insists in his book *Secrets of Mayan Science/Religion* (Santa Fe, NM; Bear Publishing Co., 1990) that the Catholic friars coming from a European mindset could not possibly have understood Native American religion and have corrupted it in their accounts. For example, Quetzalcoatl was not a white-bearded god who departed for the east and promised to return; rather, the Quetzalcoatl myth represents the capacity for godhood that lies within each of us, for we can all become Quetzalcoatl. To what extent this accurately depicts ancient Aztec or Mayan thought, or to what extent it is an attempt by modern New Age thinkers to recreate a heritage in their own image, it is impossible to determine. I for one am more willing to trust the scholarship of the friars, who had the original accounts and could talk to native practitioners directly, rather than writers who somehow believe their racial identification with the Aztecs and Mayas gives them some special ability to intuit their true beliefs.

The Aztecs believed in a fundamental spiritual essence that unites all things into one harmony. They sometimes personified that principle as Ometecuhtli, which literally means Two-Lord; because as creator he must embody both the male and female principles into one.[8]

But they were also polytheists. They believed in a host of gods, some greater than others, and as they conquered other nations they absorbed the gods of those peoples into their own pantheon. Caso gives more information:

> ... the religion of the Aztecs was polytheistic, based on the worship of a multitude of personal gods, most of them with well-defined attributes ... There was, in addition, among the uneducated classes, a tendency to exaggerate polytheism by conceiving of as gods, also, what, to the priests, were only manifestations or attributes of one god ... there is also evidence of the efforts of the Aztec priests to reduce the multiple divinities to

different aspects of the same god, for when they adopted the gods of conquered peoples or received gods from peoples of more advanced culture, the priests always tried to incorporate them, as did the Romans, into their own national pantheon, by considering them as diverse manifestations of the gods they had inherited from the great civilizations which preceded them and from whence they derived their culture.[9]

Among these were Quetzalcoatl the god of goodness, Tezcatlipoca, the god of evil, of the night sky, and warrior of the north; Huitzilopochti, the god of the daytime sky and warrior of the south; Xochiquetzal, the goddess of love and beauty; Tlaloc, the rain god; Cinteotl, the god of corn, and others. The sun, moon, and stars were also worshipped as gods, and the Aztec emperor and certain high priests were thought to be at least semi-divine.[10]

The Aztecs believed they stood in a special relationship to the sun, Tonatiuh, and the sun god, Huitzilopochti:

The sun was very brave, the source of all brightness and glory. He had his special heaven for brave warriors who had been sacrificed and for women who had died in childbirth. These warriors, dressed as eagles, lifted the sun to the top of the sky every morning, the women lowered him down each evening into the underworld.[11]

Caso describes the role of Huitzilopochti in cosmic conflict:

According to legend, Coatlicue, the old goddess of the earth, had become a priestess in the temple, living a life of retreat and chastity after having given birth to the moon and the stars. One day while sweeping, she found a ball of down which she tucked away in her waistband. When she finished her tasks, she looked for the ball of feathers, but it had disappeared. Then she suddenly realized that she was pregnant. When her children, the moon, Coyolxauhqui, and the stars, called Centzonhuitznahuac, discovered this, they became so furious that they determined to kill their mother.

Coalicue wept over her approaching death as the moon and the stars armed to kill her, but the prodigy in her womb spoke to her and consoled her, saying that when the time came, he would defend her against all.

Just as her enemies came to slay the mother, Huitzilopochti was born, and with the aid of the serpent of fire, the sun's ray, he cut off Coyolxauhqui's head and put the Centzonhuitznahuac to flight.

So it was that when the god was born he had to open conflict with his brothers, the stars, and his sister, the moon; and armed with the serpent of fire, he puts them to flight every day, his victory signifying a new day of life for men. When he consummates his victory, he is carried in a litter into the center of the sky by the spirits of warriors who have died in combat or on the sacrificial stone. When afternoon begins, he is picked up by the spirits of women who have died in childbirth, for they are equal to warriors because they, too, died taking a man prisoner — the newborn child. During the afternoon the souls of the mothers lead the sun to its setting, where the stars die and where the sun, like the eagle in his fall to death, is gathered close again by the earth. Each day this divine combat is begun anew . . .[12]

The sun-god Huitzilopochtli, the Aztecs believed, had chosen them as his special people and had led them from the north to Mexico to dominate the other peoples of Earth. For the cosmic unity of the universe was breaking down because of the rebellion of the moon-god and star-gods, and a similar breakdown was taking place on Earth. The Aztecs believed, as did pagan people throughout the Earth, that human affairs are a microcosm of the universe and the universe is a macrocosm of human affairs; that what happens in the universe affects what happens on Earth, and vice-versa: "As above, so below," as the occult saying goes. Man was an indispensable partner with the gods as Jon White explains:

> To live was to fight. Indeed, they had early come to believe that heaven had appointed them its legionnaires on earth, and that to them had been given the divine duty and privilege of fighting on behalf of the gods against the cosmic forces of destruction.[13]

And what was the role the Aztecs were to play in this cosmic struggle? To subjugate other peoples and restore order, certainly; but it was more than that. Caso continues:

> Each day this divine combat [between the sun-god and the moon- and star-gods] is begun anew, but in order for the sun to triumph, he must be strong and vigorous, for he has to fight against the unnumbered stars of the North and the South and frighten them all off with his arrows of light. For that reason man must give nourishment to the sun. Since the sun is a god, he disdains the coarse food of mortals and can only be kept alive by life itself, by the magic substance that is found in the blood of man, the chalchihuatl, "the precious liquid," the terrible nectar with which the gods are fed.
>
> The Aztecs, the people of Huitzilopochtli, were the chosen people of the sun. They were charged with the duty of supplying him with food. For that reason war was a form of worship and a necessary activity that led them to establish the Xachiyaoyotl, or "flowery war." Its purpose, unlike that of wars of conquest, was not to gain new territories nor to exact tribute from conquered prisoners, but rather to take prisoners for sacrifice to the sun. The Aztec was a man of the people chosen by the sun. He was a servant of the sun and consequently must be, above everything else, a warrior. He must prepare himself from birth for his most constant activity, the Sacred War . . . [14]

The Aztecs thus were a society dominated by religion ad war, and the two were inseparable. Religion gave purpose to war, and war was the highest religious duty. War was the means by which the sun-god was nourished, and without the sun-god the Aztecs would die.

We see then that the Aztecs were an empire of millions of people with an advanced technology, good communications, a strong and well-organized government, and a well-armed, highly-motivated, and well-disciplined military composed of millions of warriors for whom death in battle meant eternal bliss with the sun-god. Several of Cortez's soldiers who had been in battle against the Turks and the Moors said that even these foes did not rival the Aztecs in ferocity!

To return to our original question: How was it that Hernando Cortez, having just arrived in Mexico for the first time with 553 men and no knowledge of the language and customs of the people or the terrain and climate of the land, was able to defeat and subjugate this most powerful empire of the Western Hemisphere?

Three possibilities suggest themselves. Either (1) Cortez was one of the greatest generals of all time; (2) God aided Cortez in his mission; or (3) There are some facts about the Aztecs that we aren't being told today. A fourth possibility — that the Aztecs were incredibly weak or stupid — must be rejected out of hand in light of their many accomplishments.

The Man Cortez

Let us look, then, at the character and personality of the man Cortez. One fact that stands out above all others is his faith and singleness of purpose. Cortez believed he was on a divine mission to bring the gospel, Christian civilization, and the government of Spain to the western world. One might disagree with his Christian convictions, and one might be repulsed by his methods of advancing those convictions. But that he believed them himself is beyond dispute. Robinson says this about him and his companions:

We shall fail to comprehend one of the chief objects of the expedition, and quite misunderstand the psychology of the Spaniards, unless we can contrive to catch, at this later and colder date, something of the religious enthusiasm that motivated Cortez and his followers. There is nothing in our anemic contemporary life that we can compare with it. The only emotions comparable to the religious zealotry of the sixteenth- century Spaniards are the militant instincts of the twelfth-century crusaders, and the faith of the early Christian martyrs. And in each of these periods, indeed at any peak in the religious experience of a race, it is Faith, not Morals, that claims the fealty of the strongest men. So it was with Cortez in New Spain. Concerning morals he had no conscience. Faith was the paramount consideration with him — faith that God was merciful, that Christ died to reopen heaven's door to man, that He offered His body and blood in the sacrament under the appearances of bread and wine, and that the most abject heathen in the forests of the New World could be saved if these instrumentalities of salvation were presented to him. Cortez believed, as every other Spanish Catholic of his time believed, that the Catholic Church was the true, the only medium by which mankind could assure itself of heaven. There was no hypocrisy in his attitude, no taint of doubt in his belief. His ancestors had died on Moorish spears for that belief, and Cortez himself would have died to sustain the Faith that was in him.[15]

The French historian Jean Descola agrees:

> . . . the violent acts of the Conquistadors — abduction, robberies, assassinations — though sometimes performed "in the name of" religion, were never "under the pretense of" religion.
>
> The Conquistadors were sincere. The legality of the enterprise was guaranteed them by pontifical

bulls. They had been given to understand that they were leaving for a crusade — the one against Islam having ended but recently — and that after the Jew and the Mohammedan, it was now a question of converting the Heathen. They had been born into a hatred and terror of heresy. They had wept with delight at the capture of Granada, trembled before the Inquisition, and shuddered at the very name of Luther. While still children, they had often spat at the passing of a Moor or set fire to the booth of a Jew. Spain in the sixteenth century was nothing but a vast monastery, noisy with orisons and bells. They had grown up in the shadow of cathedrals and breathed the odor of incense from their earliest years, while the first words they had uttered had been the names of the saints.

The Conquistadors, although for the most part illiterate, had no need of letters to feel the same fanatical spirit as did the horsemen of the Prophet when they invaded the old Greco-Latin world, or the Crusaders when they spread over the Syrian plains, or their own fathers at the re-conquest of Granada. They had been told — they had been convinced — that millions of Indians would burn forever in Hell if they, the Conquistadors, did not bring them the faith. They believed this quite simply. Religion was for them not a pretext but a banner. The existence of God in three persons, the immortality of the soul, sin, the Last Judgment — it never occurred to any one of them to dispute these facts or even to discuss them. These men of war and passion had retained the faith of little children. Their confessions were sincere, they participated in the Mass not only in the flesh but also in the spirit. The worst of them died in penitence. Pierced by arrows, or with a sword blade in the throat, or tied to the stake under torture, they called loudly for the last rites. So "color of religion". . . What an error! No ulterior motive colored the faith of the Conquistadors. They remained men of the Middle Ages. Religious hypocrisy had not yet been invented; it was to turn up late, covering iniquity with its black cloak. The hypocrite is a creature of the seventeenth century.[16]

This does not mean they had no other motive. The foot soldier Diaz says, "We came to serve God, and also to get rich"[17] — and saw no contradiction between the two goals. (Nor do I see a contradiction between my twin hopes that this book will, first, advance the Christian faith, and second, provide some income for my family and myself.)

Second, Cortez was decisive. He made quick decisions and regularly put his opponents on the defensive. Repeatedly, faced with an enemy force that outnumbered him two hundred to one, his response is a sudden (and successful) attack. When his troops are fearful and tempted to return to Hispaniola, Cortez cuts them off by sinking his ships. Speaking with Native American caciques, he boldly tells them their idols are false and will lead them to destruction, and as they watch he destroys their idols and leads his men in Christian worship. While a guest in the emperor's palace, he and his men take Montezuma prisoner. Trapped in Mexico City by hostile Aztecs who boast that they can afford to lose twenty-five thousand men to his one, he leads a charge and fights his way out of the city.

But while decisive, his actions were not rash. His military decisions show careful preparation and consideration of alternatives and fall-back positions.

Third, Cortez possessed keen intelligence. Like Columbus he had a quick mind, but unlike Columbus he does not seem to have gained his knowledge through books and maps. Rather, he learned from people and places. He asked key questions, and while in Mexico City under Montezuma's protection he surveyed the city with the careful eye of a military engineer. His on-the-spot innovations — the building of fortresses on wheels to facilitate the escape from Mexico City, the construction of brigantines (small boats) to battle the Aztec war canoes on the lake surrounding Mexico City — show a quick mind.

He was an optimist. Like Columbus he had faith in God and in his own part in God's plan. Like Columbus he was vigorous, robust, and enthusiastic, and he communicated this quality to others. Unlike Columbus he did not become depressed when weighed down with adversity. Adversity seemed to bring out the best in him; he remained at least outwardly cheerful and confident and responded to the adversity with a quick offensive.

And he knew how to communicate this enthusiasm to others with just the right dash of flair and showmanship. Repeatedly he exhorted his weary men to follow the "banner of the Cross" and serve Christ and the Crown of Spain, and he knew how to add just enough promise of personal wealth to turn the most dejected troops into enthusiastic soldiers of the Cross. Dealing with Native American allies and enemies alike, he seemed to possess an excellent sense of timing. He seemed to know just when to be firm, and when to be conciliatory — though he did overreach occasionally.

In short, it is hard to imagine any other commander who could have accomplished what Cortez did in conquering the unconquerable.

And so, on February 10, A.D. 1519, Cortez and his men embarked on an adventure, not comprehending the glories and dangers they would face. Cortez conducted a brief review of his troops and gave the first of his many stirring addresses:

> Soldiers of Spain, we are standing upon the verge of the greatest adventure ever undertaken by so small a body of men. We now leave the known world behind us: from this time forth we plunge into a region never before trodden by men of our race or religion. The hazards of this adventure I shall not dwell upon; they are well estimated by the bravest among you. But I speak now of the immortal glory you will bring to Spanish arms, and to yourselves, in the successful accomplishment of the mission before us. The shores we shall storm are lined with teeming millions of savages, unfriendly if not openly hostile. We have only our swords and our good right arms to protect us against their overwhelming numbers.

Therefore let no childish strife or inner dissension weaken the front we must present to the enemy. If we go as united as we go courageously, we have nothing to fear, nothing to lose. But to gain? This, men of Spain: the destiny of heroes! Years from now, in the streets of Seville and Cadiz, men will point to you and say to their children: "There is a hero, he was with Cortez in New Spain."

We are on a crusade. We are marching as Christians into a land of infidels. We seek not only to subdue boundless territory in the name of our Emperor Don Carlos, but to win millions of unsalvaged souls to the True Faith. By the force and righteousness of our own Faith, we shall gain crowns for ourselves in the heaven to come.

I have told you that we shall put on the double immortality of earthly fame and heavenly salvation. That is glory indeed, but now I tell you that you shall have riches as well as glory. Be true to me, as I am to you, and I will load you with wealth such as you have never dreamed of. This wealth will not be won easily — but who is afraid? We are few but we are inconquerable. Let us therefore enter upon our labors, so auspiciously begun, and in the name of our God and our Emperor carry them joyously, confidently to a triumphant conclusion.[18]

They then said Mass and set sail. But as Robinson says, "If Hernando Cortez could have known in detail the hazards and hardships of the years before him, it is probable that his own stout heart would have quailed as he set foot upon the vessel that bore him to the mainland of America."[19]

Signs of Divine Favor

After about three weeks of travel they arrived at the island of Consumel, a few miles off the Yucatan peninsula of southeastern Mexico. Cortez arrived two days after one of his captains, Pedro de Alvarado, having stayed behind to aid a disabled vessel. Learning that Alvarado and his men had looted some native villages, Cortez rebuked them sternly and ordered the plundered goods returned. One of his servants, named Melchorego, a native of Yucatan who had been brought to Cuba on a previous voyage, served as a rather crude interpreter, and through him Cortez won the confidence of the natives and engaged in trade. As Diaz says, "Here in this Island Cortes began to rule energetically, and Our Lord so favoured him that whatever he put his hand to it turned out well for him, especially in pacifying the people and towns of these lands, as we shall see further on."[20]

Several events took place that led the Spaniards to believe the divine hand of Providence was at work in their holy quest. As they explored the interior of the island, they discovered a large stone cross. It is possible this was a pagan fertility symbol erected by natives; but to the Spaniards it was proof that Christianity had once been preached in these parts, and it confirmed their determination to win these people for Christ. Diaz then records his commander's first sermon to these people:

> . . . many Indians both the natives of the towns near Cape Catoche and those from other parts of Yucatan came on pilgrimages to the Island of Cozumel, for it appeared that there were some very hideous idols kept in a certain oratory on Cozumel to which it was the custom of the people of the land to offer sacrifices at that season. One morning the courtyard of the oratory where the Idols were kept was crowded with Indians, and many of them both men and women were burning a resin like our incense. As this was a new sight to us we stood round watching it with attention, and presently an old Indian with a long cloak, who was the priest of the Idols (and I have already said that the priests in New Spain are called Papas) went up on the top of the oratory and began to preach to the people. Cortes and all of us were wondering what would be the result of that black sermon. Cortes asked Melchorejo, who understood the language well, what the old

Indian was saying, for he was informed that he was preaching evil things, and he sent for the Cacique [chief] and all the principal chiefs and the priest himself, and, as well as he could through the aid of our interpreter, he told them that if we were to be brothers they must cast those most evil Idols out of their temple, for they were not gods at all but very evil things which led them astray and could lead their souls to hell. Then he spoke to them about good and holy things, and told them to set up in the place of their Idols an image of Our Lady which he gave them, and a cross, which would always aid them and bring good harvests and would save their souls, and he told them in a very excellent way other things about our holy faith.

The Priest and the Caciques answered that their forefathers had worshipped those Idols because they were good, and that they did not dare to do otherwise, and that if we cast out their Idols we would see how much harm it would do us, for we should be lost at sea. Then Cortes ordered us to break the Idols to pieces and roll them down the steps, and this we did; then he ordered lime to be brought, of which there was a good store in the town, and Indian masons, and he set up a very fair altar on which we placed the figure of Our Lady; and he ordered two of our party named Alonzo Yanez and Alvara Lopez who were carpenters and joiners to make a cross of some rough timber which was there, and it was placed in a small chapel near the altar and the priest named Juan Diaz said mass there, and the Cacique and the heathen priest and all the Indians stood watching us with attention.[21]

Then it appeared that God sent another sign of His favor. A canoe approached the island, and one of the occupants was dressed as a native but had the appearance of a European. He asked them in Spanish, "Gentlemen, are you Christians?" As Gomara relates the incident:

They replied that they were Spaniards [in the narratives the words "Spaniard" and "Christian" are used almost interchangeably], and he was so overcome at their words that he burst into tears. He asked if it was Wednesday, for he was accustomed to devoting several hours to prayer on that day, and he begged them to join him, sank to his knees, and raised his hands and eyes to Heaven. Then, with tears in his eyes, he offered up a prayer to God, giving Him infinite thanks for His mercy in liberating him from those infidels and hellish men, and for restoring him to the Christians and men of his nation.[22]

He introduced himself as Jeronimo de Aguilar, a Catholic priest, and related that eight years earlier he and his companions had been shipwrecked in the area, survived thirteen or fourteen days adrift in a lifeboat, and were cast ashore on the Yucatan coast. There they came into the custody of a local cacique who enslaved them but found them useful because of their knowledge and gave them favored positions. By this time all but Aguilar and one other had died; the other had a native wife and children and wanted to remain with them.

Aguilar eagerly joined the expedition and served as the interpreter, knowing Spanish better than Melchorejo and being better able to relate Spanish ideas and customs. And the Spaniards saw the sovereign hand of God at work because they had left the island a few days earlier but were forced to return because of a leak in one ship, and contrary winds had kept them on Cozumel several days longer. Had they departed as planned, they would have missed Aguilar and all that he had to relate about the new land. And because of Aguilar, Cortez was now better able to share Christ with the people. Gomara gives the following report:

> The next day after Aguilar's arrival, Cortez again spoke with the people of Cozumel, in order to inform himself better about the island, now that he could understand them with the help of his faithful inter-

preter; also for the purpose of encouraging them in the veneration of the Cross and persuading them to put aside their idols, in the belief that this was the best way to get them to abandon the sooner their heathenish customs and become Christians . . .

So Jeronimo de Aguilar preached to them about salvation, and, either because of what he told them, or because of the beginning they had already made, they were pleased to have their idols cast down, and they even assisted at it, breaking into small pieces what they had formerly held sacred. And soon our Spaniards had left not a whole idol standing, and in each chapel they set up a Cross or the image of Our Lady, whom all the islanders worshiped with prayer and great devotion, burning incense to her and offering partridges, maize, and fruits, and other things they were accustomed to bring to their temples. Such was their devotion to the image of Our Lady that ever afterward, when Spanish ships touched at their island, they would run out to them, shouting "Cortes, Cortes!" and singing "Maria, Maria!" — which they did when Alonso de Parada and Panfilo de Narvaez passed that way. Even more, they begged Cortez to leave someone behind to teach them to believe in the God of the Christians; but he did not dare consent, for fear they might kill the preacher, and also because he had few priests and friars with him. And in this he did wrong, in view of their earnest request and supplication.[23]

Their week on Cozumel had been productive and eventful, though tame compared to what was coming. They left Cozumel around March 13 sailed around the Yucatan peninsula and headed westward to Tabasco. There he faced hostile natives, who threatened to kill them if they landed. Through Aguilar, Cortez repeatedly asked to be allowed to land. Gomara recounts this story:

Cortes endeavored to treat these barbarians with every civility, as is right and as is laid down in the instructions issued by the monarchs of Castile; that is, to offer them peace one, two, and many times before making war upon them or invading their lands and taking their towns. So he repeated his offer of peace and friendship, promising them freedom and good treatment, and to teach them so many things of profit to their souls and bodies that they would consider themselves fortunate; but, on the other hand, he warned them that if they stubbornly refused to receive and admit him (setting a limit of that afternoon before sundown for their decision), he, with the help of God, would sleep in their town that night, at whatever cost to its inhabitants, who had spurned his peace and friendship.

The Indians laughed heartily at his words and mocked him, and returned to their town to tell of the boasting and madness they had heard.[24]

The Spaniards landed, and for the next several days they engaged the Tabascans in several small battles. Then, seeing that they were gathering their forces for a major attack, Cortez decided on a quick strike, with Captain Diego de Ordaz leading the foot soldiers and artillery in a frontal assault upon the Tabascans while he himself led the cavalry in an attack on the rear. Ordaz claimed they were outnumbered three hundred to one, and for awhile the Tabascans seemed on the verge of winning; but then Cortez and the cavalry attacked. The Tabascans panicked at their first sight of horses and riders, and many dropped their weapons and fled. The rest were easily routed, and the result was a Spanish victory against overwhelming odds. Prescott summarizes the results:

The number of those who fought or fell in the engagement is altogether doubtful. Nothing, indeed, is more uncertain than numerical estimates of barbarians. And they gain nothing in probability, when they come, as in the present instance, from the reports of their enemies. Most accounts, however, agree that the Indian force consisted of five squad-

rons of eight thousand men each. There is more
discrepancy as to the number of slain, varying from
one to thirty thousand! In this monstrous discor-
dance, the common disposition to exaggerate may
lead us to look for truth in the neighbourhood of the
smallest number. The loss of the Christians was
inconsiderable; not exceeding — if we receive their
own reports, probably, from the same causes, much
diminishing the truth — two killed, and less than a
hundred wounded! We may readily comprehend the
feelings of the Conquerors, when they declared, that
"Heaven must have fought on their side, since their
own strength could never have prevailed against
such a multitude of enemies!"[25]

The Spaniards believed God had intervened on their
behalf once again. Gomara relates a legend that a horseman miraculously appeared to fight on the Spaniards'
behalf and that the Spaniards believed he was either St.
Peter or St. James while the Indians thought he was a
centaur.[26] Bernal Diaz, a devout Christian but also a realistic foot soldier, doubts this legend but doesn't flatly deny
it. Rather he wryly gives this explanation:

> I say that all our doings and our victories are at
> the hands of our Lord Jesus Christ, and that in this
> battle there were so many Indians to every one of us
> that they could have blinded us with the dust they
> raised but for the pity of God who always helped us.
> It may be that as Gomara says the Glorious Apostles
> Senor Santiago [St. James] and Senor San Pedro
> [St. Peter] came to our aid and that I, being a sinner
> was not worthy to behold them. What I saw was
> Francisco de Morla, on a chestnut horse, who came
> up at the same time as Cortes, and it seems to me
> that now as I write I can see again with these sinful
> eyes all that battle in the very way that it took place,
> and although I am a poor sinner and not worthy to
> see either of these glorious apostles, there were in
> our company over four hundred soldiers and Cortes

himself and many other gentlemen, and it would have been talked about, and evidence would have been taken, and a church would have been built when the town was founded, and the town would have been named Santiago de la Victoria, or San Pedro de la Victoria instead of Santa Maria de la Victoria. If it was as Gomara says we must have all been very bad Christians, when our Lord God sent his holy Apostle to us, not to recognize the great favour that he was showing to us, and not daily to have venerated that church. I wish to God it were as the historian Gomara says, but, until I read his history, one never heard about it among the conquistadors who were there at the time.[27]

Two days later the Tabascans approached the Spaniards and asked for peace, bringing gifts, and an offering of twenty women as servants. Cortez agreed, and he preached to them through Aguilar:

> ... Cortes told them of their blindness and great vanity in worshiping many gods and making sacrifices of human blood to them, and in thinking that those images, being mute and soulless, made by the Indians with their own hands, were capable of doing either good or harm. He then told them of a single God, Creator of Heaven and earth and men, whom the Christians worshiped and served, and whom all men should worship and serve. In short, after he had explained the Mysteries to them, and how the Son of God had suffered on the Cross, they accepted it and broke up their idols. Thus it was that with great reverence, before a large concourse of Indians, and with many tears on the part of the Spaniards, a Cross was erected in the temple of Potonchan, and our men first, kneeling, kissed and worshiped it, and after them the Indians.[28]

Cortez asked the natives to return two days later, Palm Sunday, to observe their worship service. Thousands of

them came, both men and women, and Cortez and his
priests conducted a special open-air Mass at which the
natives seemed greatly moved. Prescott briefly transcends
his own anti-Catholic bias and says the following:

> The Roman Catholic communion has, it must be
> admitted, some decided advantages over the Protes-
> tant, for the purpose of proselytism. The dazzling
> pomp of its service and its touching appeal to the
> sensibilities affect the imagination of the rude child
> of nature much more powerfully than the cold ab-
> stractions of Protestantism, which, addressed to the
> reason, demand a degree of refinement and mental
> culture in the audience to comprehend them. The
> respect, moreover, shown by the Catholic for the
> material representations of Divinity greatly facili-
> tates the same object. It is true, such representa-
> tions are used by him only as incentives, not as the
> objects of worship. But this distinction is lost on the
> savage, who finds such forms of adoration too analo-
> gous to his own to impose any great violence on his
> feelings. It is only required of him to transfer his
> homage from the image of Quetzalcoatl, the benevo-
> lent deity who walked among men, to that of the
> Virgin or the Redeemer; from the Cross, which he
> has worshipped as the emblem of the God of rain, to
> the same Cross, the symbol of salvation.[29]

The Spaniards then departed from Tabasco, again having made friends and allies. With them came the twenty
women servants, who were instructed and baptized into the
Christian faith. One of these proved to be a special blessing
and sign of God's providence.

The crew sailed west about a hundred miles and dropped
anchor at the island of St. Juan de Ulua. Two canoes came
out to meet them, and the occupants bore gifts. But they
could not communicate with one another; Aguilar spoke
Tabascan but was baffled by their language.

Then one of the servant women came forth. She understood both Tabascan and the language of these people,

which was close to that of the Aztecs of whom they were vassals. Baptized Marina, she was tall, beautiful, aristocratic and intelligent. With Aguilar and Marina, Cortez was able to communicate with these ambassadors. Cortez spoke in Spanish, Aguilar translated into Tabascan for Marina, and Marina translated into the Aztec tongue for the ambassadors. Soon she mastered Spanish and was able to translate directly without Aguilar's help. Not only was she a capable linguist, she was a skilled diplomat as well. The daughter of a wealthy chieftain from the southeastern border of the Aztec empire, her father died when she was young. Her mother remarried and had a son, and to secure the inheritance for her son, she sold Marina into slavery and pretended she had died. Eventually she was sold to a Tabascan cacique, who gave her to the Spaniards.

Dona Marina (Lady Marina), as she was respectfully called, was far more than an interpreter. She was a valuable source of information about the people, customs, and politics of Mexico. She became Cortez's advisor, confidante, and eventually his lover, and she bore him his first child, Don Martin Cortez, who became Comendador of the Military Order of St. James. A devout Christian, she was ever loyal to Cortez and the Spaniards, yet throughout her life she worked for the relief of the conquered native peoples.[30] On several occasions she saved the entire Spanish company from certain death.

Through Dona Marina, Aguilar, and the natives of Cozumel and Tabasco, Cortez and his men began to learn more about the Aztec nation. It was a mighty empire, but also a troubled empire. And the Aztec religion, which was the source and impetus of Aztec power, was also the Aztecs' downfall.

Trouble in Paradise

The reader will recall that the Aztecs believed they were indispensable partners of the gods in preserving the unity and harmony of the cosmos. As the sun-god daily warred against the moon-god and star-gods, it was their sacred duty to nourish the sun-god Huitzilopochtli to strengthen

him in his battle; the very survival of the world depended on
it. And the sun-god was on a strict diet of blood — human
blood. The result was human sacrifice, not just in Mexico
City but in virtually every village in Mexico and beyond . . .

In every village in Mexico stood a temple, of varying
sizes, often resembling the pyramids of Egypt. The lower
parts of the temples often were tombs for departed aristo-
crats. There were steps up the side, and at the top was a flat
surface on which rested a chapel-like structure. When the
time for sacrifice came, the victim was led up the temple
stairs and laid facing upwards on a slab of rock. The priest
then used an obsidian knife to slash open his chest, pull out
his still-palpitating heart, and hold it up still beating before
the sun-god. The victim was then decapitated and his body
was rolled down the temple steps, where the people dismembered it and cannibalized its flesh. Caso explains the
significance of Aztec cannibalism:

> . . . Aztec cannibalism was a rite performed as a
> religious ceremony, so much so that he who had
> captured a prisoner could not eat his flesh, because
> the captive was looked upon as his son. It should not
> be forgotten that in the minds of the Aztecs the
> human victims were the very incarnation of the gods
> whom they represented and whose attire they wore,
> and when they ate their flesh, they were performing
> a kind of communion with the divinity . . .[31]

Caso describes other forms of sacrifice:

> At other times, during ceremonies in honor of the
> god Xipe, the prisoner was tied to the upper part of
> a kind of framework and then riddled by arrows
> until he died. The prisoner's blood spilling on the
> ground was thought to make it fertile and to stimu-
> late by a sort of magical sympathy the fall of the
> other precious liquid, rain.
> We have already discussed another type of sacri-
> fice associated with Xipe and with the goddess of
> earth. In this rite the victim was flayed and the

priest dressed in his skin. Decapitation and burning were also used as methods of sacrifice.

Gladiatorial sacrifice was reserved for those who had distinguished themselves by their valor. It consisted of a real duel between a prisoner captain and several of the most distinguished Aztec warriors, two of whom must be knights of the military Order of the Eagles and two of the Order of the Jaguars. It was not an equal fight, however, since the captive was bound, and to defend himself had only a wooden sword with small tufts of downy feathers attached to its edges instead of obsidian blades. His sponsor, or second, dressed like a bear, gave him four heavy sticks of pine to serve as spears to hurl at his enemies. The captive fought with one knight at a time. If the first should be defeated, another would take up the battle. If, in spite of his inferior weapons, the captive succeeded in vanquishing the four knights, a fifth, who was left-handed, generally killed him.

We are told, however, that a Tlaxcaltecan warrior named Tlahuicole did succeed in defeating all five of the knights and was consequently pardoned.[32]

Sacrifice was not limited to enemy warriors. Children were sacrificed to Tlaloc, the rain-god; the more they cried, the more likely their tears were to induce rain.

Caso describes still another form of sacrifice:

A ceremony interesting because of its symbolism took place in the sixth month, called Toxcatl. A young warrior who had been captured in battle was selected as a symbol or incarnation of the god Tezcatlipoca. For one whole year the priests taught him how to conduct himself as a personage of the court by instructing him in the manners of a noble. They also taught him to play the clay flutes and gave him a select entourage to accompany him and attend to his wants as if he were a lord. Dressed in the attire of the god, he strolled through the city streets carrying a bouquet of flowers in the manner of the nobles and smoking tobacco from a richly gilded reed pipe. Whoever met this living representation of Tezcatlipoca paid him great reverence and held him in as much esteem as if he were the king himself.

At the beginning of the month of Toxcatl, or twenty days before the celebration of the festival, his dress was changed to that worn by the great captains and war lords. He was married to four young maidens called Xochiquetzal, Xilonen, Atlatona, and Huixtocihuatl, incarnations of the wives of the god of providence.

When the day of the festival arrived, great ceremonies, dances, and banquets were held in honor of the youth. Everyone, nobles as well as plebeians, honored and praised him as if his reign were to last forever.

On the day of the festival he, along with his new wives and court, was taken in one of the royal canoes to a small, neglected temple on the shore of a lake. Here, the wives who had been with him during the time of prosperity left him, as did the brilliant entourage that had kept him company. Now, almost alone, with only a few pages, he began to walk toward the temple, carrying in his hands the clay flutes which he had played when he was regarded as a great lord.

At the temple steps even his pages abandoned him. Alone, he began the ascent, breaking one of the small flutes, a symbol of his past grandeur, on each of the temple steps.

Slowly he ascended the steps of the temple. When he arrived at the summit, the priests were already awaiting him. Stripping him of his last finery, they stretched him out on the sacrificial stone and tore out his heart. "They said," Sahagun tells us, "that this signifies that those who enjoy wealth and pleasures in this life will end in poverty and in sorrow."

As soon as this youth had died, another was chosen to represent the god, and he, too, was regaled and cared for in the same way until the following year when the month of Toxcatl returned, bringing with it the end of his life.[33]

As Director of Archeology at the National Museum of Mexico, Caso casually and objectively records all of this and more. Then, amazingly, in the only real moral judgment of the entire book, Caso calls the Spanish conquest "a sad event, for the Aztecs' way of life was no longer to follow its own course. An alien world had come to impose its views upon these people and their civilization."[34] Civilization? Way of life? Savagery and way of death would be more appropriate!

At first the sacrifices were limited in number, but in the 1400s they began to escalate into a major holocaust. In 1487 Ahuitzotl, Montezuma's immediate predecessor, dedicated the great temple to Huitzilopochtli the sun-god and sacrificed twenty thousand victims; they stood in four lines stretching between three and four miles long, and the ceremony lasted four days and was conducted by eight teams of priests.[35] The sacrifices escalated from that point and may have reached fifty thousand per year, some say higher. As the historian Jon M. White says in *Cortez and the Downfall of the Aztec Empire,* "When we visit or study photographs of Aztec temples, we should picture to ourselves those tall staircases as they frequently appeared: covered from top to bottom with a tacky, crimson sheath of blood."[36]

The practice of human sacrifice worked to the Aztecs' detriment in many ways. Not only did they sacrifice many of their own warriors, maidens, and children and thus deplete their own resources, but also by demanding human captives for sacrifice from other nations, they incurred the wrath of their own vassal states and the undying hostility of those beyond their control. Many of these nations held beliefs and practices similar to those of the Aztecs; but if their warriors were to be sacrificed, it should be to their own gods and on their own altars, not far away in Mexico City by the hated Aztecs. Cortez thus found ready allies in his conquest of the Aztecs, for many Native Americans looked upon him not as a conqueror but rather as a liberator.

It also hindered their efficiency in battle, for the Aztec goal was not to kill the enemy on the battlefield but rather to capture them alive for sacrifice. On several occasions the Aztecs had their hands on Cortez himself and could easily have killed him had they not been determined to drag him to the sacrificial altar.

The Aztecs believed the sun-god aided them in their battles just as they nourished him in his warfare. For that reason they were reluctant to fight at night and customarily retired at sundown. This worked to their disadvantage, because with their superior numbers they could easily have fought in shifts around the clock and worn the Spaniards down. And on several occasions the Spaniards caught them unaware with surprise attacks at night.

The Aztec practice of human sacrifice galvanized the Spaniards into action. They found the practice grotesque, repulsive, and against the laws of God and man in Diaz's words; but it was more than that. As seasoned soldiers they were used to bloodshed; but these were more than just acts of violence. They were rituals performed for Satan himself as Descola says:

> The Conquistadors believed in God fiercely and unreservedly. But they believed also — above all else! — in the Devil. Now, the New World was the empire of the Devil, a Devil with multiform face, always hideous. The somber Mexican divinities, Huitzilopochtli (the Sorcerer-Hummingbird) and Tezcatlipoca (the Smoking Mirror), the horrible Kinich Kakmo of the Mayas, the Peruvian Viracocha who symbolized boiling lava, the sinister totems of the Araucanians and Diaguites . . . Why, the medieval demon with short horns, lustful eye, and a tail that was curled like a vine shoot seemed a "good devil" beside such as these! Spaniards who in Estremaduran twilights had taken the flight of a bat for the passing of the Evil One were naturally terrified before these monsters of stone, with bared fangs and gleaming eyes, that seemed to come to fantastic life as night fell. How could they have

watched an Aztec ceremony without nausea? The black-robed priests with matted hair, burrowing with their knives in the breasts of their victims, the human skulls piled up at the feet of the teocallis [temple], the cannibal feasts around statues spattered with putrid blood, and the charnel-house stench which all the perfumes of Mexico were never able to hide . . .

Such things froze the spirits of the Conquistadors, surpassing the nightmares of their childhoods. Satan himself was there, and his worship was celebrated among the dismembered corpses. His maleficent power was honored. He was no longer, as in Spain, a familiar accomplice that could be driven off by a flick of the finger, or the shameful specter slipping furtively through one's conscience but put to flight by a sprinkling of holy water. He was enthroned. Carved in granite, incrusted with precious stones and encircled with golden serpents, he was the superb incarnation of Evil. He glorified sin. Nothing was lacking in this perfect representation of Hell, not even the pots in which certain tribes of the Colombian jungle cooked their enemies alive. This indeed was Satan himself, adorned with all his lugubrious attractions.

Why, therefore, should we be astonished at the reactions of the Spaniards? In the depths of the Indian sanctuaries they could see the Prince of Darkness standing in all his macabre splendor. Looking heavenward, they could distinguish the silvery figure of Saint James galloping across the clouds. The conflict between the true and the false, between good and evil, was manifest in this double apparition. The problem was simple and their duty was clear. The Indians were possessed of the Devil, who had to be exorcised, first by destroying the material evidence of Devil worship. This is why the conquerors, activated by the same blind zeal as early Christians when they shattered the Roman statues, overturned the pre-Columbian idols and burned the ritual articles and the manuscripts that transmitted the sacred tradition — in short, showed a holy ardor to abolish the very memory of the heathen liturgy. This they counted as pious work and a salutary need.

Iconoclasts? Vandals? These epithets would have scandalized the Conquistadors. Who would have applied such words except the agents of Satan who served a vile master? But the Conquistadors did not limit themselves to casting down the idols. In order that the exorcism be fully effective, it was not enough to drive away the demons; it was proper also to set up in their places the symbols of the True Faith. Just as holy medals were laid upon flesh that was eaten away with ulcers, the soldiers of Charles V [King Don Carlos of Spain was also emperor of the Holy Roman Empire where he was known as Charles V] planted crosses on the tops of the teocallis or at crossroads. On the stones that were still spattered with blood from the sacrificial tables, they raised altars to Our Lady of Guadalupe. Tolerance was not for them. Others would follow who would use gentler methods. No one doubts that these booted and armored Christians often lacked the Christian spirit and that charity was almost always missing from their pitiless fervor; but their Faith and their good faith were whole. More even than the love of God and of one's neighbor, the horror of Beelzebub explains certain of the Conquistadors' attitudes, though of course it is understood that to explain is not to absolve.[37]

The Aztec religion affected the emperor's performance of his duties. Most of his predecessors had been warriors; Montezuma had been a priest. He was devoted to the Aztec religion in all its aspects, having performed sacrifices on a large scale as chief priest, and he personally performed at least one human sacrifice every day and frequently ate human flesh. He believed that human affairs were ordained by the gods, and he regularly consulted his personal

god Huichilobos ("Witchywolves") which may have been a
corruption of Huitzilopochtli the sun-god and a smoking
mirror in the temple. In short, Montezuma had become an
obsessed, blood-drenched, superstitious man whose decisions were dictated by demonic powers rather than by God
or human reason.

Still another aspect of Aztec religion worked to the
detriment of the empire — the legend of Quetzalcoatl. The
Quetzalcoatl legends abound throughout Central America,
and they take many forms. As the Aztecs conquered other
nations and absorbed their gods into their own pantheon,
the Quetzalcoatl stories became more varied and complex.
Essentially Quetzalcoatl was the feathered serpent, the
god of goodness, and also the god of wind and the morning
star. He is the god of light who stands against the evil god
Tezcatlipoca, god of darkness and patron of evil, and the
two are in perpetual conflict.[38]

But Quetzalcoatl was also a man, or at least a god who
appeared as a man, possibly an early Toltec king or priest.
He is described in some of the Quetzalcoatl legends as
having white hair and a beard, blue eyes, and light complexion. Eventually he was forced by political intrigue to
leave Mexico, largely because he fought against human
sacrifice, and he sailed off to the east on a raft of snakes,
promising to return to rescue his people at a time of great
oppression and adversity.[39]

When Montezuma learned of the landing of Spaniards
on the east coast of Mexico, he felt that Quetzalcoatl had
returned. He shuddered, for that meant his reign was over.
The gods had willed it, and it would come to pass. Man was
but an instrument in the hands of the gods, unable to
control his own destiny.

And many of the Native Americans on the east coast of
Mexico also believed Quetzalcoatl had returned and rejoiced that the generations of Aztec oppression were drawing to a close. In the person of Cortez, Quetzalcoatl had
returned to set his people free!

Signs and portents pointed to the return of Quetzalcoatl
and the end of Aztec rule:

For a time the night sky was lit by a northern light; a volcanic disturbance caused the water in the Mexico lake to boil up and flood the city streets; the temple of the sun god went on fire; a spirit speaking in a woman's voice wailed at night: "My children, my children, ruin is at hand." Magicians were called in to interpret these signs. They could not pretend that their meaning was good. Montezuma strangled them, for in magic it is some remedy to destroy the bearer of bad news.

Sign followed sign, a comet, an earthquake. Montezuma felt his nerve giving way. A calamity was certainly approaching. His sister, Papantzin, after lying in a coma for four days, a condition that was taken for death, revived in her grave and on being carried back to the palace declared that she had seen strange beings entering the country and bringing it to ruin. This profoundly shocked him, but not more than what he himself saw shortly afterwards. He was sitting on his mat of state in the building called the Dark House of the Cord, the monastic university inside the precincts of the great temple of the Humming Bird, as the war aspect of the Smoking Mirror was called. "The sun had inclined already towards evening, but it was still day," says Sahagun, the Franciscan friar who a few years later took down the story from those, perhaps, who were present at the time. "Some people who earned their living by catching waterbirds, got a bird of ash grey colour like a crane and brought it to show Montezuma." As he looked at it he seemed to fall into a trance, and saw on the bird's head a magic mirror in which was reflected an ill-omened constellation. This alarmed him and when he looked more closely into the mirror he was horrified "to perceive reeds like men approaching, armed as for war and mounted on deer." It seemed to him that he saw the landing of Quetzalcoatl.[40]

And the light-skinned Europeans coming in ships from

the East (the direction in which Quetzalcoatl had departed) confirmed it: the Fair God had returned, and Montezuma's reign was doomed.

Cortez, for his part, never claimed to be Quetzalcoatl, and when asked he would reply he was a man and not a god. But when he learned that the natives identified him as Quetzacoatl, he did little to discourage the thought. His answer that he represented the God of Heaven and the great emperor across the ocean was just ambiguous enough to leave open the conclusion that if Cortez was not Quetzalcoatl, he was at least close to him.

Landing at Vera Cruz

Let us now return to the Gulf Coast and to Cortez and his band of conquistadors. Cortez laid plans for the foundation of a settlement on the coast, and he called the settlement Vera Cruz (True Cross). And he claimed the land for the Christian faith and the Crown of Spain.

Note that he did not claim the land for the governor of Hispaniola. This was not merely an oversight. He was laying the groundwork for a separate colony, independent of Governor Velasquez, Hispaniola, Cuba, and the Indies, and responsible directly to the Crown. For tension had developed between Cortez and Governor Velasquez, and he feared that the governor would revoke his commission and order him back. That would be the end of this great crusade, or at least of his role in it. And many of his men were loyal to Velasquez or were sick from battle-wounds, mosquitos, or malaria and wanted to return to Cuba.

If leadership is defined as making people want to do the right thing (or what you believe to be the right thing), Cortez on this occasion clearly showed himself a leader. Responding to the cries of "Return to Cuba!", he gave orders to prepare the ships for an immediate return. Those who were loyal to him then loudly clamored (as planned) for him to rescind the order, for they wanted to remain and establish a colony. Cortez responded that he had no authority from Governor Velasquez to establish a colony and therefore could not do so. His supporters continued to demand that he establish a colony under the direct authority of the king and said they themselves would authorize him to do so in the king's interest. Cortez acceded to their demand and appointed a colony government consisting of his strongest supporters.

He then announced his resignation as captain-general, saying that his military powers from Governor Velasquez were now dissolved. The colony officials, assuming that their colony now had a status equal to that of Cuba and Hispaniola, promptly reappointed him captain-general and chief justiciar, giving him far greater powers than he had enjoyed under Governor Velasquez. Perhaps Cortez had learned something in those two years of law school after all!

During this same time period Cortez had his first communication with Montezuma, who sent messengers by runners from Mexico City. The messengers were cordial and diplomatic, but also somewhat aloof. Cortez asked to meet with Montezuma, and he sent Montezuma some gifts and also a helmet and asked that it be filled with gold, saying that Spaniards suffered from a disease of the heart that could be cured only by gold.

The messengers returned eight days later with an embassy of two Aztec nobles and a hundred slaves bearing gifts from Montezuma. The helmet was returned duly filled with pure gold dust, but other gifts were of greater value, including an immense golden disk the size of a cartwheel engraved to represent the sun. But with polished diplomacy the messenger said a meeting with Montezuma was impossible because the road to Mexico City was difficult and treacherous, and the emperor was indisposed. He urged Cortez to accept the gifts and leave Mexico, content in the knowledge that he had the emperor's friendship and good will. Cortez likewise answered with smooth diplomacy that his own king would be extremely displeased if he (Cortez) returned without seeing Montezuma. He therefore requested that the messengers ask the emperor to reconsider his position. He also seized another opportunity to proclaim Christianity, this time to Montezuma's own ambassadors:

... it was now the time of the Ave Maria, and at

the sound of a bell which we had in the camp we all
fell at our knees before a cross placed on a sand hill
and said our prayers of the Ave Maria before the
cross. When Tendile and Pitalpitoque [Montezuma's
ambassadors] saw us thus kneeling, as they were
very intelligent, they asked what was the reason
that we humbled ourselves before a tree cut in that
particular way. As Cortez heard this remark he said
to the Padre de la Merced who was present: "It is a
good opportunity, father, as we have good material
at hand, to explain through our interpreters matters
touching our holy faith." And then he delivered a
discourse to the Caciques so fitting to the occasion
that no good theologian could have bettered it. After
telling them that we were Christians and relating
all matters pertaining to our holy religion, he told
them that their idols were not good but evil things
which would take flight at the presence of the sign
of the cross, for on a similar cross the Lord of Heaven
and earth and all created things suffered passion
and death; that it is He whom we adore and in whom
we believe, our true God, Jesus Christ, who had been
willing to suffer and die in order to save the whole
human race; that the third day He rose again and is
now in heaven; and that by Him we shall all be
judged. Cortes said many other things very well
expressed, which they thoroughly understood, and
they replied that they would report them to their
prince Montezuma. Cortes also told them that one of
the objects for which our great Emperor had sent us
to their country was to abolish human sacrifices,
and the other evil rites which they practised and to
see that they did not rob one another, or worship
those cursed images. And Cortes prayed them to set
up in their city, in the temples where they kept the
idols which they believed to be gods, a cross like the
one they saw before them, and to set up in the same
place an image of Our Lady, which he would give
them, with her precious son in her arms, and they
would see how well it would go with them, and what

our God would do for them.[41]

Meanwhile, knowing he had another eight days of waiting, Cortez consolidated his position at Vera Cruz and prepared to march to Mexico City — with or without an invitation.

Captain Pedro de Alvarado was sent out to explore the nearby towns and gather maize, as there was a shortage of food in the camp. He and his men quickly lost their appetites at what they saw:

> When Pedro de Alvarado reached these towns he found they had all been deserted that same day, and he found in the cues [temples or shrines] bodies of men and boys who had been sacrificed, and the walls and altars stained with blood and the hearts placed as offerings before the Idols. He also found the stones on which the sacrifices were made and the stone knives with which to open the chest so as to take out the heart.
>
> Pedro de Alvarado said that he found most of the bodies without arms or legs, and that he was told by some Indians that they had been carried off to be eaten, and our soldiers were astounded at such great cruelty. I will not say any more of the number of sacrifices, although we found the same thing in every town we afterwards entered . . . [42]

Shortly thereafter, Cortez was informed that a group of wealthy natives from a nearby city called Cempoalla wanted to see him. He received them cordially, and they informed him that their city was of the Totonac kingdom, recently subjugated by Montezuma but wanting to be free of Aztec rule. They had heard how he had defeated the Tabascans, and how he had treated the Tabascans justly and fairly after defeating them, and they wanted to form an alliance. Cortez readily agreed.

A day or two later a cacique of Cempoalla returned. He was a large man whom Gomara and Diaz refer to as the "fat cacique," and he was obviously upset. He informed Cortez that five of Montezuma's tax-gatherers had come to Cempoalla and were angry that the Cempoallans had been friendly to the Spaniards. The war god was angry, the tax-gatherers said, and to slake his anger they had to deliver twenty Cempoallan sons and daughters for sacrifice.

Cortez saw an opportunity to drive a wedge further between the Aztecs and the Cempoallans. He ordered the fat cacique to seize Montezuma's tax-gathers and imprison them. The cacique protested, but Cortez insisted this must be done so Montezuma would learn that human sacrifice must stop. With a mixture of fear and ecstasy, the Cempoallans obeyed Cortez.

The captain-general then performed a brilliant-if-risky diplomatic feat. He ordered that two of the tax-gatherers be brought to him. He received them cordially and told them he didn't know their mission or he would have interfered when the Cempoallans seized him. He then released them, telling them to carry his good wishes to Montezuma. In a similar manner he secured the release of the other three tax-gatherers, pitting the Aztecs against the Cempoallans and making them both more favorable to him. It was duplicity pure and simple, but in Cortez's view he was at war against evil, and deception is always a tactic in warfare.

Cortez and his company then went to Cempoalla to cement the alliance. All went well until Cortez raised the issue of religion. Those who insinuate that Cortez used Christianity as a pretext for his political and military goals need to explain why, time and again, he made Christianity and idolatry an issue when it was definitely not the expedient thing to do.

The Cempoallans brought out eight damsels as their gift to the Spaniards, not as slaves but as marriage partners. Cortez insisted that before they could be received in marriage, they had to become Christians and be baptized. He went on to say that "the people must free themselves from sodomy, for there were boys dressed like women who went about for gain by that cursed practice, and every day we saw sacrificed before us three, four, or five Indians whose hearts were offered to the idols and their blood plastered on the walls, and the feet, arms, and legs of the victims were cut off and eaten, just as in our country we eat beef brought from the butchers."[43] The Cempoallan caciques and priests replied that they would take measures to end sodomy, but they refused to give up the idols and sacrifices as their gods had given them good health, good harvests, and everything they needed.

The Spaniards discussed what to do. Apparently some wanted to accommodate the Cempoallans for the time being; but Cortez was adamant: "How can we ever accomplish anything worth doing if for the honour of God we do not first abolish these sacrifices made to idols?"[44] Angry words were exchanged with the Cempoallans, and both sides prepared for a fight. But the Cempoallans finally relented, saying they were not worthy of approaching their gods, but if the Spaniards wanted to destroy them, the Cempoallans would not stand in their way. Diaz says, "The words were hardly out of their mouths before more than fifty of us soldiers had clambered up [to the temple] and had thrown down their idols which came rolling down the steps shattered to pieces. The idols looked like fearsome dragons, as big as calves, and there were other figures half men and half great dogs of hideous appearance."[45]

Diaz then describes the Cempoallan priests:

These priests wore black cloaks like cassocks and long gowns reaching to their feet, and some had hoods like those worn by Dominicans, and they wore their hair very long, down to the waist, with some even reaching down to the feet, covered with blood and so matted together that it could not be separated, and their ears were cut to pieces by way of sacrifice, and they stank like sulphur, and they had another bad smell like carrion, and as they said, and we learnt that it was true, these priests were the sons of chiefs and they abstained from women, but they indulged in the cursed practice of sodomy, and they fasted on certain days, and what I saw them eat was the pith or seeds of cotton when the cotton was being cleaned, but they may have eaten other things which I did not see.[46]

Cortez then told them they could now be brothers, ordered the temple cleansed with lime, and set up an image of the Virgin Mary and the Cross. In a debatable move he appointed the former pagan priests as priests of God, ordering them to cut their hair and keep themselves clean and wear white robes instead of black. The next morning Father Olmeda presided over Mass in the presence of the Cempoallans. The eight damsels were instructed in the Christian religion and were baptized and given to various soldiers as wives. With his usual wry humor Diaz notes that the niece of the fat cacique "was very ugly; and she was led by the hand and given to Cortes who received her and tried to look pleased."[47] The alliance firmly established, Cortez and his company returned to their colony of Vera Cruz.

At this point the Spaniards prepared to march to Mexico City. But they were now more aware of the dangers they faced, and some (particularly those who had been loyal to Governor Velasquez) wanted to return to Cuba. To cement their loyalty, to establish firmly in their minds that there was no turning back, and to demonstrate decisively to his men and to the Aztecs that he planned to see his mission through to the end, he advanced a daring masterstroke of leadership: While making it appear that the idea had come from his men, he boldly declared that he was sinking all of his ships except one, and those who wanted to desert could take that ship to Cuba. When no one chose to leave, he sank that ship also. Now, with no way of escape, the company had little choice but to follow Cortez, whether to victory and glory or defeat and death on a sacrificial altar.

The March to Mexico City

And so, on August 16, 1519, Cortez and his party began their march inland, accompanied by about fifty Cempoallans. And from his palace in Mexico City, through his ever-watchful scouts and messengers and the revelations of the Smoking Mirror and the god Witchywolves, the Emperor Montezuma watched their advance with a mixture of admiration, anticipation, fear and fatalistic determination.

Starting at sea level they ascended to a ten thousand-foot pass between a large mountain and a volcano and were chilled by the cold mountain air. They passed through several towns on the way, erecting the cross and preaching Christianity in each. Concerning the town of Xocotlanl, Diaz says, "I remember that in the plaza where some of their oratories stood, there were piles of human skulls so regularly arranged that one could count them, and I estimated them at more than a hundred thousand. I repeat again that there were more than a hundred thousand of them. And in another part of the plaza there were so many piles of dead men's thigh bones that one could not count them; there was also a large number of skulls strung between beams of wood, and three priests who had charge of these bones and skulls were guarding them."[48]

Between the coast and Mexico City lay the city of Tlaxcala, center of the Tlaxcalan nation, a powerful and warlike people whom the Aztecs had never been able to subjugate, located on a plain about seven thousand feet above sea level. Cortez asked permission to pass through the country peacefully, but the Tlaxcalans refused, saying the Spaniards came with "treasons and lies from that traitor Montezuma."[49]

Cortez then gave battle instructions and exhorted, "Sirs, let us follow our banner which bears the sign of the holy cross, and through it we shall conquer!"[50] They sighted a group of Tlaxcalan spies, and their Cempoallan allies warned that a large body of warriors were sure to be waiting in ambush. They were right; a squadron of three thousand Tlaxcalans attacked, engaged in a well-fought battle, and retreated, leaving about seventeen dead Tlaxcalans and one mortally-wounded Spaniard.

The next day they confronted an army of six thousand Tlaxcalans, and Cortez attacked. An additional army of forty thousand (Gomara says eighty thousand) was waiting in the ravines, but the Spaniards and their Cempoallan allies were able to repel them, making effective use of their artillery and cavalry. The following day the Tlaxcalans attacked with an even larger force. Diaz describes the battle:

How they began to charge on us! What a hail of stones sped from their slings! As for their bowmen, the javelins lay like corn on the threshing floor; all of them barbed and fire-hardened, which would pierce any armour and would reach the vitals where there is no protection; the men with swords and shields and other arms larger than swords, such as broadswords, and lances, how they pressed on us and with what valour and what mighty shouts and yells they charged upon us! The steady bearing of our artillery, musketeers and crossbowmen, was indeed a help to us, and we did the enemy much damage, and those of them who came close to us with their swords and broadswords met with such sword play from us that they were forced back and did not close in on us so often as in the last battle. The horsemen were so skilful and bore themselves so valiantly that, after God who protected us, they were our bulwark. However, I saw that our troops were in considerable confusion, so that neither the shouts of Cortes nor the other captains availed to make them close up their ranks, and so many Indians charged down on us that it was only by a miracle of sword play that we could make them give way so that our ranks could be reformed. One thing only saved our lives, and that was that the enemy were so numerous and so crowded one on another that the shots wrought havoc among them, and in addition to this they were not well commanded, for all the captains with their forces could not come into action, and from what we knew, since the last battle had been fought, there had been disputes and quarrels between the Captain Xicotenga and another captain . . .

The enemy were already losing heart, and knowing that the followers of the other two captains whom I have already named, would not come to their assistance, they began to give way. It seems that in that battle we had killed one very important captain, not to mention others, and the enemy began to retreat in good order, our horsemen following them at a hand gallop for a short distance, for they could not sit their horses for fatigue, and when we found ourselves free from that multitude of warriors, we gave thanks to God.

In this engagement, one soldier was killed, and sixty were wounded, and all the horses were wounded as well. They gave me two wounds, one in the head with a stone, and one in the thigh with an arrow; but this did not prevent me from fighting, and keeping watch, and helping our soldiers, and all the soldiers who were wounded did the same; for if the wounds were not very dangerous, we had to fight and keep guard, wounded as we were, for few of us remained unwounded.

Then we returned to our camp, well contented, and giving thanks to God.[51]

Cortez made several more peace overtures to the Tlaxcalans, and finally they decided to accept. They told Cortez they had assumed he was in league with Montezuma and their enemies the Aztecs, who had made war against them every year for over a century; but they now saw the Spaniards as their ally and perhaps their only hope for preserving their independence from Aztec rule. Cortez and his men then entered the city of Tlaxcala, and a firm alliance was formed. As in Cempoala and elsewhere, Cortez proclaimed the Christian faith and insisted that the natives must stop sacrificing to idols. The Tlaxcalans resisted. Their caciques responded tactfully and with apparent sincerity:

> . . . we thoroughly believe that this God of yours and this great Lady are very good, but look you, you have only just come to our homes, as time goes on we shall understand your beliefs much more clearly, and see what they are, and will do what is right. But how can you ask us to give up our Teules [idols or gods] which for many years our ancestors have held to be gods and have made sacrifices to them and have worshipped them?[52]

Cortez probably would have followed his instinct and forced the issue, even if it meant war. But at this point one of the Catholic priests advised restraint:

> When we heard that reply which they gave so honestly and without fear, the Padre de la Merced, who was a wise man, and a theologian, said, "Sir, do not attempt to press them further on this subject, for it is not just to make them Christians by force, and I would not wish that you should do what we did in Cempoala, that is, destroy their Idols, until they have some knowledge of our Holy Faith. What good is it to take away now their Idols from one oratory or cue, if they carry them at once to another. It would be better that they should gradually feel the weight of our admonitions which are good and holy, so that later on they may realize the good advice which we are giving them."[53]

Cortez relented, but he requested that they clean out and whitewash one of the temples so the Spaniards could erect a cross and an image of the Virgin and hold Christian worship, and the Tlaxcalans readily agreed. The fierce Tlaxcalans were as firm friends as they had been enemies, and they proved to be the Spaniards' strongest and most loyal allies.

And from the western horizon, Aztec scouts marked the Spaniards' progress and reported to Montezuma. Seeing their prowess in battle and realizing the Spaniards would not turn from their course, Montezuma changed his tactic. He informed Cortez through his messengers that he rejoiced at their victory over the Tlaxcalans (with some truth, since the Tlaxcalans were enemies of the Aztecs). He asked Cortez to decide how much tribute he wished each year for the Spanish emperor, and he would pay it willingly. But he asked Cortez not to come to Mexico City, because the journey would be difficult. Cortez diplomatically thanked the messengers, expressed his appreciation to Montezuma for the good will and the gifts, and said he would take their request under consideration. But his plan of marching to

Mexico City remained unchanged.

Needing sulphur for gunpowder, a team of Spaniards ascended the volcano called Popocatepetl. One of their number was lowered 400 feet into the mouth of the active volcano to collect sulphur, and then was lifted out. From the top of Popocateletl, 17,852 feet above sea level, they had their first view of Mexico City.[54]

As the Spaniards prepared to leave Tlaxcalan, another macabre sight awaited Diaz and his companions:

> . . . in this town of Tlaxcala we found wooden houses, furnished with gratings, full of Indian men and women imprisoned in them, being fed up until they were fat enough to be sacrificed and eaten. These prisons we broke open and destroyed, and set free the prisoners who were in them, and these poor Indians did not dare to go in any direction, only to stay there with us and thus escape with their lives. From now on, in all the towns that we entered, the first thing our Captain ordered us to do was to break open these prisons and set free the prisoners.
>
> These prisons are common throughout the land and when Cortes and all of us saw such great cruelty, he showed that he was very angry with the Caciques of Tlaxcala, and quarrelled with them very angrily about it, and they promised that from that time forth they would not kill and eat any more Indians in that way. I said [to myself] of what benefit were all those promises, for as soon as we turned our heads they would commit the same cruelties.[55]

Cortez then advised Montezuma's messengers that he would, after all, be going to Mexico City. The messengers were not pleased but agreed to accompany him as his guides. The Aztec messengers advised that the shortest and best route was through a city called Cholula; but the Tlaxcalans urged against that route, saying the Cholultecs were a treacherous people (They were vassals of the Aztecs and enemies of the Tlaxcalans.).

Accompanied by Montezuma's messengers, Cortez and

his company were allowed to enter Cholula, but their reception was noticeably cool. After several days in the city they noted that the women and children were leaving the city and that the streets were being undermined so they would cave in under the weight of the Spanish cannons. Something was about to happen; but what?

Then the wife of a Cholultec cacique approached Dona Marina. She was impressed with Marina's beauty and noble bearing and determined that the young lady would make an excellent wife for her son. She advised Marina that the Spaniards were to be massacred the next day, and that by marriage she could escape the slaughter. Marina pretended to go along with the proposal, elicited the details from the cacique's wife, and at the earliest opportunity slipped away (ostensibly to get her possessions and bring them to the woman's house) and promptly gave Cortez the full story.

Cortez summoned his officers for a council of war. Some wanted to leave immediately, but Cortez and the majority voted for a preemptive strike.

He sent word to the Tlaxcalans, who promptly sent five thousand warriors to wait outside Cholula. He then called the chief men of Cholula to meet with him in the courtyard to bargain for supplies, saying the Spaniards were going to leave the city and were requesting an escort of two thousand Cholultec warriors. The warriors and chieftains crowded into the courtyard, thinking this would be an easy way to trap the Spaniards and slaughter them. But the Spaniards quietly closed the courtyard gates, turned their artillery on the Cholultecs, and opened fire. The cavalry then charged and trampled the Cholultec warriors at close quarters, and then the infantry completed the slaughter. Of two thousand warriors and fifty caciques, not one was left alive.

Meanwhile the five thousand Tlaxcalans swarmed into the city and took ten thousand unarmed Cholultecs as captives. In his anger at the Cholultec treachery, Cortez departed from normal procedure and authorized his men to burn and loot as they pleased.

This continued for two days, until the remaining elders

begged Cortez to spare the city. He gave orders to stop and then appointed the brother of a slain cacique as the new mayor of the city. He then requested permission to erect crosses and statues of the Virgin in all remaining temples, and needless to say, the new mayor granted his request. Cortez also ordered the Tlaxcalans to return their ten thousand captives; they vigorously objected but grudgingly returned most of them.

Cortez then questioned survivors to determine the origin of the plot. As he suspected, Montezuma and the Aztecs were behind it. Montezuma's messengers denied the incriminating evidence revealed by the investigation, and Cortez pretended to believe them, saying Montezuma was much too great a ruler to engage in such treachery.

But later that day Cortez wrote a letter to King Charles V of Spain, declaring resolutely that "Montezuma will soon be a vassal, a captive, or a corpse."[56]

Having appointed the new Cholultec leadership, Cortez was able to make an alliance with Cholula. Then, in a rather remarkable feat of diplomacy, he managed to heal the enmity between Cholula and Tlaxcala and make them allies and uneasy friends. He then opened the Cholultec prisons where men and boys were being fattened for sacrifice and cannibalism. All this accomplished, he and his company began the final leg of their march to Mexico City.

In the Halls of Montezuma

And so, on November 8, 1519, Cortez and his company arrived at the gates of Mexico City. The characters in Arthur Koestler's *Lost Horizon* could not have been more amazed at Shangri-La than were the conquistadors as they entered the fairyland paradise of Mexico City. The plain foot soldier Bernal Diaz records his impressions and those of his companions as they entered the city of fable and legend:

> . . . we saw so many cities and villages built in the water and other great towns on dry land and that straight and level causeway going towards Mexico

[City], we were amazed and said that it was like the enchantments they tell of in the legend of Amadis, on account of the great towers and cues and buildings rising from the water, all built of masonry. And some of our soldiers even asked whether the things we saw were not a dream? It is not to be wondered at that I here write it down in this manner, for there is so much to think over that I do not know how to describe it, seeing things as we did that had never been heard of or seen before, not even dreamed about.

. . . the appearance of the palaces in which they lodged us! How spacious and well built they were, of beautiful stone work and cedar wood, and the wood of other sweet scented trees, with great rooms and courts, wonderful to behold, covered with awnings of cotton cloth.

When we had looked well at all of this, we went to the orchard and garden, which was such a wonderful thing to see and walk in, that I was never tired of looking at the diversity of the trees, and noting the scent which each one had, and the paths full of roses and flowers, and the many fruit trees and native roses, and the pond of fresh water. There was another thing to observe, that great canoes were able to pass into the garden from the lake through an opening that had been made so that there was no need for their occupants to land. And all was cemented and very splendid with many kinds of stone [monuments] with pictures on them, which gave much to think about. Then the birds of many kinds and breeds which came into the pond. I say again that I stood looking at it and thought that never in the world would there be discovered other lands such as these, for at that time there was no Peru, nor any thought of it. [Of all the wonders that I then beheld] to-day all is overthrown and lost, nothing left standing.[57]

And then, as they crossed the lake on the causeway

toward the city, Montezuma and his royal retinue came out
to meet them. Richly dressed, Montezuma descended from
his royal litter, and Cortez dismounted from his horse.
Montezuma bade Cortez welcome, and Cortez through
Dona Marina wished Montezuma good health. Cortez gave
Montezuma a necklace of multi-colored stones, placed it
around the emperor's neck, and began to embrace
Montezuma — but his retinue prevented it. They exchanged diplomatic pleasantries, and Montezuma took
Cortez by the hand and led him to his quarters, which were
most magnificent, and placed a necklace of golden crabs
around his neck.

After dinner they met again. Montezuma again expressed pleasure at the Spaniards' coming and said he was
convinced by the Spaniards' feats of valor that they were
truly the men who, according to the prophecies, would come
from where the sun rose to rule the land — in other words,
Quetzalcoatl returned.

Diaz records Cortez's answer:

> It was true that we came from where the sun
> rose, and were the vassals and servants of a great
> Prince called the Emperor Don Carlos [the Spanish
> form of Charles V], who held beneath his sway many
> and great princes, and that the Emperor having
> heard of him and what a great prince he was, had
> sent us to these parts to see him, and to beg them to
> become Christians, the same as our Emperor and all
> of us, so that his soul and those of all his vassals
> might be saved.[58]

Apparently the subject of religion was not pursued
further at that point. Montezuma asked questions about
the Spanish emperor, further pleasantries were exchanged,
and then Montezuma took his leave for the evening.

The next morning Cortez opened the subject again:

> . . . we told them we were Christians and wor-
> shipped one true and only God, named Jesus Christ,
> who suffered death and passion to save us, and we

told them that a cross (when they asked us why we worshipped it) was a sign of the other Cross on which our Lord God was crucified for our salvation; and that the death and passion which He suffered was for the salvation of the whole human race, which was lost, and that this our God rose on the third day and is now in heaven, and it is He who made the heavens and the earth, the sea and the sands, and created all the things there are in the world, and He sends the rain and the dew, and nothing happens in the world without His holy will. That we believe in Him and worship Him, but that those whom they look upon as gods are not so, but are devils, which are evil things, and if their looks are bad their deeds are worse, and they could see that they were evil and of little worth, for where we had set up crosses such as those his ambassadors had seen, they dared not appear before them, through fear of them, and that as time went on they would notice this.

The favour he now begged of him was his attention to the words that he now wished to tell him; then he explained to him very clearly about the creation of the world, and how we are all brothers, sons of one father and one mother who were called Adam and Eve, and how such a brother as our great Emperor, grieving for the perdition of so many souls, such as those which their idols were leading to Hell, where they burn in living flames, had sent us, so that after what he [Montezuma] had now heard he would put a stop to it and they would no longer adore these Idols or sacrifice Indian men and women to them, for we were all brethren, nor should they commit sodomy or thefts. He also told them that, in the course of time, our Lord and King would send some men who among us lead very holy lives, much better than we do, who will explain to them all about it, for at present we merely came to give them due warning, and so he prayed him to do what he was asked and carry it into effect.[59]

Montezuma then answered Cortez:

> ... I have understood your words and arguments
> very well before now, from what you said to my
> servants at the sand dunes, this about three Gods
> and the Cross, and all those things that you have
> preached in the towns through which you have
> come. We have not made any answer to it because
> here throughout all time we have worshipped our
> own gods, and thought they were good, as no doubt
> yours are, so do not trouble to speak to us any more
> about them at present. Regarding the creation of the
> world, we have held the same belief for ages past,
> and for this reason we take it for certain that you are
> those whom our ancestors predicted would come
> from the direction of the sunrise.[60]

To the modern mind Montezuma occupies the higher
ground in this exchange. He is broadminded, willing to let
Cortez believe as he wishes, willing even to accept the
Christian God as part of the Aztec pantheon along with
Quetzalcoatl and the others. For himself he prefers the gods
and traditions of his ancestors, so he says in effect to Cortez,
"You follow your religion and I'll follow mine. Now let's
respect each other's beliefs and not impose on one another."
(And never mind such insignificant details as the sacrifice
of thousands of innocent persons every year.)

He was like the ancient Romans and Greeks who were
willing to allow Christians to worship Christ and might
even accept Christ as divine, so long as He was only one of
their entire pantheon of gods along with Jupiter, Juno, and
the others. The problem Christians faced in Rome was their
absolutism and exclusivism: "Thou shalt have no other gods
before me."

By contrast Cortez is the brash foreigner who comes
upon a culture he doesn't understand and tells Montezuma
— in his own palace, no less — "Your beliefs are all wrong,
your gods are all false, my God is the only god, my way is the
only way, accept my religion or I'll force it upon you." In the
average American classroom today Montezuma would

emerge the winner hands down!

But in a deeper sense the two leaders represented two diametrically opposite approaches to truth. To Cortez, truth was absolute, unchanging, and divinely revealed. In Montezuma's view truth was what worked and was in accord with nature. And their differing views of truth led to differing views of God. When they spoke of God, it is doubtful that Cortez understood Montezuma any better than Montezuma understood Cortez as Madariaga says:

> Neither the Mexican Emperor nor the Spanish Captain was in a position to realize that they were discussing from two different stages of man's development, fencing so to speak on two different storeys of the fencing club. For Cortes, God was the self-revealed light which reveals all else, the one and only Creator, alpha and omega of things, surrounded by the beautiful mysteries of the Trinity, the Incarnation and the Virgin Birth as the sun loves to be surrounded with clouds to shine not the less but the more and the more beautifully. For Motecucuma, the gods were spirits of the past and of nature, not unlike what they were to the Greeks and Romans, men left in a state of mid-air life, invisible but omnipresent though hovering only over the people whose dreams they were. The ever-longing religion of the Christian, open to all, was as incomprehensible to the closed-in religion of the Aztec as the infinite sea would have been to the two Mexican lofty but landlocked lakes.[61]

In a very real sense, a Western mindset and an Eastern mindset had come up against one another. Yet ironically, Cortez represented the West, and Montezuma represented the East!

During the next several days the Spaniards learned more about this New World. Montezuma showed them his aviaries, his zoos, his architecture, the court buildings, and the city marketplace which the well-travelled among them said exceeded even the marketplaces of Constantinople and

Rome. Throughout these days Montezuma was an impeccable host, attending to their every need with utmost courtesy and pleasantness. Diaz describes him with unabashed admiration:

> The Great Montezuma was about forty years old, of good height and well proportioned, slender, and spare of flesh, not very swarthy, but of the natural colour and shade of an Indian. He did not wear his hair long, but so as just to cover his ears, his scanty black beard was well shaped and thin. His face was somewhat long, but cheerful, and he had good eyes and showed in his appearance and manner both tenderness and, when necessary, gravity. He was very neat and clean and bathed once every day in the afternoon.[62]

Religion was the only source of irritation during their visit. Unable to leave the subject alone, Cortez asked to see Montezuma's idols. As they entered the temples they discovered that everything Diaz and Gomara have described in other parts of Mexico was here in the city: the stone altars, the obsidian knives, the black-robed priests with long matted hair, the fiendish-looking idols complete with basins in which to place sacrificed human hearts, the walls and steps coated with blood and human gore, the enormous piles of skulls and bones, and there was more. Gomara described an ossuary or theater made of skulls and mortar: "Andreas de Tapia, who described it to me, and Gonzalo de Umbria counted them one day and found them to number 136,000 skulls, including those on the poles and steps. Those in the towers could not be numbered."[63] There were pits of beasts and poisonous snakes; sometimes the bodies of sacrificed victims were cast into these pits after people had eaten the arms and legs. And one very large idol was made out of seeds, ground and kneaded with the blood of babies and virgins who had been sacrificed.[64]

After seeing these things, Cortez could hold his peace no longer:

Our Captain said to Montezuma through our interpreter, half laughing [apparently to soften the message and lighten the tension]: "Senor Montezuma, I do not understand how such a great Prince and wise man as you are has not come to the conclusion, in your mind, that these idols of yours are not gods, but evil things that are called devils, and so that you may know it and all your priests may see it clearly, do me the favour to approve of my placing a cross here on the top of this tower, and that in the one part of these oratories where your Huichilobos and Tezcatepuca stand we may divide off a space where we can set up an image of Our Lady (an image which Montezuma had already seen) and you will see by the fear in which these Idols hold it that they are deceiving you.[65]

Visibly upset, Montezuma replied that he would not have shown them his gods if had known they would say such defamatory things. Cortez and his company excused themselves, but Montezuma remained in the temple to perform sacrifices to appease the gods for his having allowed Cortez to enter the temple and utter such blasphemy.

Ever since they had entered the city, the Spaniards had assembled an altar on a table in their quarters when it was time for Mass. They now asked Montezuma whether he would allow them to convert one of the rooms in their quarters into a chapel; Montezuma gave permission and agreed to supply the needed materials. They held worship services every day, Diaz says, "for one reason, because we were obliged to do so as Christians and it was a good habit, and for another reason, in order that Montezuma and all his Captains should observe it, and should witness our adoration and see us on our knees before the Cross, especially when we intoned the Ave Maria so that it might incline them towards it."[66]

So these were exciting, eventful days, and, for the most part, days of good will between Spaniard and Aztec. But some of Cortez's men were growing restless. They were hopelessly outnumbered in this city, and even though

Montezuma seemed favorably disposed toward them at present, that could change at any time. They remembered that as they advanced toward Mexico City, other natives told them that Montezuma's god Huichilobos (Witchywolves) had advised him to allow the Spaniards to enter the city and then kill them. Was there a trap waiting to be sprung?

The temperament of Cortez would not allow him to sit and wait to be trapped. Rather, the time had come for decisive action. And that very day some tidings arrived that gave him a reason to act.

When Cortez and his company left Vera Cruz to march to Mexico City, they left a detachment at the new colony with instructions to help the Cempoalans and other friendly nations as the need arose. After Cortez had left, an Aztec garrison harassed the Cempoalans, demanding tribute. The Cempoalans refused, and the Aztecs attacked. The Cempoalans turned to Vera Cruz for assistance, and Juan de Escalante and a small force of Spaniards came to their aid. For years the Cempoalans had lived in terror of the Aztecs, and in this battle they were outnumbered two to one. When the Aztecs charged, the Cempoalans fled, leaving Escalante and his band to face the Aztecs alone. The Spaniards managed to fight off the attack, but Escalante and six other Spaniards were killed, and a seventh was carried off alive. The news was brought to Montezuma. The following is a quote from Diaz:

> Montezuma asked his Captains how it was that having such thousands of warriors with them, they had not conquered such a small number of [Spaniards], and they replied that their darts and arrows and hard fighting availed them nothing, and they could not drive their enemy to flight because a great Teleciguata [great lady] of Castile marched before them, and this Lady frightened the Mexicans [Aztecs] and said words to encourage the [Spaniards]. Then Montezuma thought that great Lady must be Saint Mary who we had told him was our protector, and whose image, with her precious Son in her arms, we had given to him some time before. However, I

did not see this myself, for I was in Mexico [City], but
certain conquistadores who were present say so, and
pray God that it was so, and certainly all the soldiers
who were with Cortes believed it and so it is true,
and the divine pity of Our Lady the Virgin Mary was
with us, for which I give her many thanks.[67]

Cortez seized this opportunity and went to Montezuma's
palace, ostensibly to see him about this incident. His men
came with him, and once inside the palace they stationed
themselves in key locations. Through Marina he spoke
diplomatically but with all the righteous indignation he
could muster:

Senior Montezuma, I am very much astonished
that you, who are such a valiant Prince, after having
declared that you are our friend, should order your
Captains, whom you have stationed on the coast
near to Tuxpan, to take arms against my Spaniards,
and that they should dare to rob the towns which are
in the keeping and under the protection of the King
and master and to demand of them Indian men and
women for sacrifice, and should kill a Spaniard, one
of my brothers, and a horse . . . Being such a friend
of yours I ordered my Captains to do all that was
possible to help and serve you, and you have done
exactly the contrary to us. Also in the affair at
Cholula your Captains and a large force of warriors
had received your own commands to kill us. I forgave
it at the time out of my great regard for you, and now
again your vassals and Captains have become inso-
lent, and hold secret consultations stating that you
wish us to be killed. I do not wish to begin a war on
this account nor to destroy this city, I am willing to
forgive it all, if silently and without raising any
disturbance you will come with us to our quarters,
where you will be as well served and attended to as
though you were in your own house, but if you cry out
or make any disturbance you will immediately be
killed by these my Captains, whom I brought solely
for this purpose.[68]

Let us pause for a moment and consider this man
Hernando Cortez. He lands in an unknown and hostile land
and sinks his own ships, leaving no way of escape. Time and
again he enters pagan temples reeking with human gore —
the very citadels of Satan as he sees them — to preach
Christ before hostile priests and warriors and destroy their
idols and roll them down the temple steps, knowing that the
next headless corpse to come rolling down the steps might
well be his own. Repeatedly he faces enemy armies number-
ing hundreds of times his own and charges into battle
against them. And then, on November 14, six days after
arriving in Mexico City, he enters the palace of the most
powerful emperor of the Western Hemisphere and makes
him his prisoner! Whatever his faults may have been, it can
hardly be said that Cortez lacked courage!

Montezuma protested, and they argued for awhile. Several of the Spanish captains grew impatient and threatened to kill Montezuma on the spot. Montezuma could tell
that they were angry but couldn't understand their words,
so he asked Marina what they meant. In her consoling way
she assured him that he would be well-treated in the
Spaniards' quarters, so he agreed to accompany them.
"Cortez and our Captains bestowed many caresses on him
and told him that they begged him not to be annoyed, and
to tell his captains and the men of his guard that he was
going of his own free will, because he had spoken to his idol
Huichilobos and the priests who attended him, and that it
was beneficial for his health and the safety of his life that
he should be with us."[69]

Thus began a period of honored but enforced captivity.
Montezuma had all visitors he wished, held court, went to
the temple as he pleased, and even went hunting on his
own. When his people asked, he told them he was delighted
to be with his friends for awhile.

And as occasionally happens between a kidnapper and
his victim in a protracted hostage crisis, a genuine fondness
developed between Montezuma and his captors. The Aztec
leader stood for everything the Spaniards abhorred; they
knew he was a devil-worshipper and a mass murderer who
presided over one of history's most gruesome holocausts.

But his personality was so pleasant, his manners so gracious, his demeanor so gentle; he treated even those who were assigned to watch over him with such kindness that they couldn't help liking him. Apparently he possessed a remarkable charisma that enabled him to captivate others with his charm.

How could a man be such a moral monster in some ways and so good and likeable in others? The answer has to be human sin, which has areas of weakness and areas of strength. Some of the Third Reich leaders were devoted husbands and fathers and highly cultured, personable, charitable men.

Cortez likewise grew fond of Montezuma, but he had a mission to perform for God and country and would not allow sentiment to stand in the way. A week had passed since the seizure of Montezuma, and it was time for the next step in the conquest of Mexico.

The Aztec leaders who had led the attack on Cempoala in which the seven Spaniards were killed were brought to Mexico City for trial. At trial they blamed Montezuma for the attack, saying he had ordered them to wage war against the Cempoalans and to kill any Spaniards who came to their defense. Cortez approached the emperor and told him tenderly if in fact Montezuma was guilty of this crime, he (Cortez) would lay down his own life rather than allow Montezuma's to be taken, but that for a crime of this nature some punishment was necessary even for a king. He therefore had Montezuma placed in irons!

This seems to have broken Montezuma's spirit, and his health began to fail as well. Shortly thereafter Cortez released him from his bonds and told him he was free to go back to his palace, but Montezuma declined to do so. A few days later he called his chiefs together, announced to them that he and the Aztec nation were now vassals of the king of Spain, and urged them to be loyal subjects of Spain.

What happened? What caused this once-proud king to voluntarily become a house guest, then a shackled prisoner, then a vassal of a foreign power?

Certainly one reason is the skill by which the coup was implemented. The whole idea of the king's being placed under house arrest by a foreigner was so sudden, so incredible, so preposterous, that it caught Montezuma off guard. He was utterly dumbfounded and didn't know what to do.

And while sudden, it was also gradual. Montezuma wasn't placed under arrest exactly; he was to be the honored house guest of Cortez, just as Cortez had been his honored guest; and gentle and beautiful Marina assured him he would be well-treated in the Spanish quarters. And with the conquistadors ready with their swords to force compliance, agreeing to the "temporary" arrangement seemed the easiest and most sensible thing to do. Then came the irons, but they were to be only temporary. Then the vassalage, but that was merely a formality; Montezuma would still run the Aztec empire. He went along step by step, and each step led to another.

Another factor was the Aztec religion. Montezuma may have been convinced that Cortez was Quetzalcoatl, or perhaps that the king across the ocean that Cortez served was Quetzalcoatl, or maybe they were both human manifestations of Quetzalcoatl. At least, he wasn't convinced they weren't.

How could he spend days with Cortez and not know whether the Spaniard was a god or a man? The probable answer is that in the Aztec mind the distinction between god and man was not as clear as it is for Christians. Gods sometimes mated with humans. Emperors might be divine, or partly so. Montezuma may have been unsure of the extent of his own divinity, let alone that of Cortez.

At any rate, if Cortez was Quetzalcoatl returned, then it was the will of heaven that the god return to rule. If so, it was Montezuma's sacred duty to submit to the will of the gods and relinquish the throne to Cortez/Quetzalcoatl. After all, the Aztecs had not always ruled Mexico. They gradually displaced the Acolhuans, who displaced the Chichemecs, who displaced the Toltecs, all by the will of the gods. And now the gods had chosen the Spaniards!

A third factor might be the engaging, captivating personality of Hernando Cortez. Like Montezuma, he too was a charismatic figure, and Montezuma was genuinely fond of him even if he feared and distrusted him. Montezuma's lack of bitterness over his captivity, even over Cortez's threat to kill him, are amazing to behold. As an emperor he understood political intrigue and military necessity, and as a devoted child of the sun-god, he had little fear of death.

Another factor might have been fear of his own chiefs. Many felt he had behaved like a weakling in submitting to house arrest; in fact, some thought he should never have permitted Cortez to enter Mexico City. If, after having been placed in irons, he returned to his own palace, his own chiefs might depose him or kill him. He could have concluded that his safest course of action was to trust the protection of Cortez and the king of Spain.

Hammond Innes suggests one other factor:

> Quetzalcoatl was worshipped as the god of learning. Moctezuma was the high priest of a debased religion. Was he, like all deeply religious men, in search of the ultimate god? Did he recognize in the meek action of these hard-bitten soldiers, kneeling humbly before their cross and their images of the Virgin and Child, a higher form of religion than the worship of a whole host of idols feeding on the heart's blood of innumerable victims? The mind of Moctezuma is an enigma that will always fascinate, the motives of his actions concealed by Indian impassivity and the lonely isolation of his position as an absolute ruler.[70]

Finally, perhaps the hand of God was at work. Perhaps God allowed Montezuma to go through this humbling experience to break his iron pagan will and lead him to the true faith of Jesus Christ. Like King Nebuchadnezzar of Babylon who, according to Daniel, Chapter 4, lost his kingdom for seven years so that he might learn that the Most High rules in the affairs of men, so God may have had a similar purpose with Montezuma. But while Nebuchadnezzar humbled himself and turned to God and received his kingdom back, Montezuma apparently did not.

And as Montezuma prepared to take the oath as a vassal of Spain, there was weeping in the room — not just from

Montezuma and his aides, but from the Spaniards as well. Why did they weep? Out of love for Montezuma, certainly; but there was something more profound than that. Madariaga says it well:

> Montecucuma was not a prisoner of Cortes' military force: in fact, he was not a prisoner of Cortes at all; he was a prisoner of his own self. It was his faith that delivered him, hand and foot, into the hands of the Spaniard, and it was the faith of his compatriots which made them all accept Montecucuma's proposal of surrender. Had they wished or, rather, had their faith allowed them to wish it, the Mexicans could have made mincemeat of the Spaniards (nor would this saying ever have been an apter way of putting it); but they were held in sway, not by Cortes' horses and guns, but by "Witchywolves" and his "orders."
>
> Opposite them, a similar faith — similar in its integrity, though not in its tenets — made the Spaniards as sure of their right to exact the allegiance of the Mexicans as the Mexicans were of their duty to grant it. But both sides were men; both knew what a deep tragedy it is for a man to give up his power into a stranger's hands; both felt the awe of the occasion, because they realized that both were the instruments of bigger powers than either. When Montecucuma gave his throne away in tears, he wept because he was powerless before the gods; and when the Spanish soldiers wept out of love for him, their tears were shed over the misery of man, the toy of higher, hidden powers.
>
> On no other basis can we explain the compassion for the victim felt at the time not merely by those of the soldiers who actually wept, but by all the soldiers and captains and by Cortes himself. He was still a dry-eyed man. Grief had not searched him yet to the fountain of tears; but no man can read his narrative of the scene in his letter to the Emperor without perceiving the aroma of genuine compas-

sion in his manly heart — for whom? For the man whose grief he was causing. And as hypocrisy must be ruled out — for no man ever was less hypocritical than Cortes — it follows that he had remained capable of feeling the higher unity of all men above the plane of strife on which he was a protagonist.

And then, there was the pity of it all, the sheer waste of human life not merely of the life which flows in blood and rots away with the killed flesh, but of the life of the spirit which was pitting against each other two civilizations planted, grown and come to blossom in two different soils, under two different skies, yet out of the same seed and under the same heaven; and which could find no other way to live side by side and mutually fecundate each other than this tragic, human, all too human, spiritual oppression. That scene in Mexico, when the men of Cortes shed tears for Montecucuma, is one of the most moving moments in the discovery of man by man; a moment of profound unity, achieved not as the Christian dogmatically asserted in the belief in a common origin, but in the grief and shame of common failure before the challenge of life. On that day, man wept over himself and history wept over history. One may feel the tragedy of that sad, yet noble, day ring with other forms of the perennial grief of man, in this line, perhaps the loveliest, of Camoens: "Time, time itself, over itself doth weep."[71]

Note the fast pace of events. It was then close to Christmas time in the year 1519. Before the previous March, nine months earlier, Cortez had never even been in Mexico. Now he was the de facto ruler of the empire! The landing at Cozumel, the battle with the Tabascans, the founding of Vera Cruz, the alliance with the Cempoallans, the war and subsequent friendship with the Tlaxcalans, the conspiracy and slaughter at Cholula, the entrance into Mexico City, the meeting and enigmatic friendship with Montezuma, the coup in the Aztec palace, the human sacrifices observed, the sermons preached, the idols overthrown, Dona

Marina . . . Cortez could have composed quite a letter to send with his Christmas cards that year, had he been so inclined ("How has your year been? Mine has been pretty interesting . . ."). One year before he had been a gentleman farmer in Cuba, never dreaming that such people and places even existed!

Having lost most of his power, Montezuma offered his personal treasure to the conquistadors and a personal gift of five emeralds to the king of Spain. He then offered his daughter to Cortez in marriage (after all, there could be advantages to having the god Quetzalcoatl as an in-law); Cortez thanked him but politely declined.

The Rift Develops

At this point Cortez seemed on the verge of one of the greatest coups of modern history. A foreigner from the other side of the world, he had virtually taken over the Aztec Empire without firing a shot.

But at this point, humanly speaking, he may have overreached. The city remained steeped in idol worship and human sacrifice, and Cortez determined that it had to stop. When he demanded the destruction of the idols, Montezuma became most upset and announced that Witchywolves had told him the Spaniards should leave at that time.

From this point on relations between Cortez and Montezuma became strained, although the cordiality did not totally disappear. He was willing to surrender his throne, his power, his liberty, his wealth, even his daughter; but he would not surrender his gods. The emperor probably began to doubt whether Cortez truly was Quetzalcoatl; after all, a god would never profane the sacred temples. On the other hand, there was war among the gods, and Quetzalcoatl and Witchywolves were in some ways opposites; and according to legend the first man, Quetzalcoatl, had been forced to leave Mexico because he tried to abolish human sacrifice. But even if Cortez was Quetzalcoatl — and again let us remember that for Montezuma the distinction between god and man was not that clear — the emperor was the servant of Witchywolves and might have had to fight against Quetzalcoatl himself.

And throughout Mexico City a wave of anger arose, against the Spaniards for profaning the temples and against Montezuma for his vacillation. In twentieth-century terms, we might say that both Cortez and Montezuma dropped sharply in the polls!

Had Cortez misjudged Montezuma and the Aztecs? He may have underestimated their dedication to their gods, so firm in his own Catholic faith that he could not conceive that anyone as intelligent and cultured as the Aztecs could possibly want to continue worshipping and sacrificing to Witchywolves once they had been exposed to the Truth.

If Cortez had been willing to let the situation ride for the time being, with the Aztecs continuing their pagan practices while he and his men worshipped in their private chapel, he might have ruled the empire indefinitely through Montezuma as his puppet. But Cortez was not the kind of man who could let things ride. Swift decisive action was central to his very nature. Perhaps he knew that Christianity could not coexist with paganism, at least not with paganism of such a virulent and monstrous nature. Perhaps his own sense of moral outrage at human sacrifice and idol worship could tolerate the situation no longer. Probably he sensed that, despite his success, his numbers were few and his situation was precarious, and that even if he were willing to coexist with the pagan Aztecs, they would not coexist with him much longer. If confrontation was inevitable, he would prefer to initiate it on his terms, and the sooner the better.

Then Cortez received news of trouble on the home front. Governor Velasquez of Cuba, angry that Cortez had exceeded his orders and perhaps jealous of his success, had sent a force to the mainland, consisting of eighteen vessels and a thousand men headed by Panfilo de Narvaez, to capture Cortez and bring him back to Cuba for trial. Apparently Velasquez or Narvaez had also communicated with Montezuma, telling him Cortez was an evil man and not a true representative of Spain.

Captain Narvaez sent his officers to Vera Cruz to demand the surrender of the colony, which was defended by a detachment of eighty soldiers headed by Captain Sandoval, a capable young officer loyal to Cortez. Sandoval received the officers coldly, and when they began reading a legal document before him that contained the charge of "treason," he told them to stop reading it or he would use his sword to cut the word out of the the document and out of their hearts. He then seized the officers and forcibly transported them to Mexico City to face Cortez.

But before they arrived, Cortez knew of the plan. Montezuma had an excellent intelligence system consisting of scouts and runners, and within forty-eight hours of the landing, Montezuma's scouts had not only informed him of the landing but had sent him sketches of the ships and men. He shared these with Cortez, and the pictures were sufficiently detailed that Cortez could recognize the face of Narvaez.

As always, Cortez acted swiftly and decisively. He wrote an amicable letter to Narvaez advising him of the situation in Mexico City and urging him to approach the city amicably so the Aztecs did not conclude that a rift existed among Spaniards, for that could be fatal to them both. He also reasserted that his authority came through Vera Cruz directly from King Don Carlos of Spain, not from Velasquez or Cuba, and that he would submit to Narvaez if the latter had orders from Don Carlos — knowing full well that Narvaez had no such orders.

He then sent Father Olmeda to the Narvaez camp, giving him gold to distribute among Narvaez's men as bribes and to try to forge an alliance with Narvaez himself. Father Olmeda was successful in undermining the loyalty of Narvaez's soldiers, but he got nowhere with Narvaez himself.

Cortez then placed Captain Alvarado in charge of the Spanish forces in Mexico City, left about two-thirds of his approximately 250 surviving soldiers with Alvarado, and with the remainder he set forth for Vera Cruz. He visited Montezuma to announce his departure, and Montezuma said the following to him:

> . . . do me the favor to tell me if there is anything

I can do to assist you, for I will do it with the greatest good will. Moreover, Senor Malinche [the Aztec nickname for Cortez, based on a corruption of Marina], I do not wish any calamity to befall you, for you have very few Teules [his word for Spaniards, which actually means gods or idols] with you, and those who have now come are five times as numerous, and they say that they are Christians like yourselves, and vassals and subjects of your Emperor, and they possess images and set up crosses and say Mass and say and announce that you are persons who have fled from your King, and that they have come to capture and kill you. I do not understand it at all, so take care what you are doing.[72]

Cortez assured Montezuma that he was in the right and consequently the Lord Jesus Christ would give him the strength he needed to prevail. Montezuma offered the assistance of 5,000 Aztec warriors but Cortez declined, perhaps not trusting their loyalty. He and Montezuma then rode together to the gates of the city. He then tenderly and publicly embraced Montezuma, urged Alvarado to keep the peace and urged Montezuma to look upon Alvarado as his protector, and with eighty seasoned veterans and no horses he set out for Vera Cruz (an easy walk, only 180 miles!).

On the way to Vera Cruz he met Captain de Leon, whom he had sent out earlier with eighty men as an exploring party. They decided to split the party, de Leon and fifty of his men going to Vera Cruz with Cortez and the remaining thirty heading to Mexico City to reinforce Alvarado. De Leon's men, plus Sandoval's detachment at Vera Cruz, swelled Cortez's forces to about 200. But Narvaez had a thousand men, eighty horses (for military purposes at this time a horse was far more valuable than a man), twelve cannons, and 150 muskets.

Nevertheless, Cortez had advantages. His men were better conditioned, better trained, better motivated, better led, and were much more loyal than those of Narvaez. Some of Narvaez's soldiers were old friends of Cortez; others had been bribed; some had reservations about this expedition against a fellow Spaniard who was winning gold and glory for Christ and the Crown; and still others thought their own fortunes could be better advanced through Cortez than through Narvaez. And he showed himself a military innovator and improvisor. Not having any cavalry, with the aid of his Cempoallan friends, he fashioned eighty 20-foot copper-tipped lances with which his footsoldiers could hold Narvaez's horsemen at bay.

Cortez then sent a final letter to Narvaez demanding that he either produce orders from the king or leave the country at once, sending the message with Captain de Leon. Narvaez tried to kill de Leon as a traitor, and de Leon barely escaped with his life. He advised Cortez that a diplomatic settlement was out of the question and urged an immediate attack.

Narvaez assembled his troops on the open field outside Cempoalla, where his superior numbers could be used to greatest advantage. But Cortez delayed his attack because of torrential rains, while Narvaez's poorly-conditioned men stood in the rain all day waiting for an attack that never came. Cortez struck at midnight, after Narvaez and his men had retired. Narvaez tried to assemble his forces, but his captains (some of whom secretly supported Cortez) flung contradictory orders to the troops, and the result was total confusion. Narvaez was captured, and the word spread in the camp that he was dead. The battle was over in minutes, and as usual, Cortez had won an impressive victory against overwhelming numbers with minimal loss of life.

Cortez instinctively knew that now was the time for conciliation. He spoke kindly to the prisoners, ordered his surgeons (such as they were) to treat their wounds, and offered to release them if they would pledge their loyalty and join his force. Almost without exception they accepted.

His only harsh words were for Narvaez. When he visited the fettered prisoner the arrogant captain said, "You should consider it quite an achievement, Captain, to have captured my person and defeated my army. It must indeed be a great day for you, Senor Cortez."

Cortez smiled and answered, "Senor Narvaez, my men

and I have suffered many hardships and done many brave deeds since coming to Mexico — but I assure you the least of these was capturing you."[73]

Again Cortez had turned disaster into triumph. A few days earlier it appeared he would either be sacrificed to Witchywolves and eaten by Aztecs or taken to Cuba and hanged as a traitor. Instead, he had augmented his forces by nearly a thousand men. And to the Aztecs who had begun to wonder whether he was even a true Spaniard let alone a god, his prestige was enhanced considerably since he had defeated a much larger and better-equipped force of Spaniards.

Then news of disaster came — but the disaster was a trifle compared to what was to follow. In Mexico City the Aztecs had turned against Captain Alvarado, and he and the Spaniards were under siege in their quarters.

Exactly what happened is not clear, but apparently the Aztecs were beginning to celebrate a major festival in honor of Tezcatlipoca the fertility god of harvest, and they invited the Spaniards to observe the ceremonial dance. Suddenly the Spaniards began firing upon the crowd, and then the Spaniards charged with their swords. Over a thousand Aztec chiefs and nobles were killed, and the Aztec people then rose up in revolt.

Cortez was livid with anger, but he sent word to the garrison in Mexico City to hold out until he arrived with his augmented force, and he sent word to Montezuma that he was coming to get the facts and do justice. He and his company then set out on a hard march to the Aztec capital, arriving perhaps June 24 although some chronologies say June 21.

For one of the few times in his life, Cortez was visibly upset, in fact almost out of control. Montezuma greeted him warmly at the gates of Mexico City, but Cortez brushed him aside and strode to his quarters, demanding that Captain Alvarado appear before him at once. Flushing with anger, he shouted at Alvarado that his final instructions to him had been to keep the peace and that if they ever got out of this alive he would punish Alvarado soundly.

Alvarado hotly argued that he had done no wrong, that

the ceremonial dance was merely a ruse, and that the whole festival was staged as a plot to massacre the Spaniards. He had nipped the plot in the bud much as Cortez had done with a similar plot in Chulala. Cortez spent the entire night interviewing Aztecs and Spaniards about the massacre and uprising, but he was unable to determine whether there was any truth to Alvarado's suspicion.

The next morning Cortez remained in a foul mood, and when Montezuma sent two of his chieftains asking for an interview, he brusquely refused. His men then urged him to be more civil toward Montezuma, for without his moderating influence they would all have been killed. Cortez responded angrily, asking why he should be civil to this dog who secretly dealt with Narvaez? The chieftains understood enough Spanish to know that Montezuma was being insulted, and they circulated the remarks on the streets of Mexico City. Within a few hours the Aztecs had launched a major attack on the Spanish quarters. They had also destroyed some of the bridges linking the causeways on the lake surrounding Mexico City, thus preventing escape.

Cortez Under Siege

Cortez knew they could not hold out indefinitely, but before they could leave the city, they had to fill in the gaps in the causeway. They mostly defended the walls of their quarters but occasionally went forth in companies to engage the Aztecs in battle and fill in the causeway. At night they worked in their spacious quarters constructing "burros," moveable wooden towers that could be pulled on wheels through the streets while men at the top of the tower fired upon the enemy. One great blessing was that the Aztecs, believing the sun-god could aid them only during the day, generally retired from battle at night.

Diaz describes the Aztecs' ferocity:

> We fought very well, but they were so strong, and had so many squadrons which relieved each other from time to time, that even if ten thousand Trojan Hectors and as many more Roldans had been there,

they would not have been able to break through them.

. . . neither cannon nor muskets nor crossbows availed, nor hand-to-hand fighting, nor killing thirty or forty of them every time we charged, for they still fought on in as close ranks and with more energy than in the beginning. Sometimes when we were gaining a little ground or a part of the street, they pretended to retreat, but it was [merely] to induce us to follow them and cut us off from our fortress and quarters, so as to fall on us in greater safety to ourselves, believing that we could not return to our quarters alive for they did us much damage when we were retreating.

Then, as to going out to burn their houses, I have already said in the chapter that treats of the subject, that between one house and another, they have wooden drawbridges, and these they raised so that we could only pass through deep water. Then we could not endure the rocks and stones [hurled] from the roofs, in such a way that they damaged and wounded many of our men. I do not know why I write this, so lukewarmly, for some three or four soldiers who were there with us and who had served in Italy, swore to God many times that they had never seen such fierce fights, not even when they had taken part in such between Christians, and against the artillery of the King of France, or of the Great Turk, nor had they seen men like those Indians with such courage in closing up their ranks.[74]

At one point Cortez tried to parlay with the Aztecs, but they refused. Their numbers were so superior, they said, that they could afford to lose one thousand men for every killed Spaniard (Cortez says they boasted they could lose twenty-five thousand for every one):[75]

Look out on our terraces and streets, see them still thronged with warriors as far as your eyes can reach. Our numbers are scarcely diminished by our losses. Yours, on the contrary, are lessening every hour. You are perishing from hunger and sickness. Your provisions and water are failing. You must soon fall into our hands. The bridges are broken down, and you cannot escape! There will be too few of you left to glut the vengeance of our gods![76]

The attack upon the Spanish quarters intensified, and the Aztecs used taunts to break the Spaniards' morale:

. . . they said that not one of us should remain [alive] that day and they would sacrifice our hearts and blood to their gods, and would have enough to glut [their appetites] and hold feasts on our arms and legs, and would throw our bodies to the tigers, lions, [probably jaguars and cougars] vipers and snakes, which they kept caged, so that they might gorge on them, and for that reason they had ordered them not to be given food for the past two days. As for the gold we possessed, we would get little satisfaction from it or from all the cloths; and as for the Tlaxcalans who were with us, they said that they would place them in cages to fatten, and little by little they would offer their bodies in sacrifice; and, very tenderly, they said that we should give up to them their great Lord Montezuma, and they said other things.[77]

A new danger arose: The Spaniards were no longer safe in their own quarters. The great temple of Huitzilopotchli stood only a few rods from the Spanish quarters. The Aztecs had begun using it for military purposes because it was close to the Spanish quarters and from its 150-foot summit they could look down upon the Spanish quarters and fire arrows upon them. Storming the temple became a matter of life and death.

Cortez led the attack himself. His left hand was disabled from a severe wound, but he fastened his shield to his hand and charged up the steps of the temple at the head of three hundred Spaniards and a larger company of Tlaxcalan allies:

. . . more than four thousand [Aztecs] ascended it, not counting other Companies that were posted on it with long lances and stones and darts, and placed themselves on the defensive, and resisted our ascent for a good while, and neither the towers nor the cannon or crossbows, nor the muskets were of any avail, nor the horsemen, for, although they wished to charge [with] their horses, the whole of the courtyard was paved with very large flagstones, so that the horses lost their foothold, and they [the stones] were so slippery that they [the horses] fell. While from the steps of the lofty Cue [temple] they forbade our advance, we had so many enemies both on one side and the other that although our cannon [shots] carried off ten or fifteen of them and we slew many others by sword-thrusts and charges, so many men attacked us that we were not able to ascend the lofty Cue. However, with great unanimity we persisted in the attack, and without taking the towers (for they were already destroyed) we made our way to the summit.

Here Cortes showed himself very much of a man, as he always was. Oh! what a fight and what a fierce battle it was that took place; it was a memorable thing to see us all streaming with blood, covered with wounds and others slain. It pleased our Lord that we reached the place where we used to keep the image of Our Lady, and we did not find it, and it appears, as we came to know, that the great Montezuma paid devotion to Her, and ordered it [the image] to be preserved in safety.

We set fire to their Idols and a good part of the chamber with the Idols Huichilobos and Tezcatepuca was burned. On that occasion the Tlaxcalans helped us very greatly. After this was accomplished, while some of us were fighting and others kindling the fire, as I have related, oh! to see the priests who were stationed on this great Cue, and the three or four thousand Indians, all men of great importance. While we descended, oh! how they made us tumble down six or even ten steps at a time![78]

After the Spaniards and Tlaxcalans fought their way back to their quarters, Cortez decided that their destruction of the temple and idols might have demoralized the Aztecs to the point that they might consider a proposal for safe passage out of the city. He was sure they would not listen to him, but he thought they might listen to Montezuma. So he asked Montezuma to address his people and request peace.

By this time Montezuma had become a human tragedy. Broken in spirit and broken in health, his power evaporating and his empire disintegrating before his eyes, he had withdrawn into confused depression. It is a mystery of the human psyche that this man who could plunge the obsidian knife into a human breast without flinching, would feel so much compassion at the suffering he saw around him.

Montezuma was reluctant to address the crowd, for he doubted it would do much good. He realized, as Cortez apparently did not, that his power and influence had waned and the Aztecs already had elected a new king in his place. But he agreed to try. Montezuma was placed on a battlement of the roof surrounded by Spanish soldiers amid a hail of darts, stones and arrows. He still commanded enough respect that when he began speaking, the crowd became still and listened. His speech was simple and eloquent and went something like this:

> Why do I see my people here in arms against the palace of my fathers? Is it that you think your sovereign is a prisoner, and wish to release him? If so, you have acted rightly. But you are mistaken. I am no prisoner. The strangers are my guests. I remain with them only from choice, and can leave them when I list. Have you come to drive them from the city? That is unnecessary. They will depart of their own accord, if you will open a way for them. Return to your homes, then. Lay down your arms. Show your obedience to me who have a right to it. The white men shall go back to their own land; and

all shall be well again within the walls of Tenochtitlan [Mexico City].[79]

Montezuma seems to have elicited contempt from some and sympathy from others, but obedience from none. Suddenly a cloud of stones and arrows came forth from the crowd; whether they were aimed at the Spaniards or at Montezuma or both is unknown. Montezuma was struck by three of the missiles including a stone on the head, and he fell unconscious.

Montezuma seemed resigned to death and perhaps looked forward to it. He refused treatment, and when bandages were applied, he tore them off. When Cortez came to his bedside Montezuma commended his children to his care as the most precious jewels he could leave him, adding "Your lord will do this, if it were only for the friendly offices I have rendered the Spaniards, and for the love I have shown them — though it has brought me to this condition! But for this I bear them no ill-will."[80] After about three days he died around June 30, though some chronologies suggest June 29. Diaz recalls the following:

> Cortez wept for him, and all of us Captains and soldiers, and there was no man among us who knew him and was intimate with him, who did not bemoan him as though he were our father, and it is not to be wondered at, considering how good he was.[81]

Diaz adds that the Spaniards even thought badly of Father de la Merced because he had not persuaded Montezuma to become a Christian.[82] Throughout his stay in their quarters both he and Father Olmeda had repeatedly explained the Christian faith to Montezuma. Gomara says the emperor had expressed a desire for baptism shortly before during Lent; he was going to be baptized on Easter Sunday but this had to be postponed because of the conflict with Narvaez and the events thereafter.[83] Camargo, a Tlaxcalan convert to Christianity, claimed that several of the conquistadors told him Montezuma was baptized at his own request in his last moments, and that Cortez and

Alvarado stood by him as his sponsors,[84] but if this were true it seems likely that Cortez would have mentioned it himself.

Cortez did receive Montezuma's daughters into his family and had them baptized, he said, "agreeably to their royal father's desire,"[85] but he said nothing about Montezuma's conversion or baptism. Prescott relates that Father Olmeda knelt beside Montezuma with an uplifted crucifix and asked him to embrace the sign of redemption, but Montezuma replied, "I have but a few moments to live; and will not at this hour desert the faith of my fathers."[86] Montezuma seemed to be attracted to the image of the Virgin Mary and perhaps prayed to her, but he may have seen her simply as another goddess rather than as the Mother of our Lord Jesus Christ.

How could Diaz weep at Montezuma's death and speak of "how good he was" when the man was an idolator and mass murderer who stood for everything Diaz abhorred? Montezuma was all of that, to be sure; but he was more. Maurice Collis writes an epitaph that is worth thinking about:

> That the mystery of Montezuma's life and death is fully explained here has been disavowed, but at least we have a notion of him as a "learned [man], an astrologer and a philosopher," the description already quoted from the *Codex Mendoza*, who, confronted by events which all his erudition told him inevitably led to the ruin of his race, did not give up hope and strove amid humiliations and increasing despair to find a solution.
>
> It is a mistake to think of him as deluded because he used a vocabulary and set of concepts which belonged to magic and mythology to account for the apparition of Cortez. Could he have seen the fateful landing on the coast as an invasion in the ordinary sense and taken the ordinary measures to repulse it, he might have been successful for a while. But the landing of Cortes was far more than an ordinary invasion. It was a world event which in the long run

was certain to be irresistible and fatal. Montezuma could no more have prevented the incursion of Europe than he could have stopped the march of time. That his gods and his country's independence were doomed to wither away was part-and-parcel of a global event, Europe's domination of the world, which was ushered in by Christopher Columbus and Vasco da Gama and was destined to continue for four centuries. No wonder such an event was foreshadowed by the subconscious minds of the Mexicans and assumed the form of a transcendental cataclysm.

Had Montezuma seen nothing in Cortes' landing but a foreign invasion there would be grounds for dismissing his occult sciences as a delusion, but since they indicated correctly the landing's essential nature, which was more than did any body of ideas then current in Europe, we cannot dismiss them as a hallucination. *In a broad view Montezuma had more insight into the fundamental reality of what was happening than had Cortes.* And that he had this glimpse of the essence of what faith was bringing forth makes him the leading protagonist. But his practice of human sacrifice so revolts us that we have difficulty in conceding his greatness. So utterly was he lacking in compassion when engaged in placating and sustaining the gods, that further back the exclamation escaped that he was a monster. Yet how inadequate to explain his character has that first judgment become! His ritual inhumanities are seen to be religious mysteries. He seems to take leave of mankind and enter mythology. In the super-real he rises up like an image of a pitiless universe. In this way he resembles the masterpieces of Mexican art.

"The Great Montezuma," writes Bernal [Diaz] again and again, who saw him every day for over six months, saw him despair and saw him die. Among the many figures in the old Spaniard's book no other man is called great; no other man made such an impression. As we can never know him half as well as did old Bernal, we had better take his word for it that Montezuma was a great man. With him gone the story loses its richness. Not that dramatic incident is lacking. The most exciting adventures are to come. But the Mexican leaders seem no more than heroic boys after the strange king who with such devoted patience sought to escape a dilemma which passed understanding.[87]

La Noche Triste

Now begins what Spaniards call "La Noche Triste" or "The Night of Sorrows." They chose Saturday night, June 30, at midnight to make their dash for freedom, taking advantage of the cover of darkness and the Aztecs' reluctance to fight at night.

First Cortez offered Montezuma's treasure to his men, as he had promised. But he warned against taking it because its weight would retard their flight. Cortez's own veterans took little or none of the treasure, but the troops he had acquired from the battle with Narvaez took as much as they could carry — and many didn't live to regret it.

They chose the western watercourse that connected Mexico City to the town of Tacuba because it was the shortest. Their retreat across the watercourse, it will be remembered, was blocked because the Aztecs had destroyed the eight bridges. They could not swim across those channels because they would be easy targets for the Aztec war canoes. Their efforts to fill in the gaps in the watercourse had been at best a limited success. They had been unable to reach two of the eight bridges, and those they had filled in were subsequently retaken and destroyed by the Aztecs. So Cortez decided to abandon the bridge-building policy and proceed with a portable bridge instead.

Cortez divided his men into three detachments, with the Tlaxcalans serving as porters. Captains Sandoval, Salcedo and Ordaz were to command the vanguard of 100 Spaniards, marching directly behind the porters carrying the bridge. The central detachment included Captains Avila and Olid and six hundred soldiers plus Dona Marina, who was pregnant with Cortez's child. The rear guard, commanded by Captains Alvarado and de Leon, contained over one hundred soldiers with strict instructions to protect the porters as they removed the bridge to carry it to the next channel. Tlaxcalans were divided about evenly among the companies. Cortez himself, with a select force of one hundred, was to range throughout the march from front to rear.

At midnight they commended themselves to God and quietly left their quarters and began their retreat, protected by a heavy drizzle. All was quiet as they reached the lake.

As the last of them were crossing the first channel, the Aztec attack began with shouts, trumpets, and a shower of arrows. About a hundred men from Alvarado's rear guard were cut off from the rest of the company as they defended the bridge. They tried to retreat to the Spanish quarter but were finally overcome and held for torture and sacrifice.

As the last of the company crossed the bridge, Alvarado ordered the porters to move it to the next canal. And here the fatal flaw in the plan appeared. In part because of the drizzle, the bridge stuck fast in the mud and could not be moved. The Aztecs, meanwhile, were slaughtering Spaniards and Tlaxcalans alike. Alvarado ordered them to abandon the bridge, and the remnant rushed across the bridge and on to the next canal.

There the scene was chaos and horror. As they tried to cross the water, many were weighed down by their gold, and Aztecs in their war canoes slaughtered many and dragged others aboard for the altars. By the time Alvarado and the rear guard arrived, the channel was so full of bodies that they were able to run across this human bridge.

At the third bridge they were able to cross a narrow beam, though they made easy targets for Aztec spears and arrows. Captain Sandoval and his vanguard cavalry made it to the end of the watercourse, then turned around and charged eastward to aid their companions. And so it continued until they reached the west end of the causeway, hid in a field of maize, and then made their way to a temple on high ground in the town of Tacuba.

Wounded in four placès, Cortez took stock of his forces, anguished at the loss of so many brave companions, rejoicing at the sight of those who survived, and perhaps especially rejoicing to find Marina. But some 450 to 650 Spaniards were killed during La Noche Triste (the numbers in the accounts vary), plus two to three thousand Tlaxcalans, and three of Montezuma's children who had been entrusted to Cortez's care. They also lost all their gold, all their cannons, fifty horses, and all their firearms except seven muskets and twelve crossbows. Robinson captures the mood of Cortez as night drew to a close:

> Just as dawn was breaking after the terrible night of carnage, known in Spanish history as La Noche Triste or "The Sorrowful Night," Cortez sank down for a moment's rest beneath a huge tree, and gazed with bloodshot eyes in the direction of the Mexican capital. All that he had so laboriously, so valiantly won, all that he had wrested from the clenched fist of circumstance now lay in ruins before him. Montezuma dead . . . his imperial treasure trampled in mud and water . . . a kingdom lost overnight! A sweat of agonized rage exuded from the forehead of the thirty-four year old conquistador, and in his swelling heart was born a wild resolve to bring back the greatness that had been his. The details of that resolve were not clear to Hernando Cortez in that hour of defeat, but he knew that for him there were only two courses in life: to recapture Mexico or perish in the attempt.[88]

First he had to find safety for his company, for the Aztecs were massing outside the temple for a siege. They shuddered helplessly as they listened to the snakeskin drums, the conch-horns, and the screams of two of their captured companions as they were stretched out on stone altars and sacrificed before their very eyes.

But there was a way of escape. The Aztecs surrounded the temple on three sides; the fourth side backed against a mountain. That night they built large watchfires to distract the Aztecs and climbed out the back door of the temple and proceeded up the mountain. The Aztecs did not discover that they were gone until the following morning.

Cortez's goal was the friendly capital of Tlaxcala, seventy-five miles east of Mexico City. But he could not go directly to Tlaxcala because the lake system which surrounds Mexico City extends sixty miles north to south, and they had crossed the causeway to Tacuba on the west side of the lake. So his plan was to cross through the mountains north of Mexico City, through Toltec country around Lake Zumpago, and then southeast to Tlaxcala. But the Aztecs correctly guessed that he would go to Tlaxcala, and they knew that whatever route he took he would have to pass through the valley of Otumba. So Cuitlahuac, Montezuma's successor as emperor, gave an order for all loyal nations from Mexico City to the ocean to assemble at Otumba for the slaughter.

Unaware of the Aztecs' assemblage, the Spaniards and Tlaxcalans trekked through the mountains, surviving on wild plums and berries and horses that died on the trek, and facing continual sniping along the way. The Aztecs hid on the cliffs and overpasses and threw javelins and rocks on them. Robinson describes the incident:

> After six days of harassed marching and skirmishing, during which the guides lost the way and rations were reduced to wild plums found along the road, the crippled Spanish army limped into the plains of Otumba, wishing for nothing more than a few handfuls of dried corn and a sward to sleep on. But here, filling the entire valley with their waving plumes and copper-tipped lances, were 100,000 Aztecs and their allies — the largest army a Spanish force ever met in the New World.[89]

Cortez gave instructions to his troops: Cavalrymen were to direct their lances toward the enemies' faces; infantrymen were to thrust, not strike, with their swords; above all, they were instructed to look for the enemies' leaders and strike at them because a barbarian army, like those of the East, cannot function without its commander. He then spoke words of encouragement: Numbers were unimportant when the arm of the Almighty was on their side. And then, commending themselves to God, the Virgin, and St. James, they "descended on the plain to be swallowed up, as it were, in the vast ocean of their enemies."[90]

Though outnumbered at least one hundred-to-one (the exact number of the Aztecs' allies is uncertain), the Spaniards and Tlaxcalans fought bravely; every one of them was wounded. As Diaz says, "our friends the Tlaxcalans were very lions, and with their swords and broadswords which they captured [from the enemy] behaved very well and valiantly."[91] But after several hours they began to tire, and noticing this the Aztecs intensified the attack. At this point Cortez noticed the gold and silver plumes and banner of the captain general of the Aztec army and charged him with his horse, knocking his banner down. Another cavalryman finished off the captain general with his lance. With their leader dead, the Aztecs slackened the attack and soon fell back. Again Cortez had triumphed against overwhelming odds!

Victories in the face of such numbers may seem unbelievable. But the Aztecs seemed to lack the ability to use their superior numbers to great advantage. Their warriors were fierce, disciplined, and well-equipped, but the Aztecs do not seem to have developed the science of military strategy and tactics. Especially when fighting in close quarters, their huge armies were often poorly led, immobile, and deployed ineffectively. The Aztec leaders seemed unable to mobilize their troops to attack Spaniards all at once, and they even seemed to get in each other's way.

The Gathering Storm

One can scarcely imagine the relief they must have felt as they entered friendly Tlaxcalan territory. And then their spirits were lifted by the most heartening event in months: A host of chieftains from Tlaxcala and Huejotzingo came out to meet them with fifty thousand warriors! They knew about the Aztec revolt in Mexico City and were on the way to relieve the Spaniards, but they had not heard about La Noche Triste or about the Battle of Otumba.

There was one hitch, however. Now that they knew that the Spaniards had been driven out of Mexico City, some questioned whether they should continue the alliance. For an Aztec delegation had come to Tlaxcala, telling them Mexico City now had a new emperor after the death of Montezuma and offering to end all past enmities and forgive all past offenses if they would join together against the Spaniards.

The Tlaxcalans held a council of war. One general who had never been very friendly to the Spaniards argued that the Aztecs were more closely related to them and therefore more natural allies, and if they aided the Aztecs now against the Spaniards, the old enmity could be dissolved. Others, particularly the older caciques, argued that the Aztecs had been their enemies for generations, that the Aztecs could never be trusted, that the Aztecs would never forgive them for having helped the Spaniards thus far, and if the Aztecs drove the Spaniards out of Mexico, they would turn on the Tlaxcalans and annihilate them. The older caciques prevailed, and the alliance was preserved.

As the days progressed, more good news developed. More and more nations and towns pledged to join Cortez in throwing off the rule of the hated Aztecs: Huaquechula, Texcoco, Chalco, Iztapalapa, Tlalpan, Huaxtepec, Xiuhtepec, Yautepec, and others. From Vera Cruz came word that the Cempoallans were as loyal as ever and that Pedro Barba, a friend of Cortez from Cuba, had arrived with thirteen soldiers and two horses. By May of 1520 he had assembled a force of at least one hundred thousand, and it may have swelled as high as two hundred thousand. But even that number was small compared to the Aztecs and their vassals.

It is sometimes said that Cortez had another ally: smallpox. It is true that an epidemic of smallpox broke out in Mexico City and that many of the Aztecs died from it — including the new emperor, Cuitlahauc. It is also true that the Europeans had built up immunities to smallpox and other diseases and therefore were not affected by them as much. It is not true, or at least it is a gross overstatement, that smallpox was the Spaniards' greatest ally in the conquest of Mexico. For smallpox afflicted the Spaniards' allies as well as their enemies. Maxixque, Cortez's most loyal supporter among the chieftains of Tlaxcala and a fervent Christian, died of smallpox. Many caciques from the smaller villages died of smallpox, and Cortez was frequently called upon to conciliate disputes as to tribal leadership.

While the introduction of smallpox to America was tragic, it is as wrong and unfair to place moral blame upon the Spaniards for introducing smallpox to America, as to blame Native Americans for introducing syphilis to Europe. No one at that time understood how disease is spread. If Columbus and Cortez are to be blamed for introducing disease through the exploration and settlement and conquest of America, they should also receive credit for the medical cures that American technology has produced.

Nor is it correct to say that the Western Hemisphere was free of disease before the Europeans arrived. Among diseases which existed in America before the Age of Discovery are hepatitis, encephaliltis, polio, some varieties of tuberculosis, intestinal parasites, pinta, yaws,[92] and malaria, although these diseases did not disrupt entire societies in Europe the way European diseases disrupted America.

Most unfair of all is the implication that Native Americans converted to Christianity because of disease. When natives fell victim to disease while Europeans did not, it is suggested, they concluded that the Christian God inflicted the disease upon them because He was angry with them, or that the Christian God protected the Christians from diseare while their gods were unable to protect them. Therefore, they must have reasoned, if they became Christians, the Christian God would protect them, too.[93]

Now, I do not deny that God sometimes uses disease, hardship and the danger of death to focus our thoughts on eternity and lead us to faith in Jesus Christ. Nor do I deny that some Native Americans may have believed that they could escape disease by becoming Christians.

But is there any evidence, other than the bland assertion of a modern writer, that Native Americans converted to Christianity for that reason on a broad scale? Is there any evidence that the friars used the promise of a cure as an incentive for conversion in their sermons? Maybe such evidence exists, but I have seen none. And if Native Americans converted for that reason, why did they not abandon Christianity when they found that being Christians did not exempt them from disease? Essentially this is an assumption of modernists who, finding nothing attractive about Christianity themselves, cannot believe 16th-century Native Americans could have found anything attractive about Christianity either. They will not concede that Native Americans could have accepted the Christian religion on its own merits.

One more factor about disease should be considered: Its possible connection with cannibalism, as Paul deParrie and Mary Pride point out:

> The first white men to visit Yucatan were survivors of a shipwreck [the shipwreck that brought Jeronimo de Aguilar, Cortez's interpreter, to Mexico]. Five of them were sacrificed and eaten by Mayans. Four years later the pestilence of 1515 arrived, the mayacimil or "easy death." Could it in any way be traced to this cannibal feast? If the Indians of North America could catch diseases from white men just by trading with them, the Indians of South America certainly had a better shot at catching something by eating them.[94]

Their point is worth considering. As the USDA keeps telling us, if you eat diseased meat, you get sick!

Back to Cortez. He was pretty sick after La Noche Triste and the march to Otumba, but the Tlaxcalans, rest, good food, Mexican sunshine, mountain air, and, last but not least, Dona Marina restored him to health. He then prepared for the conquest of Mexico City.

He then knew from experience that the battle had to be won in part from the water. Plans had to be laid for filling in the channels that cross the causeway, for he knew from

bitter experience that he should never advance toward
Mexico City without a safe means of retreat; so he prepared
his native allies for that task. He also set his men to work
building brigantines, boats smaller than ships but larger
than the Aztec canoes, propelled by both oars and sails,
using metalwork from the ships he sank at Vera Cruz. He
celebrated Christmas 1520 at Tlaxcala, held a review of his
forces on December 26 (or 27), and counted forty cavalrymen, 540 footsoldiers, eighty crossbows and harquebuses (a
primitive firearm), and nine muskets. He divided the cavalry into four squadrons of ten and the footsoldiers into nine
companies of sixty, appointed captains and other officers,
and addressed the company:

> My brothers, I give many thanks to Jesus Christ
> to see you now cured of your wounds and free from
> sickness. I am glad to find you armed and eager to
> return to Mexico [City] to avenge the deaths of your
> comrades and recover that great city. This, I trust in
> God, we shall soon do, because we have with us
> Tlaxcala and many other provinces, and because
> you are who you are, and the enemies the same as
> they have been, and we shall do so for the Christian
> Faith that we proclaim . . . The principal reason for
> our coming to these parts is to glorify and preach the
> Faith of Jesus Christ, even though at the same time
> it brings us honor and profit, which infrequently
> come in the same package. We cast down their idols,
> put a stop to their sacrificing and eating of men, and
> began to convert the Indians during the few days we
> were in Mexico. It is not fitting that we abandon all
> the good that we began, rather, we should go wher-
> ever our Faith and the sins of our enemies call us.
> They, indeed, deserve a great whipping and punish-
> ment, because, if you remember, the people of the
> city, not satisfied with killing an infinite number of
> men, women, and children in sacrifices to their gods
> (devils, rather), eat them afterward, a cruel thing,
> abhorrent to God and punished by Him, and one
> which all good men, especially Christians, abomi-

nate, forbid, and chastize. Moreover, without penalty or shame, they commit that accursed sin because of which the five cities, along with Sodom, were burned and destroyed. Well, then, what greater or better reward could one desire here on earth than to uproot these evils and plant the Faith among such cruel men, by proclaiming the Holy Gospel? Let us go, then, and serve God, honor our nation, magnify our King, and enrich ourselves, for the conquest of Mexico is all these things. Tomorrow, with the help of God, we shall begin.[95]

He then announced rules of war for the government of his soldiers. Gomara lists some of them:

No one might blaspheme the Holy Name of God. No Spaniard might quarrel with another. No one might wager his arms or horse. No one might force a woman. No one might take the Indians' clothing, do violence to them, or put [their towns] to the sack, without Cortes' permission and the consent of the council. No one might insult friendly Indian warriors, or use the tamemes [porters or carriers] as gifts.[96]

On December 28 they marched to Texcoco, where Cortez established a temporary military headquarters in the palace. For the first several months of 1521 he engaged in preparation, shored up provisions, drilled and trained his troops, and conducted preliminary excursions to secure the towns surrounding Mexico City. With those towns secured, he then had freedom of movement throughout the area, while the Aztecs were holed up in Mexico City. No longer was he the besieged; he was the besieger!

On April 29 he sent messengers to his allies, telling them to be ready to march in ten days. And on May 22 the crusade to Mexico City began.

Cortez then divided his forces for a multi-front attack. Alvarado and Olid were to take the northern route around Lake Zumpango, retracing the march to Otumba after La

Noche Triste. When they arrived at the village of Tacuba, across Lake Texoco just west of Mexico City, their plan was for Alvarado to secure the Tacuba Causeway while Olid proceeded south along the shore to Coyoacan and began to secure the Small Causeway. Sandoval was to take the southern approach, following the peninsula between Lake Texoco and Lake Chalco, then cross to Mexicaltzingo, and then secure the Iztapalapa Causeway that proceeds from Mexico City southward. Cortez would command the ballistrades (boats), crossing from the eastern shore of Lake Texcoco to the island of Tepepolco, then move westward across the lake to the center of the Iztapalapa Causeway where he would join with Olid and Sandoval at the point where the Iztapalapa Causeway and the Small Causeway meet. And so, in late May, the siege began!

The Battle of Mexico City

The new emperor was named Guatemoc; he was young but courageous and capable. His wife was one of Montezuma's daughters. The size of his force inside Mexico City is unknown. It had been said that Montezuma, in addition to his own Aztec forces, had thirty vassals each of whom could produce one hundred thousand warriors. But these numbers may have been exaggerated, and in time of trouble many of the vassal states could not be relied upon for support. Cut off from regular communications, Guatemoc sent smoke signals calling upon those loyal to the Aztecs to aid the besieged capital. If the signals were seen, they apparently were not heeded. Nevertheless, Guatemoc vowed to fight to the death — preferably the death of Cortez.

Alvarado, Olid, and Sandoval took their causeways as planned, except that Olid apparently found the Small Causeway impassable and used the Iztapalapa Causeway instead. Alvarado cut off the aqueduct from Chapultapec, leaving the Aztecs without a good water supply. Cortez led the brigantine fleet, taking the island of Tepeoloco and circling Mexico City, setting fire to buildings on the shore.

Guatemoc then counterattacked on two fronts. A large and well-disciplined army rushed out across the causeway and engaged Sandoval's forces in battle for several hours, while six hundred war canoes, each with eight to ten warriors with spears and bows, filled the lake. But the brigantines were larger, faster, and higher out of the water, and they could break a canoe by ramming it with the prow. The first lake battle was a clear victory for Cortez.

Cortez then prepared to launch an assault on the city. Sandoval was to circle north to Tepeyac and attack from the Tepeyac Causeway, while Alvarado, Alderete, and Cortez were to attack from the other causeways, timing the attack so as to meet and join forces in the city plaza.

But the attack failed. Cortez had given strict instructions that his captains were not to advance across the channels on the causeways until they had thoroughly filled them in with rocks and dirt. Remembering La Noche Triste, he did not want to be trapped on the causeways without a way of escape. But Captain Alderete, eager to dash for the capital, underestimated the material needed to fill in a causeway, and the materials were washed away by a current flowing eight feet deep. Cortez discovered Alderete's error and led a desperate effort to fill in the gap, carrying rock and dirt himself along with his men. But it was too late. The result was a similar disorganized retreat, with many killed and many others taken prisoner. To add to their confusion and despair, the Aztecs threw decapitated Spaniard heads at the companies of Alvarado and Sandoval, saying, "Cortez is dead!" and to Cortez's company they threw bearded heads and said they were the heads of Alvarado and Sandoval.

The Aztecs also devised a way to combat the formidable brigantines. They carefully placed sharp wooden stakes in the lake just under the surface of the water. Ramming those stakes, the brigantines would be impaled and immobilized, and the Aztecs could then attack them and carry off their crews. Several brigantines were lost that way, but through some captured Aztec chieftains, Cortez was able to learn where the stakes were located.

The Aztec practice of capturing the enemy alive for sacrifice made them less efficient in battle. It also struck terror in the hearts of their enemies, but it made them more determined to resist capture at all costs. Diaz describes the horror of almost being captured during the retreat across the causeway:

> Concerning myself I may say that many Indians had already laid hold of me, but I managed to get my arm free, and our Lord Jesus Christ gave me strength so that by some good sword thrusts that I gave them I saved myself, but I was badly wounded in one arm, and when I found myself out of that water in safety, I became insensible and without power to stand on my feet and altogether breathless, and this was caused by the great strain that I exerted in getting away from that rabble and from the quantity of blood I had lost. I declare that when they had me in their clutches, that in my thoughts I was commending myself to our Lord God and to our Lady His Blessed Mother and he gave me the strength I have spoken of by which I saved myself; thank God for the mercy that He vouchsafed me.[97]

Cortez himself was almost captured in the same way, and only the desperate rescue by his men as he was being dragged away saved him from becoming a very special sacrifice for the sun-god.

During the many pitched battles that followed, the Aztec tactic was to engage the Spaniards and their allies in combat, pretend to fall back, and lure them further on the causeway or into the streets of Mexico City beyond the point of safe retreat, and then ambush them. In this way they frequently took live prisoners.

The sacrifices, they knew, did more than nourish the sun-god; they also terrified the Spaniards. Accompanied by the beating of the snakeskin drum (as Robinson says, "a sound that always filled the Mexican heart with courage and the Spanish heart with chilly horror"[98]), they performed their sacrifices in plain view of the Spaniards. Again we witness the scene through the horror-struck eyes and ears of Bernal Diaz:

> . . . again there was sounded the dismal drum of

Huichilobos [Witchywolves] and many other shells
and horns and things like trumpets and the sound of
them all was terrifying, and we all looked towards
the lofty Cue [temple] where they were being
sounded, and saw that our comrades whom they had
captured when they defeated Cortes were being
carried by force up the steps, and they were taking
them to be sacrificed. When they got them up to a
small square in [front of] the oratory, where their
accursed idols are kept, we saw them place plumes
on the heads of many of them and with things like
fans [in their hands?] they forced them to dance
before Huichilobos, and after they had danced they
immediately placed them on their backs on some
rather narrow stones which had been prepared as
[places for] sacrifice, and with stone knives they
sawed open their chests and drew out their palpitat-
ing hearts and offered them to the idols that were
there, and they kicked the bodies down the steps,
and Indian butchers who were waiting below cut off
the arms and feet and flayed [the skin off] the faces,
and prepared it afterwards like glove leather with
the beards on, and kept those for the festivals when
they celebrated drunken orgies, and the flesh they
ate in chilmole. In the same way they sacrificed all
the others and ate the legs and arms and offered the
hearts and blood to their idols, as I have said, and
the bodies, that is their entrails and feet, they threw
to the tigers and lions which they kept in the house
of the carnivores which I have spoken about in an
earlier chapter.

... we were not far away from them, yet we could
render them no help, and could only pray God to
guard us from such a death ...

And they cried: — "Look, that is the way in which
you will all have to die, for our gods have promised
it to us many times." Then the words and threats
which they said to our friends the Tlaxcalans were
so injurious and evil that they disheartened them,
and they threw them roasted legs of Indians and the

arms of our soldiers and cried to them: — "Eat of the flesh of these Teules and of your brothers for we are already glutted with it, and you can stuff yourselves with this which is over, and observe that as for the houses which you have destroyed, we shall have to bring you to rebuild them much better with white stone and well worked masonry, so go on helping the Teules, for you will see them all sacrificed."[99]

Some of the allies were discouraged by the reverses and frightened by the Aztecs' psychological warfare, and some of them left the battle and returned to their homes; but nearly all of them returned a few days later, plus some additional tribes from the North. These northern tribes were being terrorized by marauding bands of Aztecs, and they sent word to Cortez that if he would send some Spaniards to help them, they would come down and join the battle against Mexico City. Against the advice of his captains, Cortez decided to help them even though he could not afford to spare the men; but it paid off, for many thousands of them came to help.

But for all their bravado, the situation of the Aztecs was becoming desperate. They were suffering great losses, and they were running out of food and water. The Spaniards now controlled the causeways and made regular cavalry forays into the city. Cortez's brigantines, aided by native canoes newly-supplied by friendly villages around the lake, now had complete control of the water. The lake itself was salt water and undrinkable. So when Cortez once again offered terms of peace, Guatemac called a council to consider the proposal. He himself was inclined to accept the offer, but the priests, who knew their positions would be eliminated under Spanish rule, urged that the battle continue because for three nights in a row their gods had promised them victory. So the Aztecs firmly resolved to defend Mexico City to the death.

The Aztecs fought fiercely, even impaling themselves on enemy lances to get their hands on the Spaniards. And sometimes they succeeded. Fighting continued in the city, house to house. Diaz relates that "in one of the houses there were some beams set upright and on them many of the heads of our Spaniards whom they had killed and sacrificed during the recent battles, and their hair and beards had grown much longer than when they were [last seen] alive, and I would not have believed it if I had not seen it. I recognized three soldiers as my comrades, and when we saw them in that condition it saddened our hearts. At that time we left them where they were, but twelve days later they were removed, and we took those and other heads that had been offered to idols and we buried them in a church that we made, which is now called The Martyrs . . ."[100]

But atrocities were committed on both sides. Cortez had given his troops strict orders to avoid harming civilians and not to loot and pillage, and his own Spaniards, being a disciplined force, obeyed the orders quite well. He did not have to instruct them against cannibalism, as that was totally foreign to them. But try as he might, he was unable to restrain his native allies. The Tlaxcalans in particular were proud warriors, fewer in number but every bit as fierce as the Aztecs. Destruction, slaughter, sacrifice and cannibalism had been their way of warfare for generations, and as the tide of battle turned against the hated Aztecs, the Tlaxcalans were not about to let Cortez deprive them of the just rewards of victory. On several occasions Gomara makes notations like this one: "Five hundred Mexicans died and many others were captured. Our Indian friends had a good dinner that night, for they could never be persuaded to give up the eating of human flesh."[101]

On the last day of the siege a mass slaughter took place: "Cortez begged his Indian lords not to kill these poor wretches, for they were giving themselves up; but the temptation was too great, and some fifteen thousand were killed and sacrificed."[102] Without excusing the Tlaxcalans, we must remember that they were avenging many generations of real or imagined wrongs. Cortez found all of this repulsive, but in the heat of battle he had little choice but to accept his allies as they were and hope to reform them later.

After Cortez made several peace offers, that were sometimes rebuffed and sometimes ignored, he decided the siege had to come to an end. He had hoped to take the city with minimal destruction, but then he ordered his troops to raze as much of the city as necessary to bring about a surrender. Throughout the city death was rampant from hunger, disease, and the swords of the Spanish and their allies.

Finally, on August 13, Guatemac came forth in a royal canoe and asked to be taken to Cortez. Proud in honest defeat, he said,

> "I have done all that I could to defend myself and my people. I am now reduced to this state. You will deal with me, Malintzin, as you list." Then, laying his hand on the hilt of a poniard [dagger], stuck in the general's belt, he added, with vehemence, "Better despatch me with this, and rid me of life at once."[103]

And Cortez was magnanimous in victory:

> Fear not. You shall be treated with all honour. You have defended your capital like a brave warrior. A Spaniard knows how to respect valour even in an enemy.[104]

He then inquired about the emperor's wife, a daughter of Montezuma. She was brought to him, and he provided the exhausted royal couple with refreshments and spacious quarters to rest for the night. And that day the course of history wound further, as Mexico became a territory of Spain.

Cortez gave thanks to God and ordered that a festive banquet be held that night to celebrate their victory. The party became somewhat rowdy (as Diaz says, "because this plant of Noah's made some people behave crazily,"[105] an apparent reference to drunkenness as described in Genesis 9), and Father Olmeda protested that this was not a fitting way to show their gratitude to God. Prescott says, "Cortes admitted the justice of the rebuke, but craved some indulgence for a soldier's license in the hour of victory. The following day was appointed for the commemoration of their successes in a more suitable manner."[106]

The following day the entire army was assembled for a Spanish victory ceremony, the procession of the Cross. Led by Father Olmeda, the army marched through Mexico City behind the Cross, the image of the Virgin Mary, and the banner of Spain, much as the army of Ferdinand and Isabella had done in Granada in 1492. Father Olmeda preached a brief sermon reminding the troops that God was the ultimate source of their victory, that because they had conquered Mexico they now had a grave responsibility, and that they should not abuse the rights of conquest but rather should treat the natives with humanity. They then received Holy Communion, and the service closed with thanksgiving to God.[107] In this way they set the tone for Spanish rule, for as rulers of Mexico or New Spain they were to be vassals of Spain, and in turn Spain was to be the vassal of God. Unfortunately their actions and the actions of some who came after them did not always measure up to their intentions (but then, mine don't always measure up either; do yours?). The native allies were given due honors and their share of the spoils of war, and then they were dismissed to return to their homes.

Governor Cortez

Winning the peace is sometimes just as difficult as winning a war. Now that the Aztecs had surrendered, Cortez and his companions had an empire to run, and a city to rebuild. About seven-eighths of Mexico City had been destroyed during the conquest; the rest was covered with starved, diseased, and mangled bodies. Cortez had not wanted it that way, but once the war had begun, he had little alternative but to see it through to a victorious conclusion. Prescott says this of the conquerors of Mexico:

> . . . their swords were rarely stained with blood unless it was indispensable to the success of their enterprise. Even in the last siege of the capital, the sufferings of the Aztecs, terrible as they were, do not imply any unusual cruelty in the victors; they were

not greater than those inflicted on their own countrymen at home, in many a memorable instances, by
the most polished nations, not merely of ancient
times but of our own. They were the inevitable
consequences which follow from war, when, instead
of being confined to its legitimate field, it is brought
home to the hearthstone, to the peaceful community
of the city, — its burghers untrained to arms, its
women and children yet more defenceless. In the
present instance, indeed, the sufferings of the besieged were in a great degree to be charged on
themselves, — on their patriotic, but desperate, self-
devotion. It was not the desire, as certainly it was
not the interest, of the Spaniards to destroy the
capital, or its inhabitants. When any of these fell
into their hands, they were kindly entertained, their
wants supplied, every means taken to infuse into
them a spirit of conciliation; and this, too, it should
be remembered, in despite of the dreadful doom to
which they [the Aztecs] consigned their Christian
captives. The gates of a fair capitulation were kept
open, though unavailingly, to the last hour.[108]

The first necessity was to cleanse the city so it could be
rebuilt, and before it could be cleansed it had to be evacuated. In fact, it was evacuated at Emperor Guatemoc's
request. With unfeigned sympathy, Diaz described the city
just after the surrender:

    . . . as there was so great a stench in the city,
Guatemoc asked permission of Cortes for all the
Mexican forces left in the city to go out to the
neighboring pueblos, and they were promptly told to
do so. I assert that during three days and nights they
never ceased streaming out and all three causeways
were crowded with men, women and children, so
thin, yellow, dirty and stinking, that it was pitiful to
see them. When the city was free of them, Cortes
went to examine it and we found the houses full of
corpses and there were some poor Mexicans, who

could not move out, still among them, and what they excreted from their bodies was a filth such as swine pass which have been fed upon nothing but grass, and all the city was as though it had been ploughed up and the roots of the herbs dug out and they had eaten them and even cooked the bark of some of the trees, and there was no fresh water to be found, only salt water. I also wish to state that they did not eat the flesh of their own Mexicans, only that of our people and or Tlaxcalan allies whom they had captured, and there had been no births for a long time, as they had suffered so much from hunger and thirst and continual fighting.[109]

Cortez and his men then repaired the aqueduct, restored the water supply, and burned or buried the corpses and debris. He then laid plans for the reconstruction of the city, which was accomplished in remarkable fashion over a period of seven years, so that, by 1528, no city in Europe had more buildings or was more beautiful.

The work of rebuilding, of course, was done through the slave labor of the Aztecs. We have already discussed the slavery issue at length, and while slavery cannot be justified, it must be understood in light of the time and circumstances. The enslavement of a conquered people was in accord with the universal custom of the Old World. In Christian nations, Christians were forbidden to enslave other Christians, and they were further forbidden to enslave infidels who had voluntarily surrendered. But it was considered legitimate to enslave infidels who had been conquered in war; and Muslim nations followed similar policies toward Christians and others whom they considered infidels. The Aztecs themselves had a widespread and well-defined system of slavery, and captured people who became slaves rather than sacrifices were fortunate indeed.

And slaves have been put to worse tasks than rebuilding their own city and under the supervision of their own caciques. Note, too, that in keeping with Old World custom the Aztecs and their allies were enslaved not just in Mexico

City but throughout the land, while the Tlaxcalans and others who had supported the Spaniards were exempted from slavery — though it is possible that in subsequent years this tribal distinction was sometimes conveniently overlooked.

King Don Carlos appointed Cortes Governor-General of Mexico, which was now called New Spain. He subjugated the outlying parts of the empire that were still at war with the Spaniards, and he had soon consolidated an empire larger than Spain itself.

And he brought in friars, Franciscan and Dominican, to convert the natives and instruct them in the Christian faith. Prescott notes:

> He requested the emperor to send out holy men to the country; not bishops and pampered prelates, who too often squandered the substance of the Church in riotous living, but godly persons, members of religious fraternities, whose lives might be a fitting commentary on their teaching. Thus only, he adds, — and the remark is worthy of note — can they exercise any influence over the natives, who have been accustomed to see the least departure from morals in their own priesthood punished with the utmost rigour of the law.[110]

Within a decade they had baptized over a million Native Americans and had also served as their chief defenders against Spanish abuses.

My own profession may disbar me for mentioning this, but Cortez requested, and the Crown granted, an order prohibiting "attorneys and men learned in the law from setting foot in the country, on the grounds that experience had shown, they would be sure by their evil practices to disturb the peace of the community."[111]

Cortez formulated plans to develop the natural wealth of the land. He gave land grants to conquistadors in return for their service during the conquest as well as to prominent natives. He opened mines and introduced certain crops and trees and livestock from Spain that could be productive in

the Western Hemisphere. Slaves were to be distributed
among these landowners to develop the farms and make
them productive. Madariaga, a Spanish historian and diplomat, explains the policy and the reasons behind it:

> Cortes saw the development of the country he
> had conquered as one of healthy economic growth,
> based on the content and prosperity of the native
> population. At this early stage he began to be con-
> cerned over the two chief problems raised by the
> economic and social adjustment between the two
> races: the labour question and the reward to be
> given to the conquerors for their share in the con-
> quest. There was a close relation between the two,
> for if the reward was to consist in lands, lands
> without labor are but a ruinous luxury; on the other
> hand, it was not easy to ensure an adequate supply
> of labour as long as it was possible for the natives to
> evade working for the foreigner by internal migra-
> tion. The conquerors, moreover, came from a race of
> frontier fighters who had waged an eight-century
> war against people outside the pale of civilisation. It
> was still customary for Turk or Moor in the Mediter-
> ranean to carry into slavery any Spaniard caught by
> their ships; some of Cortes' soldiers were sure to
> have relatives in slavery. A victory so hardly won,
> over a people more heathenish by far than Moor or
> Turk, should in the normal course of things have
> resulted in wholesale slavery; and only a complete
> failure to adjust our historical vision to the century
> we are observing can explain how the greatness of
> Cortes' attitude in this respect has not been ad-
> equately understood . . .
> Cortes was most averse from introducing any
> form of compulsory labour amongst the natives,
> because, as he explains to the Emperor, he held
> them "much more capable than those of the
> Islands . . . and for this reason I thought it a grave
> matter to compel them to serve the Spaniards in the
> manner it is done in the Islands; yet, short of it, the

conquerors and settlers would not be able to support themselves." He recalls how he suggested to the Emperor that the Spanish settlers should be subsidized out of he Crown's rights on the conquest . . .

He defends the scheme, one might think, as a necessary evil; for on the one hand he explicitly declares that he was "practically compelled" to adopt it, while on the other he argues that "it was not possible to find a better way to ensure both the support of the Spaniards and the survival and good treatment of the Indians." And in his fourth letter, he gives an earnest of his concern for the native population in words which carry conviction: "As it is in my interest to seek all the best possible means for populating these lands, and for ensuring that the Spanish settlers and the natives remain and propagate . . . I enacted some laws. The Spaniards who dwell in these parts are not very pleased with some of them, in particular with those which bind them to strike root in the land; for all, or most, of them intend to deal with these lands as they did with the Islands first populated, namely to exhaust them, to destroy them, then to leave them. And as I believe that it would be a grave guilt for those of us who have experience of the past not to remedy the present and the future by forestalling the evils which have caused the loss of those Islands, particularly as this land is so great and so noble . . . and where God Our Lord may be so well served and Your Majesty's income so much increased, I beg Your Majesty to look into it."[112]

But his record was not without blemish. One black mark concerns his treatment of Guatemoc, the defeated Aztec emperor. Cortez had promised that Guatemoc would be treated kindly and would rule Mexico as the vassal of Spain, and he undoubtedly made the promise with all sincerity. But he had also promised his men that they would become wealthy through the conquest.

On the night of La Noche Triste, as the Spaniards fled

from the city, they left much of Montezuma's treasure behind in their quarters. Most of that which they took with them was lost along the way, often in the channels along the causeways. When the Spaniards returned to their quarters after the surrender of Mexico City, they could find none of the missing treasure. They demanded that Cortez obtain the treasure for them and insisted it was rightfully theirs, both as gifts from Montezuma and as spoils of conquest. They further insisted that Guatemoc had hidden it or at least knew where it was.

Guatemoc either denied knowing anything about the treasure or refused to disclose where it was hidden. The Spaniards demanded that he be put to torture to force him to disclose its location. When Cortez refused, they pressed their demand relentlessly; and Alderete, the royal treasurer, accused Cortez of having a secret understanding with Guatemoc to defraud his men and the king of Spain. Finally, in a weak moment, Cortez acceded to their demands and the torture of Guatemoc began.

Under torture Guatemoc revealed only that much of the treasure had been thrown into the lake. Divers searched the lake but found very little treasure. What happened to it — and whether Guatemoc knew more than he was telling — remains a mystery.

The torture of Guatemoc cannot be excused or justified. All that can be said in defense of Cortez is that it was out of character for him, that he agreed to it only under enormous pressure from others, that it was mild compared to the treatment Cortez would have received had he been Guatemoc's prisoner, and that Cortez, ashamed of his role in this sordid affair, cut off the torture before it was finished.[113]

From this point on, the relationship between Cortez and Guatemoc deteriorated. Not long thereafter, a native informed Cortez that Guatemoc, a cacique of Tacuba, and other Aztec chiefs had formulated a plot to massacre the Spaniards. The Aztec chiefs admitted that plot existed but said it was instigated by Guatemoc and that they had refused to join it. Guatemoc and the cacique of Tacuba were arrested. The sources conflict as to how they responded to the charges. Cortez says they refused to answer but Diaz says they denied guilt, saying that a plot had been discussed but that he (Guatemoc) had discouraged it. Cortez ruled that they were guilty and ordered them hanged. Before his execution Guatemoc reminded Cortez of his words on the day of the surrender:

> I knew what it was to trust your false promises, Malintzin; I knew that you had destined me to this fate, since I did not fall by my own hand when you entered my city of Tenochtitlan [Mexico City]. Why do you slay me so unjustly? God will demand it of you![114]

Diaz adds that they received the rites of the Church through the friars before they died. While Diaz normally praises the character and actions of his commander, he says on this occasion, "this death which they suffered very unjustly was considered wrong by all those who were with us."[115]

Another blemish on the record of Cortez concerns his wife and Dona Marina. Shortly before leaving Cuba on the expedition to Mexico, Cortez entered into an arranged marriage with a lady named Catalina Xuarez. During the conquest of Mexico, various caciques frequently made native women available to the conquistadors. Cortez tolerated this as sort of a military necessity, so long as the women were duly baptized as Christians; but he seems to have been so absorbed in the conquest that he took little interest in native women himself. When the Tabascan cacique gave twenty women including Marina to the Spaniards, Cortez took none of them for himself. But when he became aware of her intelligence and skills as a linguist and diplomat, she became his interpreter, aide, advisor, confidante, and eventually his lover, bearing him his first child. Cortez professed to be a Christian, and such a relationship is contrary to the teaching of the Bible and the Church; but as Robinson said, Cortez was a man of faith and not necessarily a man of morals. As the conquest progressed their relationship deepened, and judging from the chronicles he seems to have almost forgotten that Catalina existed.

Then, in the summer of 1522, about a year after the

Aztec surrender, Dona Catalina unexpectedly came to Mexico City to join her husband. They had not seen one another, and so far as we know they had had no communication since Cortez left Cuba for Mexico over three years earlier. Whatever his emotions may have been, Cortez received her hospitably and treated her in a kindly if restrained manner, and she was accorded the respect and station of a governor's wife. But apparently the climate did not suit her, being dry table-land instead of subtropical Cuba; and she died about three months after her arrival. Diaz attributes the death to asthma.[116]

On October 12, 1524, Cortez left Mexico City on an expedition to explore and subdue Honduras which, it turned out, lasted nearly two years. Dona Marina accompanied him as his interpreter. On the way they traveled through her childhood home and she met her mother who had sold her into slavery as a child. Knowing her daughter's powerful position with Cortez, the mother was afraid; but Marina tenderly embraced her and forgave her much as Joseph had forgiven his brothers for selling him into slavery, saying that if her mother had not sold her into slavery, she would have been brought up in the Aztec religion and would never have become a Christian.

On the same expedition Cortez arranged for Dona Marina to marry Juan Xamarillo, a Castilian knight. It was a strange marriage. She and Xamarillo hardly knew one another before the marriage, and by some accounts they did not live together thereafter, though other accounts say they had one daughter.

Why, after the death of Dona Catalina, did Cortez not marry Dona Marina? No one knows. Their racial difference was not the reason; Spaniards were far more willing than other Europeans to marry Native Americans. Possibly, when Dona Catalina came to Mexico City, Cortez and Marina ended their romance and never resumed it. Maybe, because of the rumors associated with Catalina's return and subsequent death, Cortez decided he had to put some distance between himself and Marina. Or possibly their relationship was such that marriage was never in their plans. However, she did continue to serve as his interpreter

after her marriage to Xamarillo, and she declared late in
life that she would rather have held the position of servant
of Cortez than any other position on Earth.

Not marrying Marina may have been the worst mistake
of Cortez's life as Robinson suggests:

> [Cortez] conceived the idea that marriage to
> some worthy Christian gentleman was the ultimate
> service he could render her. At any rate, he arranged
> her marriage to a man she scarcely knew, cared
> nothing for, and never lived with afterward. It was
> a queer procedure, no matter how we look at it, and
> gives substance to the theory that Cortez was not
> quite sound in judgment during the trip to Hondu-
> ras. It is indisputable, also, that from the moment
> Cortez parted with his faithful and beautiful mis-
> tress, he had very little luck in life. True, he pro-
> jected great deeds and struggled mightily to encom-
> pass them; he was later to receive the adulation of
> the court of Spain and the hand of a great lady. But
> his epic period was over. His real achievements and
> his miraculous luck ended on the day Dona Marina
> was married.
>
> As for Marina herself, she soon retired, without
> her husband, to the interior of Mexico, where she
> was greeted by her people as being a little short of
> divine. Her political influence upon the natives had
> always been tremendous; she now augmented it by
> her missionary labors, wise counsels, and other good
> works among the remoter tribes of Mexico. The
> natives regarded her as the living voice of their
> racial destiny; they frankly called upon her for
> political and spiritual guidance, and she responded
> to their call by preaching the doctrines of submis-
> sion and Christianity.[117]

Their son, Don Martin Cortez, was legitimized by a
special papal bull and became Comendador of the Military
Order of St. James and a political figure in Mexico, though
he and two other sons of Cortez were temporarily banished

from Mexico in 1568 for suspected involvement in a plot to set up a new Mexico independent of Spain. His son, Don Fernando Cortez, delivered a lecture in Spain in the year 1605 detailing the contributions of his grandmother Marina during the conquest of Mexico. Mt. Malinche in east-central Mexico is named after her, and Prescott adds the following tribute to her:

> [She] has been always held in grateful remembrance by the Spaniards, for the important aid which she gave them in effecting the Conquest, and by the natives, for the kindness and sympathy which she showed them in their misfortunes. Many an Indian ballad commemorates the gentle virtues of Malinche — her Aztec epithet. Even now her spirit, if report be true, watches over the capital which she helped to win; and the peasant is occasionally startled by the apparition of an Indian princess, dimly seen through the evening shadows, as it flits among the groves and grottos of the royal Hill of Chapoltepec.[118]

Cortez did not return to Mexico City until 1526, having been away for nearly two years. The expedition to Honduras had involved great hardship and considerable disaster — losing sixty-eight horses in a twenty-four-mile mountain passage that took six days to cross, crossing a swirling river half a mile wide on a floating bridge, hostile natives, tropical disease. Cortez was ill during much of the expedition, and by the time he returned his appearance had aged so much that he was difficult to recognize. Except for the exploration of new territory, the expedition had produced no really significant results.

In Mexico City the situation had degenerated into chaos, as things had a way of doing whenever Cortez was absent. He was a national hero, but any strong-willed and decisive man has enemies. One of those enemies, an official named Gonzalo de Salazar, was running the government as a virtual dictator. Rumors had been circulated that Cortez had died in Honduras and his property had been seized. It was also said that his men had perished on the expedition, and their wives back home in Mexico City were ordered to remarry. One who refused to believe her husband was dead was flogged and forced to leave the city. Natives were being mistreated, robbed and killed, and as a result they were revolting in three provinces. Hearing this news, Cortez vowed by the Virgin Mary that he would return to Mexico City if he had to float there on a log. He set sail, landed near Vera Cruz and sought refuge in a convent while he planned his attack.

A disguised agent was sent to Mexico City to tell the friends of Cortez that he was alive and on his way back. These friends would muster their supporters, and they would meet outside Mexico City and march against the Salazar faction.

All the friends needed, it turned out, was the name of Cortez. Armed with that news, they quickly gathered support, overcame the Salazar faction, and put Salazar in a cage to await the return of Cortez.

Cortez then made the 180-mile trek from the coast to Mexico City, greeted in every village by bonfires, cheers, and shouts of thanksgiving, with triumphal arches across the roads and flowers strewn in the streets. Learning that Cortez was back, the natives ceased their revolt and promised him their support.

In June 1526 Cortez made a triumphal entry into Mexico City, with singing and dancing in the streets and a victory procession to the convent of St. Francis where services of thanksgiving were rendered for his return.

He began to set things in order, but a few days later emissaries from Spain arrived announcing that Cortez had been temporarily suspended as governor. His enemies had friends in Spain, and they had worked to undermine his influence with the royal court. They had charged him with cheating the Crown out of its rightful share of the gold by hiding the treasure of Montezuma, falsifying reports, wasting money in fortifying Mexico City, showing favoritism in the distribution of political offices, acquiring excessive influence over the natives, and planning to establish Mexico as an independent nation.

Back to Spain

An investigator from the Crown soon arrived to evaluate the charges, but the proceedings dragged on through 1527 into 1528. Weaker in health but still the man of decisive action, Cortez resolved to return to Spain to answer the charges. In a letter to the emperor he announced his own coming, writing in lofty third-person language that regardless of the outcome, "the world will at least be assured of his loyalty, and he himself shall have the conviction of having done his duty; and no better inheritance than this shall he ask for his children."[119]

As he arrived in Vera Cruz and prepared to sail, news from Spain arrived that his father had died — a crushing blow because he had not seen his father since leaving Spain twenty-two years earlier and had looked forward to a reunion on his return.

He made the return voyage accompanied by his faithful friend Captain Sandoval, several native friends, including a son of Montezuma and a son of the Christian Tlaxcalan cacique Maxixque and several other friends both native and Spaniard. He decided that if he was going to Spain to account for his actions, he would put on a first-class show for the king. He brought with him native jugglers, dancers and clowns, who made such an impression in Spain that they were taken to perform for the Pope, who was also delighted by the performance. He also brought a large collection of plants and minerals, wild animals and birds, and examples of native craft such as fabric and featherwork, all of which made the desired impression. While at first his countrymen seemed unaware that he had returned, the news soon spread, and soon he was celebrated as a hero wherever he went.

The interview with the emperor went well. Don Carlos asked him many questions and was pleased with his answers, and in subsequent conversations he repeatedly asked the advice of Cortez on colonial administration. Some of Cortez's suggestions resulted in new policies throughout the Spanish colonies to improve the condition of the natives and encourage domestic industry. Repeatedly Don Carlos appeared on public occasions with Cortez by his side, and the king even visited him in his apartment when Cortez was ill.

On July 6, 1529, the king gave Cortez the noble title of Marquess of the Valley of Oaxaca and also gave him title to large estates in Mexico. The preamble to the title declared that the lands were given in recognition of the "good services rendered by Cortez in the Conquest, and the great benefits resulting therefrom, both in respect to the increase of the Castilian empire, and the advancement of the Holy Catholic Faith," and of "the sufferings he had undergone in accomplishing this glorious work, and the fidelity and obedience with which, as a good and trusty vassal, he had ever served the crown."[120] In other words, these legal titles not only gave Cortez nobility and wealth; they also completely exonerated him of his enemies' charges!

But they also left Cortez with one major disappointment: The king declined to reinstate Cortez as governor of Mexico. Don Carlos believed the job of exploration and conquest should be separated from the job of governance because the differing tasks require different qualities, and because a conqueror inevitably makes enemies who will hinder him in governing. The failure of Columbus as governor of Hispaniola is a good example.

This is not always true; after World War II General MacArthur did an outstanding job of governing Japan, securing the love of the Japanese people and devising for them a constitution that has facilitated their return to greatness. Perhaps Cortez could have done the same. Cortez and Columbus were a lot alike; both were intelligent, ambitious, energetic, determined, and dedicated to Christ and country. But they were also different. Both were men of vision, but unlike Columbus, Cortez was not a dreamer but a realistic man of action, and the depression, despondency and self-pity of Columbus were foreign to Cortez.

Columbus was a great seaman and explorer but a poor governor. Cortez was a great conqueror and explorer, and he might also have made a great governor. But he couldn't do both at the same time. Leading the expedition to Honduras for two years, while retaining the reins of government in Mexico, was a mistake. But mistakes like that are easy to see with half-a-millennium of hindsight.

Other important events happened on the visit to Spain. One was the reunion with his mother, who swelled with pride at the accomplishments and honors of her son. Another was the meeting with his mother's kinsman Francisco Pizarro, who was soon to imitate the exploits of Cortez by conquering Peru, though in some ways it was a rather poor imitation. They met at the convent of La Rabida, where Cortez had gone for repose and rest; and they prayed together in the chapel: Cortez, in thanksgiving for victories won and Pizarro, in petition for battles to come.

A tragic event was the death of his comrade Captain Sandoval. Of all his companions in the conquest of Mexico, Sandoval was probably his favorite (except, of course, Dona Marina). Sandoval accompanied him on the return to Spain and became ill shortly after they arrived. Apparently the tremendous strain of the years of conquest had weakened his constitution, and he was unable to resist the illness. As his condition declined, Cortez was called to his bedside, and Sandoval died in his arms.

Shortly thereafter, he traveled to Guadalupe for a nine-day nouvena of prayer at the shrine. He prayed for the souls of Sandoval, his father, his wife, and for forgiveness for his own sins.

And he became betrothed to a beautiful young countess named Dona Juana de Zunigar. She was a spirited young woman, somewhat like Cortez himself. Unlike Dona Catalina, she captured his complete love. Unlike Dona Marina, she also captured his hand in marriage. Together they had four children, a son and three daughters.

But how could a man like Cortez go through all those glories and tribulations in Mexico and then be content with the life of a Spanish gentleman? He thirsted for adventure. Don Carlos would not restore him as governor but did give him the military title of Captain-General of Mexico and the Southern Sea (the Pacific). The king suggested that Cortez continue the exploration of the Pacific, and they agreed that Cortez would build and equip vessels at his own expense, lead expeditions through the Pacific, and receive title to one-twelfth of all his discoveries. It is unfortunate that the king did not give Cortez the job of conquering Peru, as he would have done it far more effectively and humanely than did Pizarro.

Explorations in the Pacific

In 1530 the Marquess and Marquessa Cortez returned to Mexico and took up residence in Texcoco, receiving a joyous reception from the natives and most of the Spaniards. The natives admired his prowess as a conqueror, and they also knew they could lay their grievances before him with some hope of obtaining justice. The Spaniards valued him because they knew he could keep the peace.

He and the marquessa lived in Mexico for ten years, during which time he tended his estates, engaged in agriculture, and tried to conduct explorations of the Pacific. In 1532 he sent out two vessels from what is now Acapulco; one mutinied and landed at Xalixco, and the other was never heard from again. He sent out a second expedition in 1534, and these ships were wrecked on the coast. One of the shipwrecked vessels was seized by Nunez de Guzman, governor of that region and an old enemy of Cortez, dating back to the old days in Mexico City when Cortez consistently sided with the friars in their complaints against Guzman's treatment of the natives. When Guzman seized his ship, Cortez "assembled a compact little army, marched two-hundred-and-fifty miles overland, and thundered at the gate of Guzman's castle. The governor of Galicia had no stomach to face the grizzled conqueror, and sent out word that if he really wanted his ship back he could have it."[121] (Note: Perhaps Cortez should have reconsidered his prohibition against lawyers! On the other hand, perhaps his method of replevin was more effective.)

The next year, 1535, Cortez decided to lead an expedition himself. Fifty years old by then, he departed from what is now Acapulco and sailed northward into the Gulf of California, or as it is sometimes called, the Sea of Cortez. He sailed up the gulf expecting to find a passage to the coast of California. Instead he proved that there is no such passage and that what we commonly call Baja California is not an island but a peninsula. He tried to establish a colony on the coast in an area that was said to be rich in pearls, but probably his real hope was to find another empire to conquer for Christ and for Spain. Finally, at his wife's request he abandoned the attempt and returned home.

Spain: The Final Years

In 1540 Cortez returned to Spain to resolve a dispute over his Mexican estates. While he was there, Don Carlos prepared an expedition against Algiers to try to break Muslim power in the Mediterranean. Ever eager to fight the infidel and perhaps hoping to regain some of his former glory as well, Cortez joined the expedition along with two of his sons: Don Martin the son of Dona Marina, and Don Martin the son of Dona Juana. Because of a storm and shipwreck they never engaged in actual combat.

Then fifty-six years old and in declining health, Cortez began to set his affairs in order. In his will he provided for his wife and for all of his children, legitimate and illegitimate. In addition to the two Don Martins and his three daughters, this apparently included the child of one of Montezuma's daughters. His will also provided for the establishment of a convent and a theological seminary to train missionaries to preach the gospel to the natives and a hospital, in Mexico, which are still in operation today. He then declared the following in his will:

> It has long been a question whether one can conscientiously hold property in Indian slaves. Since this point has not yet been determined, I enjoin it upon my son Martin and his heirs that they spare no pains to come to an exact knowledge of the truth, as a matter which concerns the conscience of each one of them no less than mine.[122]

And his old fellow-soldier Bernal Diaz then says, "After he had settled it [his will] as was fitting and had received the Holy Sacraments, Our Lord Jesus Christ was pleased to take him from this toilsome life, and he died on the second day of December in the year fifteen hundred and forty-seven,"[123] at 62.

He was buried in Seville, Spain; but in 1562 his son, Don Martin, removed his body to Mexico and reburied it beside his mother, Dona Catalina Pizarro, and one of his daughters, at the Monastery of St. Francis in Cojohuacan. They were moved again in 1629, this time to the Monastery of St. Francis in Mexico City. Then they were moved still again, this time to the Hospital of Our Lady of the Conception which he had endowed in his will. And then, during the revolution of 1823 it was feared that an anti-Spanish mob would desecrate his remains; so his body was removed again and possibly reburied in an unmarked spot somewhere in the building or grounds of the hospital, which is probably where it rests today.

So what is the epitaph of Hernando Cortez today? The enemy of Native Americans? Yes, he went to war with the Aztecs. But of the force of 200,000 that besieged Mexico City, Spaniards constituted about one-fourth of one percent. The other 99.75% were Native Americans. Prescott explains:

> The Indian empire was in a manner conquered by Indians. The first terrible encounter of the Spaniards with the Tlaxcalans, which had nearly proved their ruin, did in fact insure their success. It secured to them a strong native support, on which to retreat in the hour of trouble, and round which they could rally the kindred races of the land for one great and overwhelming assault. The Aztec monarchy fell by the hands of its own subjects, under the direction of European sagacity and science.[124]

Remember, too, that Cortez had repeatedly commanded his troops and begged his native allies to use restraint. How many Native Americans are alive today whose ancestors would have perished on sacrificial altars were it not for Hernando Cortez? And regardless of which side of the sacrificial knife you happen to be facing, how many would really prefer to live in a pre-Cortez Aztec society?

With his usual keen insight and eloquence, Madariaga

summarizes the triumph and tragedy of Cortez in the unresolved crises that have marked the history of Mexico:

> ... that nation has not yet succeeded in finding its soul. A graft of one race upon the stem and root of another, it does not yet know its true meaning and destiny, and lives an agitated life in a perpetual struggle between two bloods, so that Montezuma dies and Guatemoc is hanged every day, and every day the white man conquers and humiliates the Indian within the soul of every Mexican.

This is the deepest failure of all. Three years before his death. he had written to the Emperor: "This work which God did through me is so great and marvelous . . ." He knew that he had been just an instrument. But of what or of whom? Of God, of course, he would have answered unhesitatingly. Yes, of God. But men are not dead instruments, like hammers and saws. They have a freedom of their own, a freedom to err. He had gone over in the name of God, dreaming of a new Christian nation made up of the natives, whom he would save from heathenism, and of the Spaniards who would settle, develop, enlighten and ennoble it. He had started this nation on its new path of economic prosperity, respect for the natives, education of native and white and the "ennobling" of the land by the queen of civic arts — architecture. Within his lifetime, there were enough Latin scholars and theologians amongst the natives to frighten some timorous priests at their progress; and the first printing press of the Continent was at work. Noble buildings had made Mexico the chief capital of the New World. Shortly after Cortes' death, Cervantes de Salazar records the prosperity of Tlaxcala, the beauty of the buildings and the fertility of its lands, the wealth, contentment and well-being of the natives, and tells how one of Cortes' captains, who governed it, had built thirty-three stone bridges in the vicinity to ensure communications. This was the work he meant to achieve and had undertaken according to his lights, which were those of the best men of his day: the native Emperor, order and faith had to be removed, and in their stead the Christian Emperor, State and faith were to be finally established. It was quite simple. As for the two races, they were both born of Adam and Eve, children of God.

So he thought. So thought everybody in his day. Could he guess that, in the depths of races and nations, there lie hidden oceans of instincts, emotions, obscure memories, and that he was preparing for New Spain centuries of mental and moral storms? Could he guess that a day would come when his ashes, buried by his express desire in New Spain, would have to be protected by secrecy from the infuriated crowds of the nation he had founded, turned in a frenzy of self-negation against the man to whose vision they owed their existence? That Mexico would erect a statue to Guatemoc, less to honor Guatemoc than to insult him? That a painter of that race he did so much to ennoble and liberate would one day smear the walls of his own house in Cuernavaca with so-called scenes of the conquest distorted by a prejudice of which the painter himself is innocent since it comes from the racial depths?

He had risen by high endeavour to be one of the heroes of mankind. But, as such, what could he do but err? Poor mankind, seeking her peace and unity through the tortuous ways of history, groping almost blindly under the feeble light of her reason through the uncharted ocean of her soul, in a world which stubbornly conceals the complex secrets — mankind is a cruel devourer of her own heroes, whom she condemns to throw away treasures of energy and of self-denial in gestures tragically irrelevant to the very aims she seeks.

Cortes, great in his achievement, was even greater still in that his tragic life is a fit symbol of the tragedy of man on earth.[125]

In calling Cortez great, what do we mean by greatness? Certainly there are many kinds of greatness. The greatness of Cortez lies in his single-minded zeal, his willingness to take any risk and undergo any hardship to advance the Christian faith and the Castilian civilization that he believed to be based on Christian principles. Because of that determination, God used Cortez to change the world.

And the change was for the better, even if it was in many ways derailed from his original vision. The Christian values Cortez preached have not always been practiced, even by Christians (perhaps especially by Christians), but they have made the Americas a better place in which to live. And even more significantly for eternity, millions of precious human souls have been saved as a result.

Those who condemn Cortez would do better to examine the man and his vision and purpose of a Christian society of Europeans and Native Americans, see where it has gotten off track, and restore it and bring it to full flower.

For myself, I can only say that if I were recalled to active duty to fight a war against overwhelming odds, I know of no commander I would rather have than Hernando Cortez and no better first sergeant than Bernal Diaz. And if I were in command, I can think of no finer junior officer than Captain Sandoval, no braver company of men than the gallant band who marched into Mexico in 1519, and no trustier allies than the Tlaxcalan warriors.

Hernando Cortez inscribed on his coat of arms the words "Judicium Domini apprehendit eos, et fortitudo ejus corroboravit bracchium meum." (The judgment of the Lord overtook them; His might strengthened my arm.) When he died in 1547, his fifteen-year-old son, Don Martin Cortez, wrote an epitaph which says it all:

> Father, whose fortune an ungrateful world undeserving shared, whose valor enriched our age, rest now in eternal peace.[126]

And so, as scenes of Mexican temples fade from our eyes, we return to the shrine of Guadalupe and view once again the shadowy figure kneeling so earnestly in penitential prayer.

"Sins in Mexico?" asks the pilgrim. "I thought Cortez was the hero who won Mexico for the Cross and the Crown. Of course there was killing, but that's what war is all about. Were his actions really sinful?"

"I'm not sure I know," answers the friar. "It's pretty hard to judge that unless you were there."

ENDNOTES

[1]Samuel Eliot Morison, *Admiral of the Ocean Sea* (Boston: Little, Brown & Co., 1942), pp. 393-94; cf. Salvador de Madariaga, *Hernan Cortez: Conqueror of Mexico* (Chicago: Regnery, 1955), p. 453; Bernal Diaz del Castillo, *The True History of the Conquest of New Spain by Bernal Diaz del Castillo, One of Its Conquerors* (London: Hakluyt Society, 1568, 1908), Vol. V, Chapter 195, pp. 143-44. This eyewitness account by Bernal Diaz, a foot soldier who accompanied Cortez throughout the conquest, will be cited in this chapter more than any other source. It has been been translated and reprinted, abridged and condensed in many forms. The edition I have used, the Maudslay translation published by the Hakluyt Society, is perhaps the best and most complete. Readers using different editions will find different volume, chapter and page divisions. For the convenience of the reader, all Diaz citations herein will include volume, chapter and page in that order; for example, for this endnote, Diaz, V: 195: 143-44. The reader will note that Spanish and Native American names and places in this chapter are spelled in different ways: Cortez, Cortes; Montezuma, Mocteczuma, etc. Transliterating a name or place from one language to another, or in some cases from one alphabet to another, and in some instances from the Aztec language to Spanish to English, results in different spellings, and in many instances there is no one standard spelling. For clarity and ease of understanding I have endeavored to use consistently the spelling that is most common in the English language, except when quoting another writer, in which instance, with few exceptions, I have preserved the spelling that writer used. The nine-day novena of Cortez at the shrine of Guadalupe is historical fact; the conversation between the pilgrim and the priest is my own poetic license.

[2]Jon Canning, *100 Great Events That Changed the World* (New York: Hawthorn, 1965), pp. 230-36. Canning's work should be titled "100 Great Works of Fiction" for all its inaccuracies. To cite only a few, Canning ignores the fact that thousands of Native Americans joined the Spaniards in fighting the Aztecs, and his statement that the Aztecs' "only crime was that they had tried to defend their country" utterly ignores the Aztec human sacrifice and other crimes against humanity. His statement that "Every Aztec leader who fell into his hands he burned at the stake" is simply false.

[3]Gregory Cerio, "Were the Spaniards That Cruel?", *Newsweek*, Columbus Special Issue, 1991, pp. 48-51; see also John Francis Bannon, *The Spanish Conquistadors: Men or Devils?* (New York: Rinehart & Winston, 1960), esp. pp. 323-41.

[4]William Hickling Prescott, *The Conquest of Mexico* (London: Dent & Sons, 1843, 1908, 1965), Vol. I., p. 135 (hereafter cited as Prescott, I: 135).

[5]Pizarro y Orellana, quoted by Prescott, I: 146.

[6]Francisco Lopez de Gomara, *Cortes: The Life of the Conqueror by His Secretary* (Berkeley, U of California Press, 1552, 1964), Chapter 44, p. 95. Like that of Diaz, Gomara's work has been reprinted many times and in many forms; consequently

I will cite it by chapter as well as page, as Gomara, 44: 95. Some of the sources claim the Aztec ambassador said each of Montezuma's thirty vassals could produce 50,000 warriors rather than 100,000 as Gomara reports. The sources vary slightly as to the number of Cortez's soldiers, some saying the number was between 550 and 600 rather than 508. The reason for the discrepancy may be that those sources that gave the larger figure were including the sailors on the ships as well as the soldiers.

[7]Possibly the best analysis of Aztec religion is found in *Alfonso Caso, The Aztecs: People of the Sun* (Norman, Oklahoma: U of Oklahoma Press. 1958, 1968).

[8]*Man, Myth & Magic: An Illustrated Encyclopedia of the Supernatural* (New York, Cavendish, 1970), C.A. Burland, "Aztecs: Blood Feast of the Sun," Vol. II, pp. 200-01.

[9]Caso, p. 7.

[10]Id., pp. 23-58.

[11]*Man, Myth & Magic,* II: 202.

[12]Caso, pp. 12-13.

[13]Jon M. White, *Cortez and the Downfall of the Aztec Empire* (New York: St. Martin's Press, 1971), p. 114.

[14]Caso, pp. 13-14.

[15]Henry Morton Robinson, *Stout Cortez: A Biography of the Spanish Conquest* (New York: Century Co., 1931), pp. 52-53.

[16]Jean Descola, *The Conquisadors* trans. Malcolm Barnes (New York: Viking Press, 1957); selections reprinted by Bannon, pp. 36-37.

[17]Diaz, I: 1: 9.

[18]Robinson, pp. 47-48.

[19]Id., p. 48.

[20]Diaz, I: 26: 92.

[21]Id., I: 27: 97-98.

[22]Gomara, 12: 31.

[23]Id., 13: 33.

[24]Id., 18: 40-41.

[25]Prescott, I: 179-80.

[26]Gomara, 20: 46-47.

[27]Diaz, I: 34: 121-22.

[28]Gomara, 23: 51.

[29]Prescott, I: 181-82.

[30]Id., I: 184-85.

[31]Caso, pp. 74-75.

[32]Id., pp. 73-74.

[33]Id., pp. 68-69.

[34]Id., p. xv.

[35]*Man, Myth & Magic,* II: 200.

[36]White, p. 129.

[37]Descola, pp. 37-38.

[38]Caso, p. 14.

[39]Prescott, I: 42, 194-95; *Man, Myth & Magic,* II: 204-05; Hammond Innes, *The Conquistadors* (New York: Knopf, 1969, 1970), p. 92; Charles Michael Boland, *They All Discovered America* (New York: Permabook, 1961, 1963), pp. 297-313; William Weber Johnson, *Cortes* (Boston: Little, Brown, 1975), p. 52; Robinson, p. 111. Robinson suggests the human side of the Quetzalcoatl legend may have its

roots in a Norse voyage, the timing of which could easily have coincided with the Toltec culture. The fact that the legend, in at least some surviving forms, describes Quetzalcoatl as having light skin and departing across the ocean to the East on a raft of snakes (suggestive of a viking ship) lends some support to that possibility. The possibility of a Norse voyage to Central America is not as far-fetched as it may sound. If Norsemen did establish a colony at L'Anse aux Meadows, on the coast of Labrador around A.D. 1,000 as is now universally conceded, they would probably explore the east coast of North America, and they would only have to follow the coastline to reach Mexico. See Chapter Two for more information on the Norse voyages and the L'Anse aux Meadows sites.

[40]Maurice Collis, *Cortes and Montezuma* (London: Faber & Faber, 1954), pp. 56-57.

[41]Diaz, I: 40: 148-49.

[42]Id., I: 44: 161.

[43]Id., I: 51: 186.

[44]Id.

[45]Id., I: 51: 187-88.

[46]Id., I: 52: 189.

[47]Id., I: 52: 191.

[48]Id., I: 61: 222.

[49]Id., I: 62: 227.

[50]Id., I: 62: 228.

[51]Id., I: 65: 239-40.

[52]Id., I: 77: 280-81.

[53]Id., I: 77: 281.

[54]Id., I: 78: 287-88. Maudslay, the translator, in a footnote on page 287, suggests that the ascent of Popocatepetl probably took place a little later than Diaz places it. Maudslay places the ascent at the time the Spaniards left Cholula about a month later. Prescott, I: 224-28, essentially agrees with Maudslay. The fact that it happened is more important than precisely when it happened. Besides getting sulphur for gunpowder, another reason the Spaniards ascended the volcano was to further the aura of Spanish invincibility, since the superstitious Tlaxcalans (or Cholultecs) refused to go near the summit.

[55]Diaz, I: 78: 288-89.

[56]Robinson, p. 136.

[57]Diaz, II: 87: 37-38.

[58]Id., II: 89: 54.

[59]Id., II: 90: 56-57.

[60]Id., II: 90: 57-58.

[61]Madariaga, pp. 245-46.

[62]Diaz, II: 91-60.

[63]Gomara, 82: 167.

[64]Id., 81: 166-67.

[65]Diaz, II: 92: 78.

[66]Id., II: 93: 84.

[67]Id., II: 94: 91-92. I am simply reporting what Diaz said without drawing any conclusion as to whether the event actually occurred.

[68]Id., II: 95: 93-94.

[69]Id., II: 95: 95.

[70]Innes, p. 136.

71Madariaga, pp. 277-78.

72Diaz, II: 115: 172-73.

73Robinson, p. 204.

74Diaz, II: 126: 230-31.

75Prescott, II: 78.

76Id.; cf. Gomara, 109: 216-17.

77Diaz, II: 126: 232-33.

78Id., II: 126: 234-35.

79Prescott, II: 70-71.

80Id., II: 86. It has been claimed that the Spaniards killed Montezuma, but as Prescott says (II: 72), "It is hardly necessary to comment on the absurdity of this monstrous imputation, which, however, has found favour with some later writers." He notes that the Spaniards would not have killed Montezuma if for no other reason than that it was not in their interest to do so; Montezuma was much more valuable to them alive than dead. Juan Cano, husband of Montezuma's daughter and defender of the Aztecs and a bitter enemy of Cortez, confirmed that Montezuma died as Diaz, Gomara, and Prescott describe the event (Madariaga, p. 528).

Jon Canning's assertion that Cortez "murdered him and all his sons and daughters" (p. 236), is so ludicrous as to transcend the bounds of irresponsibility and enter the world of fantasy. Several of the children whom Montezuma commended to the care of Cortez at his death, perished at the hands of the Aztecs during the Spaniards' flight from Mexico. Others survived into adulthood, became Christians, and had children. Two became founders of noble houses in Spain. A daughter was married to Guatemoc who became the Aztec emperor after Montezuma and his successor Cuitlahuac died; after Guatemoc was killed she successively married three Spaniards of honorable families. Another daughter of Montezuma, Dona Leonor, married Cristoval de Valderrama, from whom descended the Sotelos de Montezuma family. Still others married into aristocratic families in Spain, and one descendent of Montezuma, Don Joseph Sarmiento Valladares, Count of Montezuma, ruled as viceroy over parts of Mexico from 1697 to 1701. Another descendent became Governor of New Mexico, and still another, in the early 1800s when Mexico was seeking independence from Spain, came back to Mexico from Spain to try (without success) to claim the throne based on his ancestry. See Prescott, II: 89-90). It is fortunate for Mr. Canning, but unfortunate for Cortez and the cause of truth and responsible journalism, that dead men can't sue for libel!

81Diaz, II: 126: 238.

82Id., II: 127: 239.

83Gomara, 107: 213.

84Prescott, II: 85.

85Id., p. 86.

86Id.

87Collis, pp. 191, 192.

88Robinson, p. 231.

89Id., p. 234.

90Prescott, II: 114.

91Diaz, II: 134: 253, 290-91.

92Alfred W. Crosby, *Ecological Emperialism: The Biological Expansion of Europe 900-1900* (London: Cambridge University Press, 1986), p. 197; quoted by Zvi Dor-Ner, *Columbus and the Age of Discovery* (New York: Wm. Morrow, 1991), p. 216.

93William McNeill, Taped Interview, quoted by Dor-Ner, p. 233. Please note that when I say this view is the assumption of modernists who can see nothing attractive about Christianity themselves and therefore cannot believe Native Americans could have been attracted to Christianity on its own merits, I do not mean to imply that either McNeill or Dor-Ner personally hold that attitude toward Christianity. Their religious beliefs are unknown to me.

[94]Paul deParrie and Mary Pride, *Ancient Empires of the New Age* (Westchester, Illinois: Crossway, 1989), pp. 115-16.

[95]Gomara, 120: 240-41.

[96]Id., 120: 241-42.

[97]Diaz, IV: 151: 126-27.

[98]Robinson, p. 266.

[99]Diaz, IV: 152: 149-51.

[100]Id., IV: 155: 172.

[101]Gomara, 141: 287.

[102]Id., 143: 291.

[103]Prescott, II: 277.

[104]Id.

[105]Diaz, IV: 156: 188. Maudslay, the translator, notes that this passage was blotted out of Diaz's original manuscript.

[106]Prescott, II: 281.

[107]Id.

[108]Id., II: 284-85.

[109]Diaz, IV: 156: 187.

[110]Prescott, II: 311-12.

[111]Id., II: 312.

[112]Madariaga, pp. 404-06.

[113]Prescott, II: 293-94.

[114]Id., II: 322-24; Diaz, V: 177: 26-27.

[115]Diaz, V: 177: 27.

[116]Diaz, IV: 160: 237-38; Prescott, II: 310, 348. A rumor arose that Cortez was responsible for the death of Dona Catalina, and later writers have capitalized upon it. Prescott best refutes the rumor, pointing out, among other things, that the charge never advanced beyond the stage of rumor, that 16th-century writers including those critical of Cortez like Las Casas attached no credence to the rumor, and that the royal courts of Spain, where Cortez had enemies in abundance, never took the rumor seriously.

[117]Robinson, pp. 308-09.

[118]Prescott, II: 327.

[119]Id., II: 338.

[120]Id., II: 343-44.

[121]Robinson, p. 334.

[122]Hernando Cortez, Last Will and Testament, 1547; quoted by John C. Abbott, *Hernando Cortez* (New York: Brunswick Subscription Co., 1916), pp. 285-86.

[123]Diaz, V: 204: 211.

[124]Prescott, II: 286-87.

[125]Madariaga, pp. 484-86.

[126]Don Martin Cortez, Epitaph for Hernando Cortez, 1547; quoted by Gomara, 252: 409.

CHAPTER SIX

AMERICA: PURGATORY OR PARADISE?

In October 1991 Dr. Cortez Cooper, pastor of Trinity Presbyterian Church of Montgomery, Alabama, and past national moderator of the Presbyterian Church of America (PCA), travelled to St. Petersburg, Russia (formerly Leningrad, U.S.S.R. His mission: to lecture in Russian universities about the Christian principles and motivations that underlay the founding of the American republic.

As he prepared to return to the United States, a Russian student commented, "I suppose, Dr. Cooper, you must really enjoy lecturing on Christian principles for American universities."

Sadly, Dr. Cooper replied that at most American universities there would be little interest in such a lecture, and that some would even consider a Christian lecture on state property to be unconstitutional.

The Russian student was incredulous. "When you Americans are blessed with such a wonderful heritage," he asked, "why would you throw it away?"

His question hits home. Why, when nations oppressed by atheistic Communism are earnestly trying to rediscover the Christian foundations that were forcibly taken away from them, do Americans take this heritage for granted, or ignore it, or forget it, or in some cases vilify it?

Ignorance is part of the reason. Most Americans have an appreciation for the freedom they enjoy and the institutions that make that freedom possible, even if they don't understand how those institutions work. But they utterly fail to understand that Christian values shaped the institutions they live under, because they see no connection at all between religious beliefs and civic institutions. Part of the fault, it must be admitted, rests with the Church; for the Church has failed to teach these basic truths for the past several decades. (When was the last time your church offered a class or seminar on biblical principles of government?)

This misunderstanding has led to the mistaken view of separation of church and state that has relegated religious expression to, at best, a second class status in the public arena. As a result, the religious aspects of America's heritage are often ignored, and students grow up not realizing that this dimension of history even exists. Dr. Paul Vitz, Professor of Psychology at New York University and principal author of a federally-funded study titled "Religion and Traditional Values in Public School Textbooks," concluded that textbook authors "have a deep-seated fear of any form of active contemporary Christianity, especially serious, committed Protestantism" [Dr. Vitz is Catholic], and the result is an "obvious censorship of religion" much like sex was censored during the victorian period.[1]

Sometimes this avoidance of religion is motivated by anxiety and uncertainty as to how to handle a delicate and controversial subject. Sometimes it is caused by a misunderstanding of the first amendment. Sometimes the reason is a genuine belief that the best way to be neutral about religion is to say nothing about it. In any event, the practical result is that the religious motive in history is downplayed as nonexistent or unimportant. The secular is exalted at the expense of the sacred, and students are given an incomplete and distorted picture of their heritage.

But in some cases the hostility toward our Christian heritage is motivated by a desire to replace the Christian religion with another.

Of all the major Columbus-bashers, the most vitriolic is Kirkpatrick Sale, author of *The Conquest of Paradise: Christopher Columbus and the Columbian Legacy* (New

York: Knopf, 1990). On the jackets of his various books and in *Contemporary Authors*, Sale lists himself as a founder of the New York Green Party, a member of the advisory board of New Age University, the author of a documentary history of the Students for a Democratic Society, and a contributor to various liberal publications, such as *The Nation, New Republic, Village Voice, Dissent, Evergreen Review, New York Times Magazine, Mother Jones, Commonweal,* and *Green Revolution.*

Sale's book drips with venomous dislike for Columbus, and he misses no opportunity to degrade the Admiral. Even though Columbus virtually shouts his Christian motivations throughout his journals and letters, declaring "It was the Lord who put into my mind to sail to the Indies," Sale says blithely, "It is hard to know from his later writings exactly what impelled those dreams . . ." (p. 17). Ferdinand Columbus's biography of his father is, according to Sale, "known [by whom besides Sale?] to be full of inaccuracies" (p. 21). Repeatedly he chides Columbus for not supplying more detail in his journals, conveniently ignoring the fact that we no longer have the actual journals and are forced to rely upon abridgements. When Ferdinand says his father and the crew knelt on the shore of San Salvador and gave thanks to God, Sale says Ferdinand enlarged upon his father's journal, "presumably on the authority of his imagination alone."(p. 95) Such a conclusion is indeed presumptuous since Sale does not have the missing journals any more than the rest of us.

Columbus, it will be recalled, kept a secret mileage log on his first voyage. He frankly acknowledged having done so and stated his reason clearly: If the crew had known how far they actually were from shore, they might have mutinied and demanded a return to Spain. But to Sale this is more than dishonesty; it is the mark of a pathological liar, an inability to distinguish fact from fantasy that has led to "that failure to distinguish the real world from the illusory, the experienced from the imagined, which we call madness."(pp. 49-50).

Columbus tried to explain his Christian motivations through the many Scripture quotations in his *Book of*

Prophecies, but Sale simply labels the book "bizarre" (p. 188). He even denies that the English defeat of the Spanish Armada took place, offering no data or documentation whatsoever for this startling conclusion. Such dramatic evidence-defying leaps of faith may produce gasps of admiration at New Age University, but they hardly qualify as objective scholarship.

Nevertheless, Sale has perceived the real issue more clearly than most. His book is not really about Columbus; the Admiral is merely a convenient whipping boy. Sale's real target is not Christopher Columbus, not even the Spanish nation, but rather the values of European civilization and the Christian religion that produced those values. The fundamental evil, Sale believes, is the so-called "dominion mandate" of Genesis, Chapters 1, 2, and 9, by which Christians and Jews believe God has given the human race dominion over Earth and, acting on that mandate, have proceeded to exploit and despoil the environment. Far preferable, Sale believes, are Native American religions and pre-Christian European religions which teach that man is part of nature and therefore must live in harmony with nature, changing it as little as possible.

The dominion mandate has impelled the European Christian to believe he should "make his mark" upon the land, leaving it better than he found it — "better" being usually defined in terms of productivity or hospitality to human habitation. By contrast, the pagan viewed nature as perfect in its pristine untouched beauty; therefore his home and lifestyle should blend in with the environment as much as possible, and when his life is over and he returns to the earth, he should blend back into nature leaving no trace that he had ever been here. Believing themselves to be part of a divine plan that unfolded through the ages, Europeans saw themselves as builders of a civilization that needed to advance and develop with each succeeding generation. Many of the Native Americans saw no such divine plan in human history and no reason to do anything different from their ancestors.

It may be a misconception and part of the general "noble savage" myth that gripped romantic Europeans in the sixteenth and seventeenth centuries, that Native Americans took such good care of the environment. It is true that many of them worshipped gods or spirits that personified forces of nature and that most of them interacted with nature more directly than most of us do today.

But many Native Americans did not permanently despoil the environment only because they lacked the technology to do so. More technologically-advanced nations such as the Aztecs and the Mayas left imposing structures that stand out in the jungles of Central America, and the stench and covering of human blood on those altars was hardly aesthetically pleasing. And the practice of placing a fish over each corn plant to fertilize it and help it grow might seem marvelous to a stalk of corn but downright cruel if you're a fish! I am not denying that Native Americans cared greatly about nature; I am simply saying that the myth of the noble savage is probably idealized somewhat.

On the other hand, the Christian or biblical view of nature is often misrepresented to mean that God has authorized man to ravage and destroy the environment all he wants with no sense of responsibility whatsoever. It is probable that some professing Christians have utilized the dominion mandate to justify doing exactly that. It is also possible that the Church has failed to correct that misimpression. These may well be valid criticisms of Christians and of the Church. However, these abuses are not a basis for criticizing Christianity itself, for they are an aberration of true Christian teaching.

Sale says the medieval Church did not encourage the study of nature (p. 75). His criticism is, at best, an oversimplification. The Church has never taught worship of nature as though nature were God. Nor has the Church ever taught that nature is a self-contained unit that can exist and function without the aid of a transcendent Being.

Rather, the Church has taught that nature is the creation of God and as such reflects the handiwork of God. Thus we look to nature to learn of God, just as we learn about an artist by looking at his paintings and learn about a contractor by looking at his buildings. "Consider the lilies of the field," Jesus told us (Matt. 6:28). And David says,

"The heavens declare the glory of God; and the firmament sheweth his handiwork"(Ps. 19:1). Through nature man learns of the orderliness, constancy, harmony, beauty, variety, infinity, design, and power of God. The Christian appreciates nature, but he does not worship nature.

The Christian looks at wilderness, nature in its unaltered state, in a variety of ways. The wilderness is a place of evil and of purity, of danger and of refuge. Jesus goes to the wilderness to be tempted of the devil (Matt. 4); but the woman and her child flee to the wilderness for sanctuary from the dragon (Rev. 12:6). John the Baptist is the voice crying in the wilderness, and Moses and others go to the wilderness to commune with God. The Pilgrims and Puritans who came to this country saw the New England wilderness in much the same light; it was a place of unspoiled innocence and unrestrained evil, a place of danger from the elements and the natives, yet also a place of sanctuary from England and of nourishment and growth.

In general, however, the state of wilderness, or unaltered naturalness, was less than desirable in Scripture. Being condemned to wander in the wilderness, as the Israelites were, was a discipline from God. As a sign of God's blessing and restoring grace, He says through Isaiah, "I will make the wilderness a pool of water" (41:18), "I will plant in the wilderness the cedar" (41:19), "I will even make a way in the wilderness" (43:19). As a sign of God's displeasure, lands are reduced to wilderness: "and Edom shall be a desolate wilderness" (Joel 3:19). While the word for wilderness, "midbar," can mean desert or wasteland, it commonly refers to pastureland; and when the authors of the Old Testament wanted to speak of a wasteland or desert, a stronger word, "arabah," was used.

Leaving nature in an unaltered condition, then, is not praised as a virtue in Scripture. The natural state is not necessarily the ideal state.

But while the dominion mandate authorizes man to utilize nature for his benefit and to improve upon conditions of nature, it must not be misinterpreted as carte blanche permission to despoil and waste the environment. For ultimately all things belong to God: "The earth is the

Lord's, and the fulness thereof" (Ps. 24:1). God has made man His steward to manage His creation; He placed Adam in the Garden "to dress it and to keep it" (Gen. 2:15). Man's duty is to use sound conservation practices in managing the environment, but not necessarily to leave everything in its original state.

The Hebrew terms used for dominion ("radah") and for subdue ("kabash") in Genesis 1:26-28 do not carry the implication of oppression, exploitation, or waste. Rather, they imply bringing an object under one's rule or control. Man is to control the environment; and in keeping with Genesis 2:15 he is to control it using sound conservation practices rather than wasting the resources of God.

Ironically, the Christian worldview which sees man as specially created in the image of God and given dominion over nature, provides a much firmer basis for sound conservation practices than does the evolutionary humanist model which sees man as a product of nature and therefore as part of nature.

Consider the matter of saving endangered species. The evolutionary humanist model teaches Darwin's theory of natural selection, that in the struggle for survival the fittest should survive and the unfit should die; in this way life improves as the millennia unfold. Why save the whales? If they are unfit to survive, they deserve to become extinct according to Darwin's theory. And if man is just another animal, what difference does it make whether the whales are killed off by men, or by sharks, or by bacteria? It's all part of the general struggle for survival of the fittest.

On the other hand, the Christian model sees man as created specially in God's image and entrusted with the responsibility of exercising wise stewardship over creation. Using this model, one is much more motivated to save endangered species because such species are God's precious resources.

The Christian position on nature, then, is a middle-ground position which neither countenances wholesale exploitation of the environment nor advocates leaving the world in its natural state. The Christian model sees man managing natural resources in the name of God, changing the world to make it more productive and beautiful and habitable while not wasting or destroying resources.

It is entirely possible that Christians have failed to follow the dominion mandate as it is given. It is also possible that the Church has failed to teach the dominion mandate correctly. If so, the solution is not to reject Christianity because it has been imperfectly applied, but rather to discover where we have been wrong and correct that with sound teaching from the Word of God.[2]

Even if man has dominion over nature, what right did Spaniards have to exercise dominion over the Native Americans? It is a troublesome question, as our discussion of Christopher Columbus demonstrated. To their credit, the Spaniards themselves were troubled over the matter, even the Spanish monarchs. And their attempts to address the issue led to great advances in the development of international law.

Francisco de Vitoria (circa 1480-1546), a Dominican priest and Prima Professor of Theology at Spain's leading university (Salamanca), could be called Spain's leading theologian of his generation and the leading authority on international law of the 16th century. During the years 1538-39 he presented a series of lectures focusing the Spanish conquest of the Americas as a means of addressing the larger issues of just war and conquest.

International law did not begin with Father Vitoria; it goes back at least to the ancient Romans. They spoke of a universal body of laws which all people recognized and called it the jus gentium or law of nations. Since those nations which had been conquered by Rome were not, strictly speaking, bound by Roman law, legal matters concerning those nations were judged according to the jus gentium, which was not a written statutory code but rather a form of common law based on reason and common sense. Interestingly, lawyers seldom appeared in the courts of jus gentium — theoretically because they were unnecessary, but actually, some have suggested, because lawyers would feel out of place in a court governed by reason and common sense!

But the authority behind the jus gentium was the

Roman Empire, which was thought to be universal over all nations. After the collapse of Rome and the discovery of lands and peoples outside the pale of Roman or European authority, a different basis for international law was needed. Medieval thinkers found that basis in the jus naturae, or law of nature, which Augustine and Aquinas identified with the higher law of God. And since God was supreme over human government, no human law was valid if contrary to this higher law of nature.

Father Vitoria then analyzed the various theories advanced by Spain to justify the conquest of the Americas, rejecting most but ultimately accepting two.

First it was argued that Native Americans had no legitimate governments and therefore no legitimate claims to sovereignty, because of their status as infidels and idolators. Father Vitoria rejected this argument, noting that civil authority does not depend upon personal regeneration and that even Christian monarchs do not lose their authority because of mortal sin.

Next he considered the argument, adopted from Aristotle, that Native Americans lacked the intelligence or power of reason to govern themselves and therefore were rightfully slaves of others. Not so, Father Vitoria declared:

> There is a certain method in their affairs, for they have politics which are orderly arranged and they have definite marriage and magistrates, overlords, laws, and workshops, and a system of exchange, all of which call for the use of reason: they also have a kind of religion. Further, they make no error in matters which are self-evident to others; this is witness to their use of reason.[3]

He attributed the fact that they seemed naive in some matters to their upbringing and isolation from the rest of the world.

Next he looked to the authority of Rome. Don Carlos, King of Spain, was also known as Charles V because he was also Emperor of the Holy Roman Empire, a rather loose connection of city-states in what is now Germany and

Northern Italy that claimed to be the successor to the great Roman Empire of old. Since the Roman Empire was supreme power on Earth, it was argued, the Emperor of the Holy Roman Empire was the de facto ruler of the world. Negative, says Father Vitoria. Since the dispensation of nations after the Tower of Babel (Gen. 11), each nation has been independent. The only universal reign is that of Christ, and that is a spiritual reign to which all civil authorities, including the Holy Roman Emperor, are subject. Roman claims to worldwide authority are therefore groundless, both historically and now.

Then can the Pope, as the Vicar of Christ on Earth, grant dominion over the Americas to the King of Spain? "No," Father Vitoria answers, "the Pope has only spiritual authority, not civil authority; and even his spiritual authority extends only to those princes who have accepted the Christian faith." While Church authorities should resolve disputes among Christian princes, unbelieving Native Americans are outside his jurisdiction.

Some tried to compare the Spanish conquest of the Americas to the Israelite conquest of Canaan, and indeed some similarities do exist. The Canaanites were infidels who engaged in widespread human sacrifice, particularly sacrificing babies to the altars of the fertility god Baal in the midst of sex orgies. But that was different, Father Vitoria insisted: God had given direct revelation ordering the Israelites to conquer Canaan; Spain had received no such direct revelation. Thus the conquest of Canaan could not be used as precedent to justify the conquest of the Americas.

Father Vitoria then turned to two bases which he said could justify the conquest. One such justification arose when innocent persons were unjustly condemned to death, as in the widespread Aztec human sacrifices.

The second justification concerned the right to preach and hear the gospel. Since all men and women have a common ancestry in Adam and Eve, all people have a basic right to travel and sojourn among other nations and communicate and trade with people of those nations. This right applies equally regardless of religion; Christian princes may not prevent Muslims or Jews from trading in Christian lands, any more than Muslims or Jews may prevent Christians from trading in their lands. If foreign princes try to prevent Spaniards from exercising these rights, Spaniards must first use peaceful means to try to persuade them to follow this law of nations. But if they are unable to persuade them, they may secure these rights by force.

This principle especially applies to the preaching of the gospel. Christians have a basic natural right to preach the Word of God to pagan nations, and the people of those nations have a basic natural right to hear the gospel. If pagan princes refuse to allow Christians to preach, or persecute Christian converts, and peaceful attempts to remedy the situation fail, Christians may defend themselves or even make war to secure safety and freedom for the preaching of the gospel. He added that such force should be used only with great caution because its practical effect may be to harden the pagan people against the gospel.

In fact, Father Vitoria makes the Great Commission the basic foundational principle of the law of nations: "Go ye therefore, and teach all nations, baptizing them in the name of the Father, and of the Son, and of the Holy Ghost: Teaching them to observe all things whatsoever I have commanded you: and, lo, I am with you alway, even unto the end of the world"(Matt. 28:19-20). The law of nations maintains peaceful and equitable relationships among the peoples of the world and freedom to preach the gospel is preserved, by force if necessary, as Ruben Alvarado explains:

> ... the gospel message cannot be received unless it be freely preached and the peoples be free to accept it. Compulsion is simply out of the question here. With the growth of the Church International the spiritual Kingdom of Christ expands into all the world, in fulfillment of the Great Commission. Thus the ultimate purpose of international law, which Vitoria clearly perceived, is to enable the fulfillment of that Commission.[4]

Another Spanish Jesuit theologian picked up where

Father Vitoria left off. Father Francisco Suarez (1548-1617), Professor of Theology at the Portuguese University of Coimbra (appointed to this position by the King of Spain after the Spanish conquest of Portugal), developed many highly systematic works of theology. One, *A Treatise on Laws and God the Lawgiver*, analyzed the relationship between natural law, the law of nations, human law and custom. Another, *A Word on the Three Theological Virtues: Faith, Hope, and Charity*, analyzed such issues as just warfare and the means which may justly be used for the conversion of unbelievers. For the most part Suarez agreed with Vitoria, but went beyond Vitoria in asserting that the Church may protect those whom it sends out to preach the gospel and may punish those who persecute preachers.[5] While maintaining that Christian princes may not force their subjects to become princes, at least by direct coercion, he agreed with some hesitation that Christian princes may force their subjects to hear the preaching of the gospel so that they may bear the consequences of their rejection of Christianity. However, Christian nations may not force the people of other nations to hear the gospel; but they may force the princes of other nations to at least allow the gospel to be preached and allow their people to hear the gospel.[6]

What about the reverse? Must Christian rulers allow Muslims to preach their religion in Christian countries? Vitoria and Suarez do not address this question. The law of nations, they say, clearly allows Muslims to sojourn and trade in Christian countries, but they are silent about whether Muslims must be allowed to proselytize. Firm believers in the absolute truth of the Christian revelation and the eternal consequences of acceptance or rejection of the gospel, modern notions of the complete equality of all ideas and religions were quite foreign to their minds.

Father Las Casas, the eloquent and forceful defender of Native American rights and critic of Spanish abuses, denounced forced conversions to Christianity as futile because it is not possible to wean the natives away from paganism in a few short days. He insisted,

The only way of doing this, is by long, assiduous,

and faithful preaching, until the heathen shall gather some ideas of the true nature of the Deity, and of the doctrines they are to embrace. Above all, the lives of the Christians should be such as to exemplify the truth of these doctrines, that, seeing this, the poor Indian may glorify the Father, and acknowledge him, who has such worshippers, for the true and only God.[7]

But while Las Casas repeatedly argued that the only legitimate reason the Spaniards had for being in the Americas was to preach the gospel of Jesus Christ, he never denied that military force could be used if pagan rulers refused to allow their people to hear the gospel.

Father Francisco Lopez de Gomara, Cortez's chaplain and secretary and biographer, expressed a somewhat different view. While he did not argue that Native Americans should be forced to abandon their pagan beliefs and convert to Christianity, he did believe certain pagan practices such as widespread human sacrifice created an atmosphere in which the preaching and hearing of the gospel was practically impossible. Before the gospel could be preached effectively, these practices had to be halted:

> Truth to tell, it is war and warriors that really persuade the Indians to give up their idols, their bestial rites, and their abominable bloody sacrifices and the eating of men (which is directly contrary to the law of God and nature), and it is thus that of their own free will and consent they more quickly receive, listen to, and believe our preachers, and accept the Gospel and baptism, which is what Christianity and faith consist of.[8]

In other words, while human sacrifice and cannibalism are commonplace, the atmosphere is such that the gospel cannot receive a decent hearing. First abolish these atrocities, by force if necessary, then people will be ready to hear the gospel. Father Suarez expressed a similar view, holding that Christians may not force heathens to give up pagan practices simply because those practices are contrary to the Christian religion; but they may force heathens to give up practices that are contrary to the law of nature, such as human sacrifice, cannibalism, and sodomy.[9]

Do these justifications make sense? The liberty to preach and hear the gospel may mean little if one believes Christianity is just one more viewpoint among many others. If this one viewpoint is excluded, the general marketplace of ideas will not be shortchanged too much.

But Jesus declared, "I am the way, the truth, and the life: no man cometh unto the Father, but by me" (John 14:6). If He truly is the Son of God who died for the sin of the world, and if faith in Jesus Christ is truly the essential and only way of salvation, then the issue becomes far more significant than mere competition among equally valid ideas. For a complete answer to this question it would be necessary to consider the views of the millions of Americans who are in heaven today because explorers and evangelists dared to bring the gospel to the New World.

And those who insist the Spaniards had no right to intervene to put an end to the Aztec sacrifice of up to fifty thousand innocent human beings per year, most of whom were unwilling victims from other Native American nations, might have difficulty justifying Allied intervention at Auschwitz and Dachau.

Nor is it fair to condemn evangelism as imposing the "white man's religion" upon Native Americans. Christianity is not a white man's religion. It began with the Jews, but in Christ there is neither Jew nor Greek (Gal. 3:28); rather, the gospel is for "whosoever believeth" (John 3:16).

For most of the first century of the Christian era the Middle East was the primary center of Christian activity. Shortly after the destruction of Jerusalem in AD 70, the center of Christianity moved to northern Africa, particularly Alexandria and Carthage. Northern Africa remained the center for two centuries, producing such Christian leaders as Origen, Tertullian, Cyprian, and Augustine.

Shortly after AD 300 the center of Christianity shifted to southern Europe where it remained for over a thousand years. Then, after the Reformation, it shifted to northern

Europe and eventually to North America.

Currently Christianity is undergoing a revival in parts of Africa, Asia, and eastern Europe, while western Europe seems cold to the gospel, and the future spiritual direction of America seems uncertain. The day may soon come when Africa, Asia, and Russia will send Christian missionaries to the West!

Justifying the conquest is one thing; justifying the means by which the conquest was accomplished is another. We may laud the motives of the conquistadors, but pass judgment upon their acts individually.

Columbus and Cortez were sincere in their desire to bring Christianity and Christian civilization to this western world. Other explorers shared their evangelistic fervor and are berated for it today. Consider Ferdinand Magellan, who in 1519-1522 commanded the first expedition to sail around the world. The *World Book Encyclopedia* says this of him:

> Magellan took special pride in converting many of the people to Christianity. Unfortunately, however, he involved himself in rivalries among the people. On April 27, 1521, Magellan was killed when he took part in a battle between rival Filipino groups on the island of Mactan [in the Philippines].[10]

Now, all of this is factually true, but *World Book* has given it a nasty twist by the choice of words. Note how it is stated: "Magellan took special pride in converting ..." Not that he sought to glorify God by preaching His Word; not that his love for the Filipinos led him to earnestly seek the eternal salvation of their souls; as far as *World Book* is concerned it is simply a matter of "pride," Western imperialists imposing their culture on others.

And it is true that Magellan became involved in a dispute among Filipinos, but there is more to it than that. Magellan and the priests who accompanied him had converted Datu Humabon, the rajah of the Philippine island of Cebu and his people to renounce their idols and accept Christianity. The chief of another tribe, Cacique Cilapulapu, announced that he would not accept Christianity and would wage war on any chief who did. As war between the two tribes became imminent, several of Magellan's officers advised an immediate departure; but Magellan insisted that since he had been responsible for the rajah's conversion, he could not abandon the rajah now that he was being persecuted for his faith. In the battle he was killed by a poisoned arrow.[11] But he prevailed in his cause, for the Filipinos remain overwhelmingly Christian to this day.

Other famous Spanish explorers, such as Coronado and Balboa, shared this fervor for evangelism. Others, such as Pizarro, DeSoto, and Ponce DeLeon, probably shared the Christian beliefs of Columbus and Cortez but lacked their evangelistic fervor — but there may be a spiritual side to their character that historians have missed.

But however noble their goal of evangelism may have been, this does not justify every means of attaining the goal. Were the means employed by the conquistadors justified?

To fully understand the conquistadors, we must consider the time in which they lived. It was a time when violence was more accepted than in recent memory (although that is changing as we enter a new age of barbarism) and when war was a way of life. Throughout their lives and those of their ancestors, war with the Muslim Moors or the Muslim Arabs or the Muslim Turks had been national policy and even religious duty.

The same was true in America. Native tribes and nations regularly displaced or enslaved one another, and warfare was common although often practiced on a smaller scale and with fewer casualties than in Europe and Asia. John Greenway relates the following account:

A Polynesian chief once observed to a white officer: I don't understand you English. You come here and take our land and then you spend the rest of your lives trying to make up for it. When my people came to these islands, we just killed the inhabitants and that was the end of it.[12]

Considering the practice of the times coupled with the

overwhelming numerical odds the conquistadors faced in the Americas, we must conclude that the Spaniards at least tried to exercise considerable restraint. Columbus, it will be recalled, expressed the belief that the natives he encountered were gentle people who could be won for the Lord better by love than by force. He gave his men strict orders that they were to bargain fairly with the natives and not take advantage of their ignorance of the value of European goods. In their letters to Columbus, King Ferdinand and Queen Isabella repeatedly gave strict orders that natives were to be treated kindly, and Columbus gave similar orders to those under his command — orders which, unfortunately, were not always obeyed.

Cortez commanded his troops, under threat of strict penalties, to treat the natives with courtesy and respect and not to loot their homes and villages. On the battlefield he acted decisively, for his main responsibility as a commander was for the success of his mission and the safety of his men and their allies. Even in battle his men were forbidden to sack villages or harm civilians. He tried to apply the same standard to his native allies but had only limited success.

Cortez is often criticized for two alleged massacres: that of Choulala around November 1, 1519 and Alvarado's slaughter of the festival celebrants around June 1520. The first was a response to a Choulatec plot to massacre the Spaniards and a necessary means of self-defense. The second took place while Cortez was away at Vera Cruz; Alvarado insisted the celebration was simply a ruse to capture the Spaniards and sacrifice them, and he and his men had fired upon the celebrants in self-defense. The truth will probably never be known.

Before engaging the enemy in battle, Cortez's practice was to offer the enemy an opportunity to surrender, promising liberal terms, good treatment, and semi-autonomy. At the final siege of Mexico City Cortez repeatedly entreated Guatemac and the Aztecs to surrender, but they refused. The result was a lengthy siege with mass starvation, disease and death, but not necessarily the fault of Cortez or Guatemac or anyone, but rather an unfortunate consequence of war. In Iraq today there is widespread disease, hunger and malnutrition as a consequence of the war in the Persian Gulf and subsequent embargo which most Americans (including this author) believe was justified. The point is that human tragedy often takes place in war, even in just wars; but this does not mean moral blame can necessarily be attached to any particular person or group.

Some of the Spaniards' actions after the discovery and conquest are more difficult to justify or excuse. Without a doubt acts of cruelty and injustice occurred. The accounts of these injustices conflict and range from sweeping generalities to isolated instances, making it impossible to know whether these injustices are the rule or the exception.

Note, however, that many of these problems occurred while Columbus and Cortez were away on business or voyages of discovery. Perhaps it was a mistake to make them governors in the first place; perhaps they could have served the realm better on further voyages.

One of the chief problems, though, resulted from a failure to follow the advice Columbus and Cortez gave to the Crown. Columbus, you will recall, had written that Spain should send no one but true Christians to the Indies because it was so important that people of good Christian character be in the New Land to win the natives to Christ by their lives and testimonies. Cortez emphasized that colonial policy should be to grant land to colonists only on condition that the colonists stay in Mexico and work the land, to discourage the get-rich-quick mentality. Unfortunately, these recommendations were not followed. Colonists were in some cases convicted criminals who were promised remission of sentences for time served as colonists. In other cases Spanish hidalgos, gentlemen who did not want to do physical work and looked down upon those who did, wanted to make a quick fortune and return to Spain. With colonists such as these it is no wonder the policies which sounded good in theory broke down in practice.

Certainly Spain should have practiced more quality control over the colonists sent to the Americas and should have kept a tighter rein on the colonies. But the Americas were an ocean away, and Spain was only beginning to comprehend the nature and vastness of this new enterprise. Pressing problems at home were given first priority. Certainly this was shortsighted, but Ferdinand and Isabella were neither the first nor the last to suffer from that malaise.

The Spaniards held a basic view of God and man, that man was created in the image of God, that provided a basis for believing in human equality even if they did not fully realize all of the implications of that view. They knew from Scripture that "God is no respecter of persons" (Acts 10:34), that in Christ "there is neither Jew nor Greek" (Gal. 3:28), and the Old Testament injunctions that judges were to judge impartially without favoritism. By contrast the pagan world view which sees our race as specially favored of the gods, or the evolutionary world view which leaves people free to conclude that their race has evolved above all others opens the way for all sorts of "super-race" theories. Both of these views fueled the Third Reich.[13]

At the same time, the Christian view of man should be humbling, for it should keep one ever mindful of his own sinful nature. While ending human sacrifice on the pagan altars, we must remember that we are capable of committing atrocities ourselves. Phillip Yancey tells of a pastor who served in the U.S. Army at the end of World War II. His detachment had charge of a group of German prisoners, former Nazi SS prison guards at Dachau. The American soldiers had contempt for these Nazi prisoners, looking upon them as war criminals. Some wanted to annihilate the prisoners on the spot, but their orders were to hold them for trial. When they were asked to escort the prisoners to the interrogation center, one American soldier volunteered and marched them out of sight. There came a smattering of machine gun fire, and the American returned to his detachment alone with a fiendish grin on his face, saying, "They all tried to escape." Despite his rage toward the Nazis, the pastor says he felt a sickening horror inside, for he feared that if he were ordered to escort the next group of prisoners he might be tempted to do the same. "The beast that was within those [Nazi] guards," he said, "was also within me."[14]

Looking across the centuries, what are the results of that voyage of 1492? The discovery and settlement of a new hemisphere, the establishment of over two dozen new nations with a combined population approaching one billion, have caused many blessings and curses for the world.

But the blessings outweigh the curses. The United States in particular developed a constitution and form of government that have served as a model and inspiration for nations throughout the world. The United States has established an economic system of free enterprise that has provided the greatest prosperity and the greatest freedom the world has ever seen. American advances in technology, medicine, aviation, railroads, automobiles, steamships, telephones, telegraphs, agriculture, art and literature have benefitted people on all continents.

Americans have been generous in many ways. In World War I and in a host of smaller conflicts, Americans have fought and died on foreign soil to prevent the expansion of tyranny. America has provided more foreign aid to other countries than any other nation in history, both in money and in technology and volunteer help, while American farmers have fed the world. For half a century America has stood as a bulwark against Communist expansion that threatened to engulf the world. Last and most important, America has provided freedom for the gospel and has sent more missionaries and Bibles to other lands than any other nation on Earth.

On balance, has the United States of America been primarily a force for good in the world or primarily a force for evil? The inescapable conclusion is that America, while far from perfect, has been a force for good.

But what of Americans who live south of the Rio Grande? To what extent does Latin America share in the blessings enjoyed by the United States?

In 1991 I watched a television movie about the life of General Sam Houston, who defeated General Santa Anna at San Jacinto in 1836. I enjoyed the story, but my thoughts were elsewhere. In 1836 Texas was undeveloped territory. Its settlers were striving to eke out a living, and at least some considered themselves oppressed by Mexico. Now, barely a century-and-a-half later, Texas is a dynamic, prosperous state. When one crosses the border from El Paso to Juarez or from Laredo to Nuevo Laredo or from Brownsville to Matamoros, the differences are obvious.

Why has Texas, as part of the United States, made such giant strides toward liberty and prosperity while Mexico has lagged behind? Four basic answers stand out.

The first is the United States Constitution. With its state/federal balance of powers, its separation of powers into three branches, its checks and balances, its provision for representative government of the people, and its protection of individual rights, it has established a government with enough power to govern effectively while at the same time limiting that power so that government does not become tyrannical and oppressive. Furthermore, it has established a system of orderly transition of government by the will of the people, thereby providing two centuries of political stability that much of Latin America has lacked. It is not a divine system, but it is the most successful system of government yet devised by the mind of man because it is consistent with the biblical view of human nature. James Madison, often called the "Father of the Constitution," wrote in *The Federalist No. 51:*

> But what is government itself but the greatest of all reflections on human nature? If men were angels, no government would be necessary. If angels were to govern men, neither external nor internal controls on government would be necessary. In framing a government which is to be administered by men over men, the great difficulty lies in this: You must first enable the government to control the governed; and in the next place, oblige it to control itself.

Second, the free enterprise system of the United States has provided liberty, variety and prosperity. Utilizing the profit motive, it has provided a positive incentive to produce that is lacking under state-controlled economies, and the nation as a whole has benefited from this increased productivity.

But these institutions are not the entire answer. For freedom can exist only in proportion to wholesome self-restraint. As John Adams said, "Our constitution was made only for a religious and moral people. It is wholly inadequate for the government of any other."[15] If people do not possess the discipline and civic virtue necessary to produce the self-restraint that makes a free society possible, government must supply the restraint by force.

Something else must be considered in understanding the success of Texas and the United States, because something else has made it possible for the Constitution and the free enterprise system to work in North America. The answer has its roots in the Protestant Reformation of the 1500s.

One basic Reformation doctrine was the priesthood of all believers, the belief that people need not go through a priest or bishop as an intermediary between themselves and Jesus Christ but rather may come directly to Jesus Christ themselves through faith.

This doctrine had several political ramifications. It led to congregational and presbyterian systems of church government, which gave American colonists practical experience in local self-government. This spiritual equality led, further, to notions of political equality. Finally and perhaps most significant, it led to widespread literacy. As Luther and Calvin stressed, every plowboy should be able to read or interpret the Scriptures for himself rather than having to ask a priest or pope. This meant every plowboy had to learn how to read!

Certainly Roman Catholicism emphasized literacy. Throughout the Middle Ages Catholic schools, monasteries, and universities kept learning and science alive, and during the Middle Ages and the Renaissance most of Europe's leading scientists, statesmen, and scholars were churchmen or at least were educated through the Church. But Protestants added a sacred dimension to reading, even for the common man. Every man was a priest, and part of his priestly duty was to read the Word of God.

Because of this, the population of colonial United States was extremely literate, a literacy they developed using the

Bible and the Calvinistic New England Primer as their basic texts. As a result they were able to understand their Constitution and legislative process and exercise the franchise intelligently. Montesquieu, the French Roman Catholic political scientist upon whom our founding fathers relied so heavily in developing our system of government, wrote that while Christian nations in general were more likely to have free and humane governments than Islamic nations, among Christians the Protestant nations of Northern Europe were more amenable to republicanism while the Catholic nations of Southern Europe were more amenable to limited monarchy.[16]

Another Protestant principle helps to explain North American prosperity: the Protestant work ethic, more especially the Puritan work ethic.

Roman Catholicism stressed the value of work. Employees were to work diligently for their employers, and fathers were to provide for their families, for so commands the Word of God.

But the reformers added a new dimension to work — the sacredness of all vocations. Whereas a Catholic who feels called to the priesthood is spoken of as "having a vocation," Luther and Calvin stressed that every honorable occupation is a vocation of God. One may serve God just as zealously and just as fully while practicing law or farming or serving in the armed forces or building houses or working in a factory as in being a pastor or priest. This provided a further incentive for work beyond the profit motive: One works for the glory of God and His kingdom!

And the Protestant work ethic also emphasized that it is good and right to profit from one's labor. Growing rich is not shameful; it is honorable. Catholicism did not prohibit its adherents from profiting from their labors and did not teach that there was anything wrong with being rich. But Catholicism stressed a virtue in poverty in a way that Protestantism did not.

These factors — the United States Constitution and the Protestant belief in the priesthood of all believers that made it possible, the free enterprise system and the Puritan work ethic that made it successful — account for the liberty and prosperity of the United States. And if North Americans are going to abandon the Puritan work ethic, as they seem determined to do, what will we put in its place?

If Latin America wants to enjoy the prosperity and liberty of North America, must it adopt these Protestant values and North American institutions?

What Madariaga wrote about Mexico is to some extent true of all of Latin America: That region has not yet fully discovered its own soul. Latin America is part Spanish or Portuguese, a larger part Native American, and still larger part mestizo. The land was formerly pagan but became Christian, and now seems to cling to some vestiges of Christianity while yearning to return to its pagan roots. While Protestantism has made some inroads in recent years, Catholicism is more deeply engrained in the Latin character.

As Latin America seeks its soul, it might turn to what Michael Novak calls the "Catholic Whig" tradition. Tracing the Catholic Whig tradition from Aquinas through Bellarmine, de Tocqueville, and Lord Acton, Novak says the following in *This Hemisphere of Liberty:*

> . . . the Catholic Whigs share with all other progressives a certain hope in the capacities of human beings for approaching ever more closely "the building up in history of the kingdom of God." They share with traditionalists a sharp sense of limits and a sense of sin. They believe that by God's grace and promises, through a fuller exercise of charity and practical intellect, human beings can make steady progress in arriving at more just societies, but also that, through sin, such progress is reversible and may descend even to the gates of hell — as in our century it has.
>
> In a balanced way, the Whigs value deeply all that the human race has learned and embodied, often in tacit ways, in existing habits, institutions, and traditions. They do not think that their grandparents were less wise than they. They spend much effort learning from the past, trying to put into

words its often tacit wisdom. They think of themselves as part of a living tradition and therefore are as much oriented toward the future as they are respectful of the past. They are wary of ideology, which they regard as a form of rationalism untutored by experience. They are not afraid to dream, and yet they have a special regard for things tried, tested, and found to be true. They think it foolish not to learn from the hard-won lessons of the past and foolish, too, to ignore the new needs of the human pilgrimage barely discernible in the near future.

In this respect, the classic Whig vision is rooted in the cautious optimism that springs from reflection on human experience in the light of original sin.[17]

Based upon this view of human nature, Novak recommends a basic free enterprise system based on respect for individual liberty and creativity, republican forms of government, and other proposals for Latin American liberty and prosperity that are worthy of serious consideration.

All of this discussion illustrates the folly of the notion of complete separation of church and state, a phrase which does not appear in the U.S. Constitution or its amendments and which is far from what the framers intended. Church and state should be separate offices, but each derives its authority from God.[18]

And every nation and every society has its own national character. For that reason Latin America can never be a southern counterpart of the United States, nor can all Latin American nations be the same.

The character of a nation is shaped by its ultimate values. Those values are expressed in the nation's laws, institutions, forms of government, in its art, music, literature, architecture, schools, technology, and social organizations.

And those ultimate values have their roots in religion. That is why a Christian civilization will be different from an Islamic civilization, a Hindu civilization, a pagan civilization, an atheistic, or New Age civilization. Nor will every

Christian civilization be the same. Christian values find expression in many ways in forming the character of a nation. Evangelists who bring Christianity to a pagan land must use careful discretion in determining what aspects of the pagan culture are rooted in pagan religious values and need to be changed and what aspects are simply cultural and may remain to form part of the unique Christian civilization of that people.

So there is such a thing as Christian civilization. Christianity is not only conversion and sanctification. It is that, first and foremost. Salvation is foundational; without it there can be nothing else. But Christianity should find expression in the culture of society.

And in that sense there is such a thing as a Christian nation. Not in the sense that everyone in the nation is truly regenerate, or even professes to be Christian. A Christian nation is a nation which was founded or reformed by sincere professing Christians, in which a substantial portion of the people profess the Christian faith and conduct themselves accordingly, and in which the institutions and culture of the nation reflect Christian values founded on the Word of God. In that sense the United States of America was founded as a Christian nation and remains to some extent a Christian nation today. And in fact, the U.S. Supreme Court expressly so ruled in *Church of the Holy Trinity* v. *United States*, 143 U.S. 457 (1892): "... this is a Christian nation." (If you think I've quoted the case out of context, read it for yourself.)

But there are efforts today to remove this nation from its Christian foundations and re-establish the United States as a secular state. Those who would do so should carefully consider the true character and foundation of the nation they rail against, what they would replace it with, and why.

President Theodore Roosevelt said it well in 1909:

> Progress has brought us both unbounded opportunities and unbridled difficulties. Thus, the measure of our civilization will not be that we have done much, but what we have done with that much. I believe that the next half century will determine if

we will advance the cause of Christian civilization or revert to the horrors of brutal paganism. The thought of modern industry in the hands of Christian charity is a dream worth dreaming. The thought of industry in the hands of paganism is a nightmare beyond imagining. The choice between the two is upon us.[19]

ENDNOTES

[1]Dr. Paul Vitz, *Religion and Traditional Values in Public School Textbooks*

[2]See Peter J. Leithart, "Biblical Perspectives on the Environment," Contra Mundum Winter 1992. pp. 28-33.

[3]Francisco de Vitoria, *The Principles of Political and International Law in the Work of Francisco de Vitoria,* Antonia Truyol Serra (ed.) (Madrid: Ediciones Cultura Hispanica, 1946); quoted by Ruben Alvarado, "Vitoria's New World Order: The Great Commission and the Discovery of the New World," Contra Mundum Winter 1992 p. 4. Vitoria's lectures are reprinted in *The Spanish Origin of International Law: Francisco de Vitoria and His Law of Nations,* by James Brown Scott (Oxford: Clarendon Press, 1934; see also Arthur Nussbaum, *A Concise History of the Law of Nations* (New York: Macmillan, 1947), pp. 52-85.

[4]Alvarado, Contra Mundum, Id., p. 8.

[5]Francisco Suarez, "A Work on the Three Theological Virtues: Faith, Hope, and Charity — Divided Into Three Treatises to Correspond with the Number of the Virtues Themselves," reprinted in *Selections from Three Works of Francisco Suarez,* S.J., prepared by; Gladys L. Williams, Ammi Brown and John Waldron (Oxford: Clarendon Press, 1944), pp. 742-43.

[6]Id., pp. 749-767.

[7]Bartolome de Las Casas, quoted by William H. Prescott, *The Conquest of Mexico* (New York: Dutton, 1843, 1965), p. 171.

[8]Francisco Lopez de Gomara, *Cortes: The Life of the Conqueror by His Secretary,* 1552; trans. Lesley Byrd Simpson, Berkeley: U of California Press, 1964), Ch. 13, p. 33.

[9]Suarez, p. 775.

[10]*World Book Encyclopedia,* 1985, "Magellan, Ferdinand."

[11]Charles McKew Parr, *So Noble a Captain* (Binghamton, NY: Vail-Bazllou Press, 1953), pp. 350-68.

[12]John Greenway, "Will the Indians Get Whitey?" *National Review,* March 11, 1969; quoted by Steve Wilkins, "Columbus and the New World Order," Contra Mundum, Winter 1992, p. 15 n. 14.

[13]Jerry Bergman, Ph.D., three unpublished papers, "Evolution and the Origins of the Biological Race Theory," July 6, 1990; "A Brief History of the Eugenics Movement," July 6, 1990; "Eugenics and the Development of Nazi Race Policy," July 10, 1990.

[14]Philip Yancey, quoted by Richard Exley, *Abortion: Pro-Life by Conviction, Pro-Choice by Default* (Tulsa, OK: Honor Books, 1989); pp. 85-86.

[15]John Adams, *Thoughts on Government*; quoted in John R. Howe, Jr., *The Changing Political Thought of John Adams* (Princton, NJ: Princeton U Press), p. 384.

[16]Charles Louis Joseph de Secondat, the Baron Montesquieu, *The Spirit of the Laws* (New York: Hafner, 1748, 1962), 24: 30-31.

[17]Michael Novak, *This Hemisphere of Liberty: A Philosophy of the Americas* (Washington, D.C.: AEI Press, 1990), pp. 10- 11.

[18]For a full exposition of the religion clauses of the First Amendment, see my works, *The Christian Legal Advisor* and *Christianity and the Constitution*, both by Baker Book House of Grand Rapids, Michigan, 1987.

[19]Theodore Roosevelt, 1909; quoted by George Grant, *The Quick and the Dead* (Wheaton, Illinois: Crossway, 1981), p. 134.

INDEX

An ordained minister and constitutional lawyer, Lt. Colonel Eidsmoe is available for lectures, seminars, talk shows, inspirational presentations, debates, and other presentations on this subject and others relating to the constitutional history of the United States. He may be contacted through the Thomas Goode Jones School of Law, Faulkner University, 5345 Atlanta Highway, Montgomery, Alabama 36193-4601, (205) 270-1789.

> Am I a soldier of the cross —
> A follower of the Lamb?
> And shall I fear to own His cause,
> Or blush to speak His name?
>
> Must I be carried to the skies,
> On flowery beds of ease,
> While others fought to win the prize,
> And sailed thro' bloody seas?
>
> Since I must fight if I would reign,
> Increase my courage, Lord!
> I'll bear the toil, endure the pain,
> Supported by Thy word!
>
> In the name of Christ the King,
> Who hath purchased life for me,
> Thro' grace I'll win the promised crown,
> Whate'er my cross may be.
>
> — Isaac Watts